DISCIPLESHIP FOR EVERYDAY LIVING

CHRISTIAN GROWTH, FOLLOWING JESUS CHRIST
AND MAKING DISCIPLES OF ALL NATIONS

MATHEW BACKHOLER

Discipleship For Everyday Living, Christian Growth
Following Jesus Christ And Making Disciples of All Nations:
Firm Foundations, the Gospel, God's Will, Evangelism, Missions,
Teaching, Doctrine and Ministry – Power of the Holy Spirit

IMPORTANT NOTE: The information within this book *but especially chapters 35-49* are Christian spiritual laws of Divine origin; remedies that are non-pharmaceutical. **If you are ill, have a disease or health problem (physical or mental), you should contact a doctor / physician to seek professional medical help. The author is not a mental health professional, doctor / physician or counsellor. If you think you may be suffering from depression, or any mental / physical illness please go and see a doctor / physician for professional advice. The related contents of this book cannot take the place of advice from a medical professional, and is not intended to.**

ISBN 978-1-907066-12-2 (paperback)
ISBN 978-1-907066-25-5 (eBook ePub)
British Library Cataloguing In Publication Data
A Record of this Publication is available from the British Library.
First published in October 2011 by ByFaith Media, updated in March 2014, May 2015, January 2016 and August 2017.

- Jesus Christ is Lord -

'As new born babies, desire the pure milk of the Word, that you may grow thereby, if indeed you have tasted that the Lord is gracious' (1 Peter 2:2-3).

'For everyone who partakes only of milk is unskilled in the Word of righteousness, for he is a babe. But solid food belongs to those who are of full age, that is, those who by reason of use have their senses exercised to discern good and evil' (Hebrews 5:13-14).

Contents

Page   **Chapter**

Contents

'As you have therefore received Christ Jesus the
Lord, so walk in Him, rooted and built up in Him
and established in the faith, as you have
been taught...' (Colossians 2:6-7).

'...Christ in you, the hope of glory. Him we preach, warning
every man and teaching every man in all wisdom,
that we may present every man perfect in
Christ Jesus' (Colossians 1:27b-28).

Preface

'Be diligent to present yourself approved to God, a worker who does not need to be ashamed, rightly dividing the Word of truth' (2 Timothy 2:15).

'...To present you holy, and blameless, and irreproachable in His sight – if indeed you continue in the faith, grounded and steadfast and are not moved away from the hope of the Gospel which you heard...' (Colossians 1:22b-23a).

Discipleship for Everyday Living aims to take Christian believers from milk to meat, (from babes in Christ towards maturity). It aims to educate and inform as part of the 'whole counsel of God' (Acts 20:27), covering six vital sections that are split into fifty biblical subjects. Christian advancement is not automatic; it occurs only when we team up with God and we won't grow unless we sit at Jesus' feet. The Holy Spirit can guide us into all truth, and truths applied in the many facets of our lives glorify Jesus Christ as we are being made into His image and transformed from glory to glory.

The author has not scoured theological books to collect information for *Discipleship for Everyday Living* but with more than twenty-five years of diligent study of the Holy Bible, coupled with more than a decade of full-time Christian ministry, has written from personal experience, whilst being guided by the Holy Spirit. The author has also gleaned from the experience of others with whom he has worked and who have helped train and mentor him, for which he is truly thankful. Bees gather from many flowers and in the course of the author's reading over the decades, certain thoughts have been stored in the subconscious mind. These may have come out again in different phrases in *Discipleship for Everyday Living*. This book contains many quotes from yesteryear whose grammar may differ from modern usage, this has been printed within this book unaltered. Words within brackets [like this] are the author's own additions to aid or to clarify words or a phrase within a quote.

Discipleship for Everyday Living is aimed at Christian growth, as we follow Jesus and make disciples of Christ. The book's fifty easy-to-read chapters are split into six sections: Firm Foundations, The Call of God, World Mission, Evangelism and Teaching, Ministering in the Power of the Holy Spirit, and Ministry – Being Set Free and Delivered.

> 'I fed you with milk and not with solid food; for until now you were not able to receive it...' (1 Corinthians 3:2).

This book is best read systematically from beginning to end, but can also be used as a refresher for any of the given biblical topics. Each chapter is a concise overview of a subject with Scripture references throughout the text, which will clarify and confirm what has been written. Some chapters are introduced with a question, which sets the scene for the chapter, whilst some close with 'further study' – additional Scripture references. Whatever translation of the Holy Bible you use, remember it is vitally important that you apply what you read to your everyday living, be a 'doer of the Word, and not a hearer only' (James 1:22).

The Holy Bible is a wonderful Book – the Word of God penned by men under the direct inspiration of the Holy Spirit. It is eternal truth and just as applicable today as when each of the 66 books of the Bible were written by scribes and preserved for each subsequent generation of Christians, believers who are called by Jesus Christ to "Go and make disciples of all nations..." (Matthew 28:19).

Knowledge without practical application is not beneficial. To reproduce fruit, you do not bury that which you have, but sow it into other people's lives. With the talents and knowledge that you have been entrusted with, invest wisely. Each person is responsible and accountable on the Day of Judgment for that which has been given unto them – for what they did do AND for what they knew and did not do! The author hopes that by reading this book, you will have a greater love for God, will grow in the Christian faith, be more Christ-like and go and make disciples of all nations.

Chapter One

The Good News

Jesus said, "Repent and believe in the Gospel" (Mark 1:15).

'Jesus went about all Galilee, teaching in their synagogues, preaching the Gospel of the Kingdom and healing all kinds of sickness and all kinds of diseases among the people' (Matthew 4:23).

"What is the Good News?" It is Jesus Christ and the free Gospel of salvation He proclaimed. Without Jesus Christ and the cross of Calvary there would be no Christians. Jesus came to 'seek and to save' those who are lost (Luke 19:10), for 'there is no other name under heaven given among men by which we must be saved' (Acts 4:12). We have the Holy Bible that reveals to us the Good News of Jesus Christ that includes His life and teachings. We must read and apply the Holy Bible that will allow us to build firm footings in our Christian faith, which must begin on the Rock of Christ – our immovable foundation. As we walk with the Lord Jesus Christ we build up our bodies (which are temples of the Holy Spirit) in the most holy faith and we must proclaim the Good News via our lives and testimonies, of what Jesus Christ has done for us. The Good News is for everyone!

The Gospel of our Lord and Saviour Jesus Christ
The Society for Missions to Africa and the East was founded in 1799, though renamed the Church Missionary Society (CMS) in 1812. The primary object of the Society can be seen from the opening paragraph of *The Account* that was written by John Venn, rector of Clapham. He was the chairman of the first Committee and spiritual advisor to the group of men who founded the society. He wrote: 'Of all the blessings which God has bestowed upon mankind, the

Gospel of our Lord and Saviour Jesus Christ is the greatest. It is the sovereign remedy for all the evils of life, and the source of the most substantial and durable benefits.'[1]

God so loved the world, that He gave His
Only begotten
Son, that whosoever believeth on Him should not
Perish, but have
Everlasting
Life (John 3:16).[2]

The word 'Gospel' means 'Good Tidings' that comes from two Anglo-Saxon words: 'god' = good, and 'spell' = news. Joe E. Church wrote: 'The Greek word, 'evangelism,' really means 'good message,' and is translated as Gospel in the New Testament. The Gospel is the good message entrusted to Christ's followers to tell the world that salvation is to be had. It offers this salvation and shows how it is obtained.'[3]

The Gospel Is:
- The Gospel of the grace of God (Acts 20:24).
- The Gospel of God (Romans 1:1).
- The Gospel of Christ (Romans 1:16).
- The Gospel of the glory of Christ (2 Cor. 4:3-4).
- The Gospel of your salvation (Ephesians 1:13).
- The Gospel of peace (Ephesians 6:15).
- My Gospel said the apostle Paul came through the revelation of Jesus Christ (Rom. 2:16 and Gal. 1:12).

The heart and soul of evangelism is proclamation of the Gospel – John Wimber.

Four Great Facts Define the Gospel
Selwyn Hughes wrote: 'Four great facts, said someone, define the Gospel: 'A baby in a cradle, a Man upon the cross, a body in a tomb, a King upon a throne.' Christ's mission involved an incarnation, a death by crucifixion, a resurrection, and a final triumphant ascent to the eternal throne. No one but Christ could accomplish this, and the beginning of Christian faith is the acceptance of these facts.'[4]

Born in Sin

Missionary to Africa, Joe E. Church in relation to sin wrote: 'Sin is universal. By nature we are born in sin. Sin is a natural bias to which each man is ever prone, even those who have been regenerated [converted – 'born again,' John 3:3, 7]. Sin is like a disease, an 'infection of the nature,' that must be cleansed, and even then brought daily when necessary for renewed cleansing (c.f. John 13:10). Sin is like a burden on a man's back which must be loosed from him and buried. Christ alone was sinless.'[5]

Dead in Trespasses and Sins

Evangelist, W. P. Nicholson was preaching on the subject of 'Eternal Life' from John 5:12-13, 'He that hath the Son hath life and he that hath not the Son of God hath not life....' He said, "We are all by nature dead in trespasses and sins. We may be rich or poor, good or bad, educated or ignorant, church members in good standing or non-church members, we may take the communion or preach and teach the Word of God, we may be generous and patriotic, but yet we all alike by nature, the children of wrath are dead in trespasses and sins. We were born that way and we must be 'born again' if we are to have eternal life."[6]

Salvation Scriptures

- 'All we like sheep have gone astray; we have turned every one to his own way and the Lord had laid on Him [Jesus] the iniquity of us all' (Isaiah 53:6).
- '...That they are all under sin. As it is written: "There is none righteous, no, not one...there is none who does good, no, not one" ' (Romans 3:9-10).
- 'All have sinned and fall short of the glory of God, being justified freely by His grace through the redemption that is in Christ Jesus, whom God set forth to be a propitiation by His blood, through faith...' (Romans 3:23-25).
- 'But God demonstrates His own love toward us, in that while we were still sinners, Christ died for us' (Romans 5:8).
- Jesus said, "You must be born again" (John 3:3, 7).

- 'Just as through one man [Adam] sin entered the world, and death through sin, and thus death spread to all men, because all sinned' (Romans 5:12).
- 'As through one man's [Adam's] offences judgment came to all men, resulting in condemnation, even so through one Man's [Jesus'] righteous act the free gift came to all men resulting in justification of life' (Romans 5:18).
- 'For the wages of sin is death, but the gift of God is eternal life in Christ Jesus our Lord' (Romans 6:23).
- 'For God so loved the world that He gave His one and only Son that whoever believes in Him shall not perish but have everlasting life' (John 3:16).
- 'Christ died for your sins' (1 Corinthians 15:3).
- 'For by grace you have been saved through faith and that not of yourselves; it is the gift of God, not of works, lest anyone should boast' (Ephesians 2:8-9).
- 'For there is one God and one Mediator between God and men, the Man Christ Jesus, who gave Himself a ransom for all, to be testified in due time' (1 Timothy 2:5-6).
- 'He who has the Son has life; he who does not have the Son of God does not have life' (1 John 5:12).
- 'He who believes in Him [Jesus] is not condemned; but he who does not believe is condemned already, because he has not believed in the name of the only begotten Son of God' (John 3:18).
- 'Repent therefore and be converted that your sins may be blotted out, so that times of refreshing may come from the presence of the Lord' (Acts 3:19).
- '...If you confess with your mouth the Lord Jesus and believe in your heart that God has raised Him from the dead, you will be saved. For with the heart one believes unto righteousness, and with the mouth confession is made unto salvation' (Rom. 10:9-10).
- 'If we confess our sins, He [God] is faithful and just to forgive us our sins and to cleanse us from all unrighteousness' (1 John 1:9).

Chapter Two

A True Christian

'All have sinned and fall short of the glory of God, being justified freely by His grace through the redemption that is in Christ Jesus, whom God set forth to be a propitiation by His blood, through faith…' (Romans 3:23-25).

Jesus said, "Most assuredly, I say to you, unless one is *born again*, he cannot see the Kingdom of God…. Do not marvel that I said to you, 'You *must* be born again' " (John 3:3, 7).

"Who is a true Christian?" The Holy Bible plainly declares that 'whoever calls upon the name of the Lord will be saved' (Acts 2:21 and Romans 10:13), but those who confess with their mouths are also called to profess by their changed lives; that is, 'show forth fruits worthy of repentance' (Matthew 3:8). Genuine disciples of Jesus Christ (true Christians) can be differentiated from those who come in sheep's clothing, yet inwardly are ravenous wolves because 'by their fruit you will know them,' for a 'good tree cannot bear bad fruit' (Matthew 7:15-20). *If* we abide in God's Word, we are His disciples and we shall know the truth and it will set us free (John 8:31-32). Also, people shall know that we are Jesus' disciples '*if* we have love for one another' (John 13:34-35), and *if* we 'walk worthy of the Lord, *fully* pleasing Him' and increase in the knowledge of Him which qualifies us to be 'partakers of the inheritance' (Colossians 1:10-12). By the Word of God and His grace we are able to receive the inheritance, but only 'those who are sanctified' (Acts 20:32).

Jesus also said that not everyone who calls Him "Lord" will enter the Kingdom of heaven, even though they may have done many miraculous signs and wonders in His name, but He will declare, "I never knew you; depart from Me you who practice lawlessness" (Matthew 7:21-23, see Luke 6:46-49).

The travesty of the twenty-first century is that there are many people who attend church who genuinely believe they are saved and part of God's family (John 1:12) yet they are not. They have had a counterfeit conversion – thus meaning that they are NOT converted at all, even though they sincerely believe they are saved, but tragically they are not.

Repentance, a renouncing and turning away from the works of darkness with faith in the death and resurrection of Jesus Christ is the foundation of salvation. Are you saved – saved from what? From the wrath to come, the lusts of the flesh? Saved from selfishness, greed, impure thoughts, a deceitful heart – saved from what? Jesus said, "Therefore by their fruits you will know them" (Matthew 7:20), because without holiness no man shall see the Lord (Hebrews 12:4), and we are commanded to be holy because He is holy (1 Peter 1:16). The righteous one is scarcely saved (1 Peter 4:18), and those who do not do the will of God are not part of Jesus' family (Matthew 7:21 and Mark 3:35).

Jesus declared that we are justified and condemned by our words (Matthew 12:37), and our confession of faith in Jesus Christ (Romans 10:9-10), is the crux of our faith. If the Lord will say to some, "I never knew you" – to those who even did miracles and cast out demons in His name (Matthew 7:21-23) can you really say you are saved? Jesus said, "Narrow is the gate and difficult is the way which leads to life and there are few who find it" (Matthew 7:14). Jesus said, "You must be born again" (John 3:7).

Salvation, genuine conversion, is a Divine transaction as the Spirit of God comes and indwells and seals the believer (John 14:23, 27). Jesus said, "He who hears My Word and believes in Him who sent Me has everlasting life, and shall not come into judgment but has passed from death into life" (John 5:24). A genuine convert is a 'new creation' (2 Corinthians 5:17-18), having been 'reconciled' to God through Jesus Christ (Romans 5:10). It is a passing from 'death to life' (John 5:24 and 1 John 3:14), from 'darkness to light and from the power of Satan to God' (Acts 26:18), and they now live for Jesus Christ in newness of life.

God knows who His chosen ones are and if we are not wearing the right clothes at the wedding feast we will be caught out and cast out (Matthew 22:11-14). We must accept and live by the Word of God and make Jesus not only our Saviour, but our Lord and Master. Have you? 'Examine yourselves as to whether you are in the faith. Prove yourselves. Do you not know yourselves that Jesus Christ is in you? – Unless indeed you are disqualified' (2 Corinthians 13:5).[1]

In 2007, Andy Banton, General Secretary of The Open-Air Mission wrote: 'In the work of evangelism today there is an awful lot of shallowness. It seems to be a common assumption that if people simply hear about Jesus and then make a commitment to Him, they are saved. The feeling a person experiences which bring them to that commitment are rarely asked about, let alone examined. So what does the Word of God say about what a person should experience in their coming to a saving knowledge of Jesus Christ? In Acts 2:37 we are provided with the answer. Peter had been addressing a huge crowd in Jerusalem on the day of Pentecost. Luke records that as he spoke, many were 'cut to the heart.' What does this phrase mean? In the very depths of their beings, many of Peter's hearers were convicted of their sin. They actually felt a sense of their moral dirtiness before a holy God. They were now aware of what God had already been aware of – their responsibility for the death of the Lord Jesus. This was something that was laid bare before their eyes. They not only saw it but felt a sense of horror of it. In fact the people now felt something of the enormity of their rejection of the One who had claimed to be the Messiah. Like a repentant King David they knew what it was to have hearts that were broken and contrite (Psalm 51:17).'[2]

Eight Categories of Deceived "Christians"
1. A Non-Christian: One who thinks that he or she is a Christian, yet have never put their faith in Jesus Christ's atoning death for the forgiveness of their sins. At the end times, unrighteous people will follow the deceptions of the devil (2 Thessalonians 2:7-12).
2. A Premature Christian: One who does not live the life, who constantly, deliberately and habitually sins (John 14:15, 21, Hebrews 6:1-6 and Heb. 10:26-31).

3. A Young Christian: One who is led astray. Simon (who had previously practised sorcery) wanted to buy the power of the impartation of the Holy Spirit. Peter denounced him and called him to repent as his heart was not right in the sight of God, being poisoned by bitterness and bound by iniquity (Acts 8:9-13, 18-23).
4. A Naïve Christian: One who has been taken captive by the devil to do his will (2 Timothy 2:26), or one who has been deceived by another (2 Timothy 3:1-6).
5. A Religious Christian: One who outwardly appears right before God, but in their heart they are looking for the praise and adoration of man. The Pharisees were full of hypocrisy and lawlessness (Matthew 23:1-7, 13-15, Matthew 23:23-33 and Luke 11:42-44).
6. A Traditional Christian: One who believes that their devotion to their tradition is more important than their relationship to God (Matthew 23:16-22 and Mark 7:6-13). Often doctrine comes before devotion.
7. An Apostate Christian: One who upon seeing lawlessness abound, allows their love for Christ to grow cold (Matthew 24:10-12 and 2 Thess. 2:3-4).
8. A "Manipulated" Christian: The elect who after seeing deceiving signs and wonders follow after a false Christ or false prophets (Matthew 24:23-26).[3]

A True Christian

Marie Monsen was a Norwegian missionary who arrived in China in 1901. She saw revival across China from 1927-1932, in every mission station she visited (of differing denominations) in numerous provinces. In November 1931, she arrived at Chenping, one of the mission stations of the Norwegian Lutheran Mission in Honan, and saw revival. In the second week she spoke at the Chenping annual three day conference. At the end of the day, as her custom was, she would take her stand at the door and as the people left, she pointedly asked, "Are you saved?" The next day, as the people left, with her incredible discernment, she asked, "Are you still on the road to destruction?"

Her co-worker wrote: 'Many came to see her and confess their sins, but she sent them away, some as often as three to four times. They were not in a condition of real need. "Pray that God's Spirit may enlighten you concerning your sins," was the admonition they received to take away with them. She never tired of admonishing us, "Do not gather unripe fruit." [4]

Laurence J. Crabb in *Basic Principles of Biblical Counselling* wrote: 'The effect of sin is separation. Four distinct separations summarise the total catastrophe introduced by man's wilful rebellion. First, man is separated from God – he has spiritual problems. Second, he is separated from his fellow – he has social / interpersonal problems. Third, he is separated from nature – he has ecological and physical problems. Fourth, he is separated from himself – he has psychological problems. Christians understand that the ultimate cause of every difficulty is sin, a decision to live life without regard for God's authority.' [5]

Three-fold Way of Sin
Sin is rebellion and enmity (deep-seated ill will) against God and is demonstrated in a threefold way:
1. By act – e.g. stealing is an act of sin.
2. By attitude – e.g. hypocrisy is an attitude of sin.
3. By state – e.g. being unsaved is a state of sin. [6]

Sacrifice for Sin – Jesus Christ's Death
In the Old Testament, since the days of Adam and Eve, God provided a remedy for sin. The blood of a slain animal made atonement to the one who truly repented and believed in its efficacy (belief in its power to work).

Joe E. Church wrote: 'Sacrifice in its original sense implied the offering of an innocent animal for the guilt of the individual. Where this was accompanied by true repentance, and faith, God looked upon the shed blood and granted atonement in anticipation of the cross. True sacrifice as ordained by God in the Old Testament was the shadow of which Christ's death was the reality.' [7]

Jesus is the Lamb of God who was slain before the foundation of the world (John 1:29 and Revelation 13:8), and in the fullness of time, came in the likeness of man (Jesus Christ) where He willingly died for the sins of the world and took the punishment that we deserved upon Him (see Isaiah

53). The New Testament reveals the New Covenant that supercedes the Old – a *better* covenant (see Hebrews 8). Belief in the death and resurrection of the Lord Jesus Christ and His shed blood for us is the final and *only* way of escape from the wages of sin which is death, for there is no other name under heaven given to men by which we must be saved. With faith and belief in Jesus Christ must also come repentance and then a changed life. Salvation is by God's grace, not something that can be bought or worked for, it is a gift of God (see Ephesians 2:8-9).

Repentance
Joe E. Church wrote: 'True repentance means a radical change of attitude towards God, and therefore towards sin. It is a genuine sorrow for sin, *accompanied by* a change of heart. It is an *attitude* of mind, as well as an *act*. Remorse...alone is not real repentance.'[8]

For the Truly Repentant
- He has a sincere grief for sin and a sincere hatred of sin.
- He used to live in sin, now he longs to be delivered from it.
- He used to love sin, now he loathes it.
- He used to revel in sin, now he runs from it.
- He used to delight in sin, now he detests it.

The Real New Testament Message
Bible teacher, A. W. Tozer said, "The Gospel message embraces a great deal more than an offer of free pardon. It is a message of pardon...but it is also a message of repentance. It is a message of atonement, but it is also a message of temperance and righteousness and godliness in this present world. It tells us that we must accept a Saviour, but it tells us also that we must deny ungodliness and worldly lusts. The Gospel message includes the idea of amendment, of separation from the world, of cross-carrying and loyalty to the Kingdom of God even unto death.... They are part and parcel of the total message which we are commissioned to declare. No man has authority to divide the truth and preach

only a part of it. To do so is to weaken and render it without effect."

"…To offer a sinner the gift of salvation based upon the work of Christ, while at the same time allowing him to retain the idea that the gift carries with it no moral implications, is to do him untold injury where it hurts him worst."[9]

Salvation – Concept of Wrong

Evangelist, W. P. Nicholson was preaching on the subject of 'Salvation' from Ephesians 2:8-9, 'For by grace, you have been saved, through faith…not of works…' He said, "There is no difference of opinion as to the need of salvation. Every one believes in it and its necessity. We all have a consciousness of being wrong, whether we believe in a Divine revelation or not – whether we believe in God or not. Men everywhere know they are not living according to their own conceptions, let alone according to the conceptions contained in the Scriptures and therefore they have a sense of condemnation. This asserts itself in spite of their arguments and excuses."[10]

The Process of Salvation

- The Father (God) draws us (John 6:44).
- The Son (Jesus Christ) saves us (Acts 2:38, Acts 3:19, Acts 4:12 and Romans 5:8).
- The Holy Spirit brings conviction of sin (John 16:7-11). It is the Holy Spirit that regenerates us, and seals us (John 3:3, 7, John 14:17 & 2 Timothy 2:19).
- We must respond to the call of 'the Spirit and the Bride' and 'come' (Revelation 22:17), in repentance (Matthew 3:2, 4:17). We are saved by grace, through faith and it is the gift of God (Ephesians 2:8).
- The Holy Spirit bears witness that we are children of God (John 1:12 and John 15:26).
- Our responsibility is to live holy lives (1 Peter 1:16), fully living for Christ (Romans 6:6 and Galatians 2:20); to declare the praises of Him who called us out of darkness into His marvellous light (1 Peter 2:9). We must always be ready and prepared to witness for Jesus Christ (Proverbs 15:28 and 1 Peter 3:15).

The Three Stages of Salvation Are:
1. We *have been* saved – Justification (forgiven of my sins – just as if I had not sinned).
2. We *are being* saved – Sanctification (being cleansed from sin, as sin is being put away).
3. We *shall be* saved – Glorification (in heaven).[11]

Hell – Seek the Lord Now

W. P. Nicholson after stating all the descriptions of hell from the Holy Bible (lake of fire, bottomless pit, place of weeping, everlasting destruction etc.) said, "Hell begins where man's day of grace ends here. There are so many who imagine they can be saved when they like and where. That just when they take the notion they can flee from the wrath to come and escape hell. That they can turn to the Lord God Almighty into a convenience, and make a servant of Him, so that He must be at their beck and call, and when they take the notion of seeking Him He must be found of them. This is the devil's delusion to damn your soul. The Word says, 'Seek ye the Lord *while* He may be found...call upon Him *while* He is near.' You may seek Him and not find Him. You may call when He is not near.... You may reject Christ for the last time now, then your day of grace has come and gone for you for ever. That is where hell begins for you and every other soul who has sinned their day of grace away. God is under no obligation to save you. Salvation is of purest grace. It is of the Lord. You will never deserve it, or be able to buy it or merit it. If you are to be saved you must accept it as a poor, undeserving and hell-deserving sinner. Be warned unsaved one...don't kill it by putting off accepting Christ any longer. But just now, where you are and as you are, trust Him with your soul and be saved for eternity. This is God's day of grace."[12]

W. P. Nicholson wrote: 'I am either saved or lost, a child of the devil or a child of God, on the road to heaven or on the road to hell. There is no middle ground, no neutral attitude. If we won't receive salvation from the Lord, we will have to receive damnation.'[13]

Chapter Three

Help for Christians

Jesus said, "...Ask and it will be given to you; seek and you will find; knock and it will be opened to you. For everyone who asks receives and he who seeks finds.... How much more will your heavenly Father give the Holy Spirit to those who ask Him!" (Luke 11:9-10, 13).

'Your Word [the Holy Bible] is a lamp to my feet and a light to my path' (Psalm 119:105).

The apostle Paul penned a description of a true Christian: 'If anyone is in Christ, he is a new creation; old things have passed away; behold, all things become new' (2 Corinthians 5:17). The Lord spoke to Paul that his witnessing to both Jews and Gentiles was to, 'Open their eyes and to turn them from darkness to light, and from the power of Satan to God, that they may receive forgiveness of sins and an inheritance among those who are sanctified by faith in Me' (Acts 26:18). This chapter consists of various quotes from believers that will help Christians and aid us in our spiritual growth, alongside checks and warnings. We are called to be the light of the world (Matthew 5:14), so let our light shine!

Six Short Rules for Young Christians
Brownlow North from the nineteenth century had six short rules for young Christians. They are:
1. Never neglect daily private prayer and when you pray, remember that God is present and that He hears your prayers (Hebrews 9:6).
2. Never neglect daily private Bible reading, and when you read, remember that God is speaking to you and that you are to believe and act upon what He

says. I believe all backsliding begin with the neglect of these two rules (John 5:39).

3. Never let a day pass by without trying to do something for Jesus. Every night reflect on what Jesus has done for you and then ask yourself, what am I doing for Him? (Matthew 5:13-16).

4. If you are in doubt as to a thing being right or wrong, go to your room and kneel down and ask God's blessing upon it (Colossians 3:17). If you cannot do this, it is wrong (Romans 14:23).

5. Never take your Christianity from Christians, or argue that because such and such a person does so and so, that therefore you may (2 Cor. 10:12). You are to ask yourself, how would Christ act in my place? And strive to follow Him (John 10:27).

6. Never believe what you feel, if it contradicts God's Word. Ask yourself, can what I feel be true, if God's Word is true? And if both cannot be true, believe God and make your own heart the liar (Romans 3:4 and 1 John 5:10-11).[1]

The Basics of the Christian Life

Evangelist, Dr. Reuben A. Torrey in *How to Bring Men to Christ* (1903) states that all new Christians, if they are to succeed in life, they need to be immediately told the basics of the Christian life. They are:

1. Confess Christ with the mouth before men at every opportunity you get (Romans 10:9-10 and Matthew 10:32-33).

2. Be baptised [immersed in water] and partake regularly of the Lord's Supper (Acts 2:38-42, Luke 22:19 and 1 Corinthians 11:24-26).

3. Study the Word of God daily (1 Peter 2:2, Acts 20:31, 2 Timothy 3:13-17 and Acts 17:2).

4. Pray daily, often and in every time of temptation (Luke 11:9-13, 22:40 and 1 Thessalonians 5:17).

5. Put away out of your life every sin, even the smallest and everything you have doubts about, and obey every Word of Christ (1 John 1:6-7, Romans 14:23 and John 14:23).

6. Seek the society of Christians [fellowship with Christians] (Ephesians 4:12-16, Acts 2:42, 47 and Hebrews 10:24-25).
7. Go to work for Christ (Matthew 25:14-29).
8. When you fall into sin, don't be discouraged, but confess it at once, believe it is forgiven because God says so and get up and go on (1 John 1:9 and Philippians 3:13-14).[2]

I am Not Growing Spiritually

Selwyn Hughes (founder of CWR) noted four major reasons why Christians fail to grow in grace. They are:
1. Failure to maintain a clear conscience. If any sin, or violation of God's Word is not dealt with immediately, then it lies in the heart and festers.
2. Neglect of personal prayer. We must have a quiet time before God.
3. Lack of daily Bible reading. In order to grow we must read from the Holy Bible every day and apply its teaching.
4. No clear understanding of one's place within the body of Christ. Every Christian is designed by God to fit into a special place in His body, the church. See Romans 12:6-8.[3]

Four Names For Christians

A Mr Fuller from the eighteenth century noted that the Scriptures give four names to Christians, which are taken from the four cardinal graces. They are:
1. Saints – for their holiness.
2. Believers – for their faith.
3. Brethren – for their love.
4. Disciples – for their knowledge.[4]

Evidences of Salvation

Evangelist, Steve Hill noted seven evidences of salvation. They are:
1. An inner witness that you are a child of God (1 John 5:10).
2. A new awareness of sin and sinful thoughts (1 John 1:8-9).

3. A new desire to read God's love letter – the Bible (Psalm 119:11).
4. A desire to live holy and be like Jesus (Phil. 3:10).
5. The experiencing of social pressure (2 Tim. 3:12).
6. A sense of urgency to share the Gospel (Acts 4:20).
7. A new love for other Christians (1 John 3:14).[5]

Evidences of Conversion

Evangelist, W. P. Nicholson noted nine evidences that result from genuine conversion. He wrote: 'They may not all be as evident to yourself or to others, or as fully evident as you or they would desire. But in some measure and in some degree they are there. There is first the blade and then the ear and then the full corn in the ear.' These evidences are:

1. Are you fully surrendered to Christ? Do you know, and endeavour to do His will?
2. Has the burden of sin been removed and have you now peace with God?
3. Has there come into your heart a new feeling of love to Christ and Christians! Has the enmity been slain?
4. Have you a relish and desire for God's Word? [The Holy Bible].
5. Has secret prayer not only become a necessity but a real luxury? You don't merely do it because you feel it is your duty, but you delight in it.
6. Does pain come to your heart now because of sin and sinful thoughts?
7. Do you experience deep humility and self-abasement daily? Once you were proud and boasted about your good deeds and self-righteousness. [Now you don't].
8. Have you a growing desire after holiness and likeness to Christ?
9. Is there a real desire and an honest effort to save the lost?[6]

Love (Christian Fruit and Character)

The unnamed author in *The Teacher's Visitor* (Feb. 1845) wrote: 'Charity [old English word for love] is that principle of Divine love which the Spirit of God pours into the soul of the true believer, and which evidences itself in love to God and love to man; in this second branch of it, it is generally called in the [Authorised Version of the] Scriptures 'charity.'

'God, that is God the Holy Ghost (1 Corinthians 2:13 and 1 Peter 1:12), hath taught us, by the written Word of His apostles that nothing is of any avail without charity [love] (1 Corinthians 13:10). It being the fulfilling of the law (Romans 13:10), and the end of the commandment of the Gospel (1 Timothy 1:5), for he that loves God must love his brother also (1 John 4:21).

'[Pray] that God would send His Holy Ghost, and pour into our hearts that most excellent gift of charity (1 Corinthians 12:31), which is the bond of peace of all virtues; that is, of perfectness (Colossians 3:14 and compare 2 Peter 1:5-7), without which, whosoever lives (naturally) is counted dead (in spirit) before God (1 John 3:14).

'The Holy Spirit is the Author of life (Romans 8:2-10), and so of the various Gospel principles which are evidences of it, and in which it consists; and among others, of love (Romans 5:5), especially that branch of which it relates to man (Galatians 5:22).... We may remark that it is an evidence of our being in Christ (John 13:35), and that professors [of Christianity] who are destitute of it are hypocrites (1 John 2:9, 11). It is exhibited in being kindly affected towards others (Romans 12:10), in mutual forbearance (Ephesians 4:2), in visiting the sick and afflicted (James 1:27 and compare Matthew 25:36-40), in forgiving injuries (Ephesians 4:32), in longing after the spiritual advances of others (Philippians 1:8), in feeding Christ's sheep (John 21:15-17). Joseph exemplified this charity (Genesis 45:4-5); Stephen (Acts 8:60); Dorcas (Acts 9:36); the Good Samaritan (Luke 10:33, 37), and Nehemiah (Nehemiah 5:19). Our prayer should be: 'Now may the God of peace who brought up our Lord Jesus from the dead, that Great Shepherd of the sheep, through the blood of the everlasting covenant, make you complete in every good work to do His will, working in you what is well pleasing in His sight, through Jesus Christ, to whom be glory forever and ever, Amen' (Hebrews 13:20-21).'[7]

Twenty Directions for Correct Living

In 1690, Bible commentator Rev. Matthew Henry noted twenty directions for correct living, which is phrased in old English, with some explanations added. They are:

1. Fix a right principle of true grace in your heart [have a good conscience] (2 Corinthians 1:12).
2. Eye the Gospel of Christ as your great rule [live like you are a Christian] (Philippians 1:27).
3. Set the Lord before you always (Psalm 16:8).
4. Keep your heart with all diligence (Proverbs 4:23).
5. Abide always under the rule of the fear of God (Proverbs 23:17).
6. Be not conformed to the world (Romans 12:2).
7. Live in a constant dependence upon the Lord Jesus Christ (Colossians 3:17).
8. Take your affection off from the present things [think about heavenly things] (1 John 2:15).
9. Be always standing on your watch [be ready for Christ's return] (Mark 13:37).
10. Keep a conscience void of offence toward God and towards men (Acts 14:6).
11. Live by faith (Galatians 2:20).
12. Be much in communion with your own heart [meditate on God and the Holy Bible] (Psalm 4:4).
13. Set a double watch before the door of your lips [be careful what you say – restrain your tongue] (Psalm 39:1).
14. Follow the steps of the Lord Jesus (1 Peter 2:21).
15. Lay before you the example of the saints (Hebrews 4:12).
16. Be very cautious what company you keep [be careful who your friends are] (Proverbs 13:20).
17. Make conscience how your spend your time [don't waste your day, make it profitable] (Ephesians 5:16).
18. Pray to God for holy wisdom (James 5:1).
19. Be often thinking of death and judgment [you will live how you ought to with this realisation before you] (2 Peter 3:11).
20. Converse much with heaven [we will end up in heaven, so think about it] (Philippians 3:20).[8] See *Heaven – A Journey to Paradise* by Paul Backholer.

Chapter Four

Growing in the Christian Faith

'Grow in the grace and knowledge of our Lord and Saviour Jesus Christ. To Him be the glory, both now and forever. Amen' (2 Peter 3:18).

'Now may our Lord Jesus Christ Himself, and our God and Father, who has loved us and given us everlasting consolation and good hope by grace, comfort your hearts and establish you in every good word and work' (2 Thessalonians 2:16-17).

"How can I best grow in the Christian faith?" By reading and applying the truths of the Holy Bible, spending time in prayer, and in fellowship with other Christians who can help and guide you. This chapter consists of many Scriptures in various categories, all of which are essential for growing in the Christian faith. However, Christian knowledge without application of these truths is empty knowledge. We are told to be 'doers of the Word, not hearers only' (James 1:22).

Evangelist Billy Graham, speaking to J. Edwin Orr during the Hollywood for Christ Campaign of September 1951, said, "In the past, evangelists have not always seemed willing to face the fact that the so-called 'converts' passing through their enquiry rooms are not all converts.... Furthermore, many evangelists, including myself, used to spend ninety-five percent of their efforts in persuading men to *decide* for Christ. Now I am convinced that it takes ninety-five percent of evangelistic effort [follow-up] to get men to *follow* Christ, as compared with five percent necessary for decision.'[1]

Theological Overview of Christianity
- The authority of the Holy Bible (2 Timothy 3:16-17, Hebrews 4:12 and 2 Peter 1:21).

- The problem of sin (Psalm 51:5, Isaiah 64:6, Romans 3:22-24 and Romans 6:16).
- The consequences of sin (Isaiah 59:2, Ezekiel 18:4, Romans 5:12 and Romans 6:23).
- The remedy for sin (Isaiah 53:6, Luke 5:31-32, John 10:11, 14-15 and 2 Corinthians 5:21).
- The judgment to come (John 3:36, Romans 14:12, Hebrews 9:27 and Revelation 20:11-13).
- The reality of hell (Matthew 3:10-12, Matthew 25:29-30, 41-46 and Revelation 20:14-15).
- God's love for mankind (Isaiah 55:1-3, John 3:16, Romans 5:8 and 1 Corinthians 15:1-4).
- Receiving the Saviour, Jesus Christ (Matthew 4:17, John 3:3-6, Romans 10:8-10 and Ephesians 2:8-9).
- An assurance of salvation (Matthew 12:50, John 1:12, Romans 10:9 and 1 John 5:11-13).
- The assurance of forgiveness (Matthew 6:14-15, Hebrews 8:12 and 1 John 1:7-9).
- The second coming of Jesus Christ (Daniel 7:13-14, Zechariah 14:5, Mark 13:27, Acts 1:9-11 and 1 Thessalonians 4:14-18).
- Living for Jesus Christ (Romans 12:1, Galatians 2:20 and 2 Corinthians 5:15).

'For no other foundation can anyone lay than that which is laid, which is Jesus Christ' (1 Corinthians 3:11).

The Holy Bible – The Word of God
- 'This book of the Law shall not depart from your mouth, but you shall meditate in it day and night, that you may observe to do according to all that is written in it. For then you will make your way prosperous, and then you will have good success' (Joshua 1:8).
- 'The law of the Lord is perfect, converting the soul; the testimony of the Lord is sure, making wise the simple; the statutes of the Lord are right, rejoicing the heart; the commandment of the Lord is pure, enlightening the eyes; the fear of the Lord is clean, enduring forever; the judgments of the Lord are true and righteous altogether. More to be desired than

gold, yea, than much fine gold...moreover by them your servant is warned and in keeping them there is great reward' (Psalm 19:7-11).

- 'Your Word is a lamp to my feet and a light to my path' (Psalm 119:105). See also Psalm 119:130.
- 'The heart of the righteous studies how to answer...' (Proverbs 15:28).
- 'My people are destroyed for lack of knowledge' (Hosea 4:6). See also Hosea 6:3.
- 'I am not ashamed of the Gospel of Christ for it is the power of God to salvation for everyone who believes...' (Romans 1:16).
- 'All Scripture is given by inspiration of God, and is profitable for doctrine, for reproof, for correction, for instruction in righteousness, that the man of God may be complete, thoroughly equipped for every good work' (2 Timothy 3:16-17).
- 'Holding fast the faithful Word as he has been taught, that he may be able, by sound doctrine, both to exhort and convict those who contradict' (Titus 1:9).
- 'For the Word of God is living and powerful, and sharper than any two-edged sword, piercing even to the division of soul and spirit, and of joints and marrow, and is a discerner of the thoughts and intents of the heart' (Hebrews 4:12).
- 'Sanctify the Lord God in your hearts, and always be ready to give a defence to everyone who asks you a reason for the hope that is in you with meekness and fear' (1 Peter 3:15).

The Importance of Prayer

- Jesus said, "I say to you, ask, and it will be given to you; seek and you will find; knock, and it will be opened to you" (Luke 11:9).
- Jesus said, "Whatever you ask in My name that will I do, that the Father may be glorified in the Son. If you ask anything in My name, I will do it" (John 14:13-14).
- Jesus said, "If you abide in Me and My Words abide in you, you will ask what you desire and it shall be done for you" (John 15:7).

- Jesus said, "...Whatever you ask the Father in My name He will give you. Until now you have asked nothing in My name. Ask and you will receive that your joy may be full" (John 16:23-24).
- Jesus said, "I say to you that if two or three of you on earth agree concerning anything that they ask it will be done for them by My Father in heaven. For where two or three are gathered together in My name, I am there in the midst of them" (Matthew 18:19-20).

Key Scriptures for Answered Prayer

- Confess all known sin. 'If I regard iniquity in my heart the Lord will not hear' (Psalm 66:18).
- Ask in Jesus' name. Jesus said, "...Most assuredly I say to you, whatever you ask the Father in My name He will give you" (John 16:23).
- Is it God's will? 'Now this is the confidence that we have in Him, that if we ask anything according to His will He hears us' (1 John 5:14).
- Believe, have faith and forgive everyone. Jesus said, "I say to you, whatever things you ask when you pray, believe that you will receive them and you will have them. And whenever you stand praying, if you have anything against your brother forgive him, that your Father in heaven may also forgive your trespasses" (Mark 11:24-25).
- Be persistent in prayer. 'Then He spoke a parable to them that men always ought to pray and not lose heart' (Luke 18:1).

Obedience to the Word and Full Surrender

- Jesus said, "If you abide in My Word, you are My disciples indeed. And you shall know the truth, and the truth shall make you free" (John 8:31-32).
- Jesus said, "If anyone desires to come after Me, let him deny himself, and take up his cross daily and follow Me" (Luke 9:23).
- Jesus said, "...Unless a grain of wheat falls into the ground and dies, it remains alone; but if it dies, it produces much grain. He who loves his life will lose

it, and he who hates his life in this world will keep it for eternal life" (John 12:24-25).

- 'I beseech you therefore, brethren, by the mercies of God, that you present your bodies a living sacrifice, holy, acceptable to God, which is your reasonable service' (Romans 12:1).
- 'And He [Jesus] died for all, that those who live should live no longer for themselves, but for Him who died for them and rose again' (2 Corinthians 5:15).
- '...Let us cleanse ourselves from all filthiness of the flesh and spirit, perfecting holiness in the fear of God' (2 Corinthians 7:1).

The Necessity of the Holy Spirit

- Jesus said, "You shall receive power when the Holy Spirit has come upon you; and you shall be witnesses to Me in Jerusalem, and in all Judea and Samaria, and to the end of the earth" (Acts 1:8).
- 'The Holy Spirit...given to those who obey Him [God]' (Acts 5:32).
- Jesus said, "The Helper, the Holy Spirit, whom the Father will send in My name, He will teach you all things, and bring to remembrance all things that I said to you" (John 14:26).
- Jesus said, "...Ask and it will be given to you; seek and you will find; knock and it will be opened to you. How much more will your heavenly Father give the Holy Spirit to those who ask Him!" (Luke 11:9, 13).

The Gifts and Graces of the Holy Spirit

- 'For to one is given the word of wisdom through the Spirit, to another the word of knowledge through the same Spirit, to another faith by the same Spirit, to another gifts of healings by the same Spirit, to another the working of miracles, to another prophecy, to another discerning of spirits, to another different kinds of tongues, to another the interpretation of tongues' (1 Corinthians 12:8-10).
- 'Having gifts differing according to the grace given to us, let us use them: if prophecy, let us prophesy in

proportion to our faith; or ministry, let us use it in our ministering; he who teaches, in teaching; he who exhorts, in exhortation; he who gives, with liberality; he who leads, with diligence; he who shows mercy, with cheerfulness...distributing to the needs of the saints, given to hospitality' (Romans 12:6-8, 13).

- 'God has appointed these in the church: first apostles, second prophets, third teachers, after that miracles, then gifts of healings, helps, administrations, varieties of tongues' (1 Corinthians 12:28).
- 'But to each one grace was given according to the measure of Christ's gift. And He Himself gave some to be apostles, some prophets, some evangelists, and some pastors and teachers. For the equipping of the saints for the work of the ministry, for the edifying of the body of Christ' (Ephesians 4:7, 11-12).
- 'Is anyone among you sick? Let him call for the elders of the church, and let them pray over him, anointing him with oil in the name of the Lord. And the prayer of faith will save the sick, and the Lord will raise him up. And if he has committed sins, he will be forgiven. Confess your trespasses to one another, and pray for one another, that you may be healed. The effective, fervent prayer of a righteous man avails much' (James 5:14-16).

'The Lord gave the Word; great was the company of those who proclaimed it' (Psalm 68:11).

Ministering in the Power of the Holy Spirit
- 'My speech and my preaching were not with persuasive words of human wisdom, but in demonstration of the Spirit and power, that your faith should not be in the wisdom of men but in the power of God' (1 Corinthians 2:4-5). See Acts 1:8.
- 'For the Kingdom of God is not in Word but in power' (1 Corinthians 4:20). See 2 Corinthians 12:12 and 1 Thessalonians 1:5.
- Jesus said, "My doctrine is not Mine but His who sent Me" (John 7:16). See Mark 16:15-17.

Chapter Five

What is Discipleship?

Jesus said, "Go therefore and make disciples of all the nations...teaching them to observe all things that I have commanded you; and lo, I am with you always, even to the end of the age" (Matthew 28:19-20).

'As you have therefore received Christ Jesus the Lord, so walk in Him, rooted and built up in Him and established in the faith, as you have been taught...' (Colossians 2:6-7).

"What is discipleship?" It has been said that Christianity is coming to the foot of the cross, but discipleship is about embracing the cross. When you become a Christian (you repent of your sins and put your faith in the death and resurrection of Jesus Christ, the Son of God, you are "born again" to use Jesus' words in John 3:3, 7, and pass from 'death to life'), you are introduced to Jesus. However, becoming a disciple of Jesus Christ is getting to know Him better and living for Him. In its most basic sense, discipleship is trying to live like Jesus and be obedient to Him. It is a process of coming from illumination of the Word (saving knowledge of Jesus) into a living illustration (living like Jesus) of the works of God and walking in the newness of the Spirit (Romans 7:6 and 2 Corinthians 3:6).

'...Christ in you, the hope of glory. Him we preach, warning every man and teaching every man in all wisdom, that we may present every man perfect in Christ' (Col. 1:27b-28).

J. A. Broadbelt, Principal of Cliff College in the 1930s wrote: 'Christian discipleship that thrills and satisfies is a very personal thing. Our Lord said, "If any man shall come after ME...follow ME" (Matthew 16:24 and Luke 9:23). It is different from every other kind of discipleship in that it is a passionate and personal devotion to Jesus Christ.'[1]

The problem with too many Christians in the twenty-first century is that many *play* church when they should be the Church. That is to say, that they are not fully committed to the things of God, they live for self, not for the glory of Jesus Christ and never become disciples. The apostle Paul knew that what he had performed in his own ability was as nothing in God's eyes, 'What things were gain to me, these I have counted loss for Christ' (Philippians 3:7). To truly embrace the cross and to get to know Jesus better means that you have to give your life entirely over to Him. That means that Jesus is not only your Saviour but your Lord as well.

Jesus said, "Whoever desires to come after Me, let him deny himself, and take up his cross, and follow Me. For whoever desires to save his life will lose it, but whoever loses his life for My sake and the Gospel's will save it" (Mark 8:34-35).

Jesus died so that we can live. We also need to die (to self) so that we can live to our *full* potential. If you lose your life; it means that you are willing to follow God's plan for your life. You will be led of the Holy Spirit and not led of your own desires, whims or ambitions. Either Jesus is Lord of all or He is not Lord at all. John the Baptist said in reference to Jesus, "He must increase, but I must decrease" (John 3:30). This living process of surrendering your will to God might take years, if not decades, but it all begins with the acceptance that God can control your life His way, better than you can do it without Him. It is a choice of the human will that must be surrendered and broken before God, a daily dying to self.

"If anyone desires to come after Me, let him deny himself, and take up his cross daily and follow Me" - Jesus (Lk. 9:23).

Words of Wisdom
Genuine disciples of Jesus Christ will acknowledge that in their own ability they will make mistakes, but in Him all things are possible, as they desire to have continual fellowship,

whilst doing His will and bearing fruit for His glory. It's not your ability, but your availability that God is after. God is looking for people who will be faithful and diligent in all that they are called to do, whether in their own house, the workplace or on the mission field at home or abroad. God is faithful and can be trusted. All that He said, He will do. When storms are at their darkest, the greater the victory that can be achieved. He will never leave you nor forsake you. Often you have to step out in faith and just believe and trust.

Walk in love, servant-hood, and humility. Be accountable to others who can correct, rebuke and encourage when the need arises. Most people have issues to be worked through within their lives and mercy is always better than the heavy-handed law. People are always more important than rules or structures. Don't live to please man, but live to please God. Continually be filled with the Holy Spirit and do not ignore His gentle still voice. It is very important to exercise your spiritual gifts (1 Corinthians 12:1-11), as well as daily walking in the fruit of the Spirit (Galatians 5:22-23).

Jesus said, "You have not chosen Me, but I have chosen you and ordained you that you should go and bring forth fruit, and that your fruit should remain; that whatever you shall ask of the Father in My name, He may give it to you" (John 15:16).

Study the Holy Bible and pray without ceasing. Jesus Christ never lost His focus: He knew where He came from and where He was heading and so must you. All of God's promises can be appropriated (claimed and participated of), as long as the conditions have been met. You will make mistakes and be tripped up; confess any sin as sin, get up, dust yourself off and move on. Learn to forgive and keep your heart soft and tender. Nobody is perfect and nobody has all the answers. An experience is mightier than someone with an argument and worth more than a ton of theory. Learn to respect other people's views whilst being gentle, kind and courteous. Do not major on the minors and learn to expound (to teach and apply) the whole counsel of God (Acts 20:27).

Whilst all people have natural limitations, most people never attempt to work to their full potential and would be amazed at what is possible if only they stepped out in faith. Never allow fear of the unknown to paralyse you; worse than fear is coming to the end of your life and saying, "If only?" In the walk of faith, the impossible becomes the possible and the mountain becomes a molehill. Live your life for God, and when your time is up you will not be disappointed at the eternal rewards. There is much in life to be learnt and the best education you can get is in the college of life.

> Jesus said, "I can do nothing of Myself...I do not seek My own will, but the will of the Father who sent Me" (John 5:30).

In light of what you do, ask yourself these three questions:
1. How does what I think, do or say affect me?
2. How does what I do or say affect others?
3. How does what I do or say affect God's Kingdom?

> 'Now when they saw the boldness of Peter and John, and perceived that they were uneducated and untrained men, they marvelled. And they realised that *they had been with Jesus*' (Acts 4:13).

A preacher once said, "Those who claim to be Christian, yet refuse to live as Jesus commanded are denying and dishonouring Him. Jesus' pain did not end at the cross. It continues every time when we put our interests before His." Therefore, resolve today to give your life fully and unequivocally over to God, because when you truly die to yourself, then you can fully live for Him and be a true disciple of Jesus Christ.

Attitudes and Being a Christian
Selwyn Hughes wrote: 'By our attitudes are we nullifying the Christian message? Does our behaviour contradict the very truths we are trying to get across to others? If Christians are by definition, people in whom Christ lives, then should we not be showing more evidence that the risen Christ is alive within us?'[2]

Chapter Six

Spiritual Growth

'...Christ in you...Him we preach, warning every man and teaching every man in all wisdom, that we may present every man perfect in Christ Jesus' (Colossians 1:27b-28).

'...Grow in the grace and knowledge of our Lord and Saviour Jesus Christ. To Him be the glory both now and forever. Amen' (2 Peter 3:18).

"How can I measure my spiritual growth?" One of the easiest ways is to ask myself, am I closer to God now, compared to last week, last month or last year? Is my lifestyle glorifying to God? Am I trying to live a holy life, and relinquish my rights to Him? Can those I live with and work amongst, (Christians and non-Christians) see a difference in the way I act, talk and generally work? Does my life show forth the fruit of the Spirit and do I walk in the Spirit? (Galatians 5:22-25).

'But we all, with unveiled face, beholding as in a mirror the glory of the Lord, are being transformed into the same image from glory to glory, just as by the Spirit of the Lord' (2 Corinthians 3:18).

Our Walk with God

There are many stages in our walk with God, as we desire to become true disciples for Jesus. We need to step out in service with God, we have good deeds to do (Ephesians 2:10), we must exercise our abilities, talents, and spiritual gifts; step out in faith and use them for His glory. To neglect a talent or gifting is sin. Laziness grows on us; it begins in cobwebs but ends in chains. We may think we can do things without God, but that is pride; we will fall and be humbled.

Continually be filled with the Holy Spirit who will empower us (Luke 11:13, Luke 24:49, Acts 1:8, Acts 2:4 and Acts 4:31).

> The psalmist said, "Teach me to do Your will, for You are My God..." (Psalm 143:10).

To Grow as Believers

- Seek God continually (Psalm 37:4, Proverbs 3:5-6 and Matthew 6:33).
- Love God and others (Matthew 22:37-39 and 1 Corinthians 13:4-8).
- Know the Scriptures and apply them (Hosea 4:6, Hosea 6:3, John 14:15 and James 1:22).
- Abide with God, in obedience and prayer (John 15:1-11, John 16:23, 1 Thessalonians 5:17 and Jude 20).
- Fear God (Proverbs 1:7, Proverbs 8:13, Proverbs 9:10 and Ecclesiastes 12:13).
- Have a right heart (1 Samuel 16:7, 1 Kings 3:9, 1 Chronicles 28:9, Psalm 24:3-5, Psalm 86:11, Proverbs 16:1 and Proverbs 23:26).
- Pursue peace and unity among the brethren (Psalm 133:1, Acts 1:14, Acts 2:1 and Romans 14:19).
- Continually be filled with the Holy Spirit (Luke 11:9-10, 13, Acts 1:8 and Ephesians 5:18).
- Exercise your spiritual gifts (1 Corinthians chapter 12 and 1 Corinthians 14:1).
- Acknowledge your weaknesses but trust in God (Isaiah 40:31, John 3:30, 2 Corinthians 3:5, 2 Corinthians 10:18 and 2 Corinthians 12:9-10).
- Daily surrender your will to God (John 12:24-26, 2 Corinthians 5:15 and Galatians 2:20).
- Give no offence in what you do (2 Corinthians 6:3, Colossians 3:17 and 1 Thessalonians 5:22).
- Have a vision for your life (Proverbs 29:18).
- Honour God with your possessions (Proverbs 3:9-10, Malachi 3:6-10 and 2 Corinthians 9:6-12).
- Have a desire to witness (Matthew 28:19-20, Romans 1:16 and 1 Peter 3:15).
- If called to leadership, be a good leader (1 Samuel 15:22 and Proverbs 27:23).

Words of Wisdom

We will all encounter bad situations and difficult problems in the Christian faith. Handle these situations and problems in a mature, godly and dignified manner and you will grow spiritually. What would Jesus do? As each situation comes to you, give God the responsibility of the outworking of it and the teaching for you from within it (see Job 32:8-9). Learn to deal with any negative emotions in a godly fashion.

We all need to be discipled, encouraged, instructed and rebuked (2 Timothy 3:16-17) when necessary. Everyone has much to learn, keep a check on your lifestyle, and where possible try to teach and impart to others, what you know. With the Word of God we should continually grow in grace.

We have books to read, Christian seminars or conferences we can attend, mature brethren we can chat to, Christian TV to watch, CDs and MP3s to listen to, alongside free internet downloads, Apps and Christian websites to peruse. In addition, there are numerous teaching DVDs, all of which can inform, educate and edify; to help build us up in the most holy faith (Jude 20). Disobedience is costly; we need to put truth into practice. Remember that we are valued.

Why Believers Can Fail to Mature in Christ Jesus

- Overtaken by problems and difficulties, their eyes are not on Jesus in the difficult times (Romans 12:1-3).
- The arrogance of youth (1 Kings 12:1-19).
- Greed, the desire for more (Joshua 6:18-19, Joshua 7:1-21 and Acts 5:1-11).
- Problems with lust and adultery (2 Samuel 11:1-5, 2 Samuel 13:1-15 and Romans 8:5-8).
- The desire for power and prestige (Exodus 30:11-12, 2 Samuel 24:1-10, 1 Chron. 21:1-8 and Psalm 20:7).
- Compromising and not standing firm when called to obey God (1 Samuel 15:1-30).
- Jealousy (Exodus 20:17, 1 Samuel 16:14-23 and 1 Samuel 18:5-16).
- Fear of man (1 Samuel 15:24, Proverbs 29:25 and Galatians 2:6-16).
- Disobedience to the written Word of God (Deuteronomy 17:14-20 and 1 Kings 11:1-13).

- Disobedience to the spoken Word of God or the Holy Spirit (Numbers 20:7-12 and 1 Samuel 15:18-23).
- Ignorance of the written Word of God (Hosea 4:6, Acts 18:24-28, John 14:21 and James 1:22).
- Impatience (1 Samuel 10:8, 1 Samuel 13:8-14, Proverbs 25:28 and James 1:3-4).
- Unforgiveness (Matthew 5:7, Matt. 6:14-15, Matthew 18:15-35, Luke 17:3-4 and Ephesians 4:31-32).
- Not taking personal responsibilities seriously (1 Samuel 2:12-17, 22-33 and 1 Samuel 3:13-14).
- Lack of leadership, a leader should lead and not be led! (Exodus 31:18-32:35).

Issues That Can Hinder Spiritual Growth
- Cultural, historical and emotional bondages. These issues may not necessarily be sin, but wrong attitudes and ways of thinking which do not line up with biblical precepts.
- Past hurts, curses, abnormal fears, and poor theology will also send you down the wrong road and can be a hindrance or stop you dead.
- There is also a big danger of building a lot on a little, but especially when that little happens to be a preconceived idea. Any doctrine must come from God's Word and not your own ideal, culture or ideology (Romans 15:4, Romans 16:17, 1 Corinthians 10:11 and 2 Timothy 3:16-17).
- Focussing on a single doctrine to the neglect of others, we need to know the whole counsel of God.

Am I maturing in Christ Jesus? Am I closer to God now than one year ago? See Isaiah 28:9-10.

Further study: Psalm 84:4-5, 11, Psalm 119:105, 130, Luke 14:25-35, Acts 20:27, 1 Corinthians 3:1-2, Galatians 5:16-26, Ephesians 4:11-16, Hebrews 2:11-12, Hebrews 5:11-14, Hebrews chapter 6, 2 Peter 1:3-8 and 2 Peter 3:14-18. Paul's letters: (1 Corinthians to Colossians) and the Pastoral Epistles (1 Thessalonians to Titus).

Chapter Seven

Discerning the Voice of God

Jesus said, "...He who does not enter the sheepfold by the door, but climbs up some other way, the same is a thief and a robber. But he who enters by the door is the shepherd of the sheep. To him the doorkeeper opens, and the sheep hear his voice; and he calls his own sheep by name and leads them out...the sheep follow him, for they know his voice.... *My sheep hear My voice*, and I know them, and they follow Me and I give them eternal life..." (John 10:1-4, 27-28).

'Your ears shall hear a word behind you, saying, "This is the way, walk in it," whenever you turn to the right hand or whenever you turn to the left' (Isaiah 30:21).

"Sometimes I feel that God is speaking to me, but I am not always sure." Discerning the voice of God comes through experience, but even mature Christians make mistakes and get things wrong on occasions. God will never tell you to do anything that contradicts His Word as revealed in the Holy Bible. Any so-called 'word' can be from God, the devil or from one's own imagination (wishful thinking) (Jeremiah 14:14 and Jeremiah 23:25-36). Some people speak with two spirits; the Holy Spirit, but are also influenced by another spirit (Job 26:4), this is often because their lives are polluted and they have compromised in an area.

The Holy Spirit speaks lovingly, reassuringly, encouragingly and will guide you into all truth and inform you of things to come (John 14:26 and John 16:13). God's Word will bring peace into your life even if it is a rebuke (Colossians 3:15). Whereas the devil accuses, nags, and speaks in a mocking manner; he will try to confuse you with regards to God's will by sowing doubt, fear and discouragement into your mind, "Did God really say?" (Genesis 3:1-4).

Hearing God

Hearing God is sometimes only possible when you have taken, or are forced to take times of quietness. You may not be able to hear or discern properly when you are busy so learn to be quiet in His presence, during times of prayer. Be still and ask God to speak to you (Psalms 46:10 and Isaiah 40:31). As you continue in fellowship and daily communion with God you will gradually become more sensitive to His voice. However, it is not just being able to hear God's voice that it is important, so is obedience (James 1:22. See also John 14:15, John 14:21 and 1 John 5:2-3). This includes doing things that you may not like to do or want to do. Obedience to God at whatever cost should be at the forefront of your heart and mind at all times.

God's Guidance

God has promised to guide the believer, but there are conditions that need to be met (Psalm 25:9, Psalm 32:8 and Isaiah 42:6). It is foolish to think that God will reveal things to you when you are in deliberate and wilful sin, because your prayers will get no higher than the ceiling (Psalm 66:18, Proverbs 28:9, Isaiah 59:2-15 and Ezekiel 14:3). Also, do not expect God to reveal His will to you if you have not obeyed the basic revealed will of God as found in the Holy Bible.

Prayer and abiding in the Father's will is essential for discerning what God wants to reveal to you in whatever walk of life you are in (John 15:1-11 and Acts 2:42). If you are not sure (and we are all like that sometimes, see 1 Samuel 3:1-11), ask God to confirm what He has said; Gideon asked for a sign by using a fleece, and received extra confirmation (Judges 6:15-40 and Judges 7:7-15). Consider asking for advice from your pastor, elder, respected prophet or a mature Christian who knows you well (1 Corinthians 7:17-24). Continually seek God's presence, and you will understand His will for your life. Work hard and be diligent.

'Trust in the Lord, and do good; dwell in the land, and feed on His faithfulness. Delight yourself also in the Lord, and He shall give you the desires of your heart. Commit your way to the Lord, trust also in Him, and He shall bring it to pass' (Psalm 37:3-5).

How God Can Speak to You

- Through the Scriptures, His Word the Holy Bible.
- The Holy Spirit's small still voice (1 Kings 19:9-18, John 14:26, Acts 10:19, Acts 13:2 and Romans 8:16).
- Your inner witness, conscience (Acts 15:28 and 1 John 3:20-21).
- Audibly like another person speaks (Exodus 3:4 and Exodus 33:11), though this is not common.
- Being rebuked by others (even via non-Christians), "Christians shouldn't do that!"
- Through Christians, by means of the gifts of the Holy Spirit, a word of wisdom, a word of knowledge or a prophecy etc. (Jeremiah chapter 42 and 1 Corinthians chapters 12-14). If you receive a word from God via another believer then weigh it and pray it. Test the spirits whether they are of God or not (1 Thessalonians 5:19-21 and 1 John 4:1-3). If you are not sure then ask God for confirmation (1 Corinthians 14:26 and 2 Corinthians 13:1b).
- Through nature or inanimate objects, e.g. a book, the television, magazine, etc., something just sticks out or jumps out and grabs your attention.
- By a dream, a vision or a trance (Genesis 41:8, 15-16 and Acts 10:16).

'Your Word is a lamp to my feet and a light to my path' (Psalm 119:105).

Four Choices in Life

There are four kinds of choices in life that Christians need to make and of which God is clear:

1. Those which God has said an emphatic *no*.
2. Those things which God has said an emphatic *yes*.
3. Those in which He wants us to consult our own sanctified preferences.
4. Those few and rare matters about which we cannot acquire enough information to permit us to make intelligent decisions and so special guidance from God must be sought.

In relation to the above four points A. W. Tozer noted:

1. Never seek the leading of the Lord concerning an act that is forbidden in the Word of God.
2. Never seek the leading of the Lord concerning an act that has been commanded in Scripture.
3. Except for those things that are specifically commanded or forbidden, it is God's will that we be free to exercise our own intelligent choices.
4. When we are forced to choose between two possible courses in life then look at James 1:5-6 (asking for wisdom) and Isaiah 48:17 (the Lord will lead you in the way to go) – here we have God's faithful promises to guide us in the right way.[1]

Checks From God

- The Holy Spirit may forbid you (Acts 16:5-10, until Acts 19:10).
- Lack of peace (Colossians 3:15).
- Lack of opportunity, doors open or close (1 Corinthians 16:8-9, Colossians 4:3 and Revelation 3:8), but in 2 Corinthians 2:12-13, even though a door had opened for Paul in Troas, he had no peace.
- Lack of a direct Word from God, a *rhema* Word (Psalm 119:105 and Isaiah 30:1-2, 21).
- If you have the mind of Christ then the correct fruit and attitude will be manifested within your spirit (1 Corinthians 2:16 and Galatians 5:22-23). Do you have joy or peace about a given decision or will? (Psalm 16:11, Isaiah 55:12, 2 Corinthians 5:7 and Philippians 4:7). Is there doubt or faith, love or fear, joy or unhappiness, patience or impatience?

Conviction of the Holy Spirit / Condemnation of Satan

- The Holy Spirit is gentle and loving. Satan condemns and generates fear.
- The Holy Spirit gives encouragement. Satan brings discouragement.
- The Holy Spirit helps to discipline us. Satan tries to destroy us.
- The Holy Spirit convicts us of sin. Satan encourages us to sin.

- The Holy Spirit points us to God. Satan focuses on our weaknesses and failings.
- The Holy Spirit confirms that confessed sin is forgiven. Satan tells us it is not.
- The Holy Spirit reminds us there is hope. Satan tells us there is no hope.
- The Holy Spirit encourages fellowship with believers. Satan discourages it.
- The Holy Spirit points us to God's Word. Satan points us to our feelings.
- The Holy Spirit reminds us of the cross. Satan reminds us of our own works.
- The Holy Spirit reassures us of God's love. Satan accuses and says we're hated and rejected.

How God *May* Get Your Attention

- A dream (Genesis 41:8, 15-16, 32), especially when it is confirmed!
- Disappointments (Genesis 40:14-23).
- Circumstances (Exodus 2:11-15).
- Unusual circumstances (Exodus 3:1-7).
- Plagues (Exodus chapters 7-11). Not common!
- Judgments (Numbers chapter 16).
- A tragedy (Numbers 21:4-9).
- Lack of provision, due to theft (Judges 6:1-10).
- Lack of resources (1 Kings 17:5-10).
- Failure or presumption (Joshua 7:1-26). See also Numbers chapter 13 and Psalm 19:13.
- Through someone else (1 Samuel 3:15-18).
- Unanswered prayer, often because of sin (2 Samuel 12:9-23 and Psalm 66:18).
- Restlessness, unable to sleep (Esther 6:1-3).
- Sickness (Isaiah chapter 38). This is an extreme method of which most Christians will not encounter. However look at Genesis 32:24-32, 2 Chronicles 21:6-19, Psalm 119:67, 71, 75, Luke 1:11-20, 57-64 and Acts 13:6-12 for extreme cases!
- Affliction (Acts 9:1-9 and Acts 13:11).
- Through God's goodness (Romans 2:4).

- Through a prophecy (1 Corinthians 12:10 and Acts 11:27-30).

Please note: this list is not exhaustive.

The Truth

- Jesus is the Truth (John 14:6).
- God's Word is truth (John 17:17).
- The Holy Spirit is Truth (1 John 5:6).
- Buy the truth (Proverbs 23:23).
- Abide in the Word of truth (John 8:31-32).
- Be guided into truth (John 16:13).
- Love the truth (2 Thessalonians 2:9-12, this Scripture is in a negative form).
- Obey the truth (1 Peter 1:22).

'The entrance of Your Words gives light; it gives understanding to the simple' (Psalm 119:130).

Do Not Deny Truth

It will cost you something to acknowledge the truth, but truth can save you. The ultimate judgment of God is to turn people over to error because of their deliberate and wilful rejection of the truth!

- Beware of the "spirit of slumber" because of the hardening of one's heart toward the things of God (Isaiah 29:9-13 and Romans 11:8).
- King Saul had an evil spirit sent from God because of his continual disobedience (1 Samuel 16:14-15).
- Those who suppress the truth in unrighteousness, God has given up to the defilement of the flesh; they have been given over to a debased mind, and have exchanged the truth of God for a lie, they serve the creature rather than the Creator (Romans 1:18-32).
- God will send a strong delusion on those who do not receive the love of the truth, who have pleasure in unrighteousness (2 Thessalonians 2:7-12).

Further study: Psalm 37:23, Proverbs 3:5-6, Habakkuk 2:20, Acts 8:29 and Acts 11:12.

Chapter Eight

Finding God's Will

'...We also, since the day we heard it, do not cease to pray for you, and to ask that you may be filled with the knowledge of His will in all wisdom and spiritual understanding; that you may have a walk worthy of the Lord, fully pleasing Him, being fruitful in every good work and increasing in the knowledge of God' (Colossians 1:9-10).

'I beseech you therefore, brethren, by the mercies of God, that you present your bodies a living sacrifice, holy, acceptable to God, which is your reasonable service. And do not be conformed to this world, but be transformed by the renewing of your mind, that you may prove what is that good and acceptable and perfect will of God' (Romans 12:1-2).

"How can I know the will of God for my life?" By spending time with God you will gradually get to know His will for your life. However, do not run ahead or lag behind in His plans and purposes for you. You may only know what is around the corner for the next few months (and that is fine) because most people don't know the *entire* plan that God has for them, but take one day at a time (Matthew 6:34 and Proverbs 27:1). For most Christians, they continue in their trade, occupation or calling until God says otherwise (1 Corinthians 7:20), doing it all for the glory of God. The most important thing in any Christian's life is to become more like Jesus and to fully surrender to, and obey the Holy Spirit. As we continue on in fellowship we will gradually discern what is from God and what is not and get used to hearing His voice, and will know whether or not we are in His good pleasing and perfect will. Sometimes even the best Christians are not one hundred percent sure about certain things, but over time, God's will always becomes clearer for those willing to hear and obey. It is advisable to ask God to clarify to you His will or desire for the future. God has promised to guide the believer, but there are conditions that need to be met – don't live a sinful life (Psalm 25:9, Psalm 32:8-9, Proverbs 28:9, Isaiah 42:6 and John 16:13). You may wish to ask advice from your pastor, a respected prophet, elder or mature Christian who knows you well (1 Corinthians 7:17-24).

'Trust in the Lord with all your heart and lean not on your own understanding; in all your ways acknowledge Him and He will direct your paths' (Proverbs 3:5-6).

Four Calls of God
- A general call of salvation – 'Whosoever wills' (Revelation 22:17). God has no pleasure in the death of the wicked, but desires all mankind to be saved.
- An appointed call – The five-fold ministry of apostles, prophets, evangelists, pastors and teachers (Ephesians 4:10-13). The Bible also notes other gifts and graces of the Holy Spirit, see pages 31-32.
- An open call – "Who will go?" on missions etc. (Isaiah 6:8) or 'stand in the gap' in intercession on behalf of another (Ezekiel 22:30).
- A specific call – Saul was called to be King of Israel (1 Samuel chapters 9-12), you will probably not be called to be a king or queen of a country! But may be called to other things.

Being Faithful
If we are serious about desiring to do God's will, then we need to be considered faithful; not perfect or sinless, but having a heart after God, seeking Him and desiring to do that which is right in His eyes. If we cannot be faithful in the small things of life like cleaning, tithing, managing our finances, loving the brethren, witnessing to those in our home town etc., then God will not put us in charge of bigger things. Always commit the day to God, and any works that you know that you will be doing. God will guide you, and ask for wisdom and discernment as you commit the day's affairs to Him. God does give abilities and talents for specific jobs.

Words of Wisdom

Whatever your occupation, do not suddenly hand in your notice (or leave your studies), unless God has told you very clearly to do so. Is it His will? Sometimes it can be wishful thinking (you really dislike your job), your flesh or the devil trying to confuse you. Pray for God's will to be revealed (Colossians 1:9). Sometimes we want to run away when God has something to teach us through our job, a situation or event. If you start a God-given project, job, vision, task or objective then finish it with Him. If you have a God-given task to do, try to set a clear goal or specifics to aim at, not too big or too small, something that can be within your reach. Goals can always expand but you have to start somewhere. Don't allow circumstances or friends to dictate to you how it should be done. Take godly counsel, but well meaning people can give wrong advice (Job 12:12 and Job 32:6-10).

Seeking God for His will to be Revealed

- God has a good plan for your life (Jeremiah 29:11-13 and Romans 8:28-39).
- Prepare your heart to seek God (Ezra 7:10).
- Seek God and repent of all known sin (2 Chronicles 7:14 and Psalm 66:18).
- Seek God first, and then everything else will fall into place (Matthew 6:31-34 and Mark 12:30).
- Seek God's presence (Psalm 27:4, 8, 1 Chronicles 16:11 and 1 Chronicles 22:19a).
- You must have faith; God rewards those who diligently seek Him (Hebrews 11:6).
- Be meek and humble; seek righteousness (Zephaniah 2:3 and Psalm 51:17).
- God wants deeper fellowship with you (Rev. 3:20).
- Have fellowship with God (abide in Him) and receive answers to prayer (John 15:7, 1 John 1:6 and 3:24).
- Ask, seek, knock; persevere in prayer and receive (Matthew 7:7-8).
- Pray that God will bless you, believe it and pray for it. Jabez asked and he received! (1 Chronicles 4:10).
- Serve God wholeheartedly, He knows your thoughts (Psalm 119:21 and Chronicles 28:9).

- Stay close to God, otherwise, forsake Him and be forsaken (2 Chronicles 15:2b and Psalm 51).
- Ask in faith to be a wiser person (James 1:5-6), and forsake sin (Hosea 10:12).

The Call to Missions

In relation to missions – and you may receive a call to go on a short-term mission (STM) at home or abroad, though we should all evangelise as and when opportunities arise. The world is a needy place and the fields are white unto harvest, but most people can only work in one field (Matthew 9:38 and John 4:35). The question is 'what is my calling and field?' The need does not necessarily constitute a call. We can do many good things for God without Him, and He may even bless it, but when we do what He says, then He will anoint us for the task to bear fruit for His glory (John 15:7-8). There is a big difference between a blessing and an anointing (compare Acts 16:6 with Acts 19:10). God can speak to you in many ways. The Lord may burden your heart, or open your eyes to the needs of a certain people group (Psalm 37:23), or your church may be leading a STM.

Additional Steps of Obedience

- Fear God and He will teach you the way to go (Psalm 25:12, Proverbs 1:7, Proverbs 8:13a and Prov. 9:10).
- Move in step with God, not too quick or too slow (Psalm 32:9 and Galatians 5:25).
- God's timing is always critical and essential for any work (Isaiah 55:8-9 and Acts 16:5-10).
- Trust God entirely (Psalm 37:4-7, Psalm 37:22 and Proverbs 3:5-7).
- Yield / surrender yourself fully to God that you will know His will (Romans 12:1-2 and 2 Cor. 5:15).
- Obey God when He makes His will known to you, even when called *not* to do a good thing (Acts 16:6-10); the timing may be out (Acts 19:10).

Further study: Psalm 25:4-5, Psalm 123:2, Psalm 143:8, Psalm 143:10, Proverbs 8:17, Proverbs 20:24, Jeremiah 33:3, Acts chapter 16 and Ephesians 5:8-10.

Chapter Nine

Finding God's Direction

'I, wisdom, dwell with prudence, and find out knowledge and discretion. The fear of the Lord is to hate evil...counsel is mine, and sound wisdom; I am understanding, I have strength. I love those who love me, and those who seek me diligently will find me' (Proverbs 8:12-14, 17).

'I will instruct you and teach you the way you should go; I will guide you with My eye' (Psalm 32:8).

"I know God's will for my life, but how can I go about fulfilling it?" If God has shown you what to do, then He will also show you how to accomplish it. Sadly, all too often when God shows us something, we want to shout it from the rooftop and tell the world, but this is not wise (Nehemiah 2:12, Proverbs 12:23, Proverbs 14:33 and Luke 2:19). We must recognise that God's timing is right and that we must not run ahead, lag behind or reject the call that God has for us. The shepherd boy Joseph had a dream that was not fulfilled until nearly three decades later (Genesis 37:4-10 and Genesis 45:7-8). What God has revealed to you may be for an appointed time and not within the next day or two (Habakkuk 2:2-3). God spoke to Abram (later called Abraham) and Sarai (later called Sarah) and promised them a child. After many years had passed they tried to accomplish God's plan by natural means through Hagar. Ishmael was born; but he was not the son of the promise and this led to strife and continual conflict. The promised seed of Isaac was not birthed until all natural hope was lost (Genesis chapters 15-19 and 21). Sometimes we have to get to the end of our tether, before we are ready to accomplish God's will. At other times, the direction of God is one way and because of various Divine circumstances and events in our lives we end up somewhere different. Getting from A to B as we follow God may not be in a straight line or how we think it should be done. We may also get sidetracked along the way or because of our future work or ministry, we may have to pass through various experiences and tests.

Jesus said, "…I must be about My Father's business" (Luke 2:49b).

God speaks to different people in different ways. He directed Joseph by several dreams. He spoke to Moses from the burning bush in an audible voice (Exodus 3:2-4). He led the Israelites in the wilderness by a pillar of cloud and fire (Exodus 13:21). He spoke to the Israelites via the Urim and Thummim (Numbers 27:21). He showed David his calling through the prophet Samuel (1 Samuel 16:3-13), and through Nathan a word of rebuke (2 Samuel 12:1-14). God also spoke to King David with regard to battle tactics because he asked for advice (1 Chronicles 14:10, 14). He sent words to the prophet Jehu for others (1 Kings 16:7, 12). He whispered to Elijah in a still small voice (1 Kings 19:11-12). God sent the Archangel Gabriel to Mary with a very important message (Luke 1:26-35). Jesus appeared personally to Paul in a glorified body (Acts 26:14-19 and 1 Corinthians 15:3-8). In the early days of the Church, Agabus the prophet warned the disciples of an impending famine (Acts 11:28-30). The Holy Spirit told Philip what to do (Acts 8:29), and spoke to others (Acts 10:19, Acts 13:2 and Acts 16:6-7). Timothy was directed through the laying on of hands by the presbytery (1 Timothy 4:14 and 2 Timothy 1:7). See also Romans 1:11.

Obedience is Key
Very often an act of obedience is required before a word from God can be fulfilled (Acts 8:29 and Acts 9:6). Abram had to leave his homeland (Genesis 12:1-3), before his seed could eventually possess the Promised Land nearly five hundred years later! God may ask you to do something before He reveals the full plan (1 Samuel 16:1-3). King David made preparation for the building of the temple, but it was his son Solomon who built it (see 2 Samuel 1:7-17 and 1 Chronicles 22:1-5). During the Israelites forty years of

wanderings in the desert, Moses had to strike the rock before water would come out (Exodus 17:5-7). However, on another occasion he had to *speak* to the rock, but instead, he hit the rock and so was not allowed to enter the Promised Land (Numbers 20:7-12). The incident with Moses reveals to us that disobedience is costly. Disobedience is extremely foolish. It cost King Saul his dynasty (1 Samuel 13:13-14 and 1 Samuel 15:10-31). If God calls you then it will cause change, and sometimes it can cause disturbances; others may want to tag along with you, like Lot did when Abram left Ur of Chaldeans, but this led to strife and confrontation (Genesis 13:4-11). Abram later had to rescue Lot who had been taken captive (Genesis 14:11-16). God is always willing to point someone in the right direction, especially when He knows that they will be obedient to Him.

Jesus said, "...Not what I will, but what You will" (Mark 14:36b).

J. Hudson Taylor founded the China Inland Mission in June 1865. To a friend who needed guidance he wrote: 'Light will no doubt be given you. Do not forget, however, in seeking more, the importance of walking according to the light you have. If you feel called to the work, do not be anxious about the time and way. He will make it plain...I desire increasingly to leave all my affairs in the hands of God, who alone can and who assuredly will, lead us aright if humbly and in faith we seek His aid.

'...I urge on you...the importance of seeking guidance from God for yourself personally apart from the movements of others. Each one of us has an individual duty and responsibility towards Him. The conduct of others cannot make duty, for me, of that which is not so; nor can the claim of duty be lessened because of the action, right or wrong of others. We may and should thank God for all the help He gives us through others in performance of duty. But let us seek to see our own way clearly in the light of His will and then in trial and perplexity we shall be 'steadfast, unmoveable,' not having trusted to an arm of flesh. The Lord guide and bless you and give you ever to lean unshaken on His faithfulness.'[1]

Two Right Choices (see also page 44)

A choice between right or wrong is not difficult for a disciple to make, but when the choice is between two right things then we need some extra help. Godly council will go a long way (Proverbs 11:14, 12:15, 15:22, 19:20, 20:18 and 24:6). God may speak to you directly, through the Word (a passage from the Holy Bible) or directly to your spirit. A prophet or someone with a word of wisdom or knowledge may speak into your situation (Jeremiah chapter 42 and 1 Corinthians chapters 12-14). However we should all be led of the Holy Spirit and therefore we will ultimately glorify Jesus (Acts 16:6-7). If you have the mind of Christ then the right fruit will be manifested within your spirit (1 Corinthians 2:16 and Galatians 5:22-23). Do you have joy or peace about a given decision? (Psalm 34:13, Isaiah 55:12, 2 Corinthians 5:7 and Philippians 4:7). Is there doubt or faith, love or fear, patience or impatience? The Holy Spirit can guide us into all truth, (John 14:26 and John 16:13). On one occasion, the apostle Paul was forbidden by the Holy Spirit to preach the Gospel in Asia Minor (Acts 16:6-7) – simply because the *time* was not right. When he was permitted to go, everyone in the area had heard the Good News within two years (Acts 19:10). Remember, the Holy Spirit can give us specific directions and commands (Acts 8:29, 10:19, 11:12 and 13:2).

'Those who seek the Lord understand all' (Proverbs 28:5b).

Team Decisions

Stepping out in faith on your own is one thing, but if there is a spouse (or a ministry team) involved and they also help shape decisions, then there needs to be unity. God will not be saying opposing things, though individuals may be acting out of confusion, fear, wishful thinking, delusions or grave disagreement. When everyone who are involved in making decisions are in unity with God and each other, then the right course of action can be determined and the blessing can and will prevail (Psalm 133).

Further study: 1 Samuel 28:6, 1 Chronicles 15:13, Nehemiah 7:65, Proverbs 16:9, Psalm 31:3 and Psalm 123:2.

Chapter Ten

Knowing the Way to Fulfil God's Direction

'A man's heart plans his way, but the Lord directs his steps' (Proverbs 16:9).

'As the eyes of servants look to the hand of their masters, as the eyes of a maid to the hand of her mistress, so our eyes look to the Lord our God...' (Psalm 123:2).

"How can I accomplish the work that God has called me to do?" In many respects, it all depends on what God has called you to do. It may be quite simple, like put a wrong right, or go and speak to someone. On the other hand, God may be calling you to be part of a specific group, attend other church meetings, change career or go on a short-term mission (STM).[1] It is important not to be paralysed by fear. Fear of the unknown or fear of what people may think, but be obedient to God. If you do step out in believing faith and get it wrong (it does happen) you will have learnt a good lesson (or two) and God will not punish you for it; you may just feel a little embarrassed – we've all been there.

The saddest words ever spoken or written were, "It might have been." William Carey was a shoemaker by profession who became the Father of Modern Missions. He sailed to India in 1793 and translated the Bible (or portions of) into 40 languages. He said, "Few people know what may be done till they try and persevere in what they undertake." Thomas Edison was the inventor of the light bulb who patented over one thousand inventions. He said, "If we did all the things we were capable of doing we would literally astonish ourselves."

The Way of God

God's timing is different from man's and His ways are much higher. What may seem very illogical or even humanly irresponsible can only be understood in the light and revelation of God's infinite wisdom and knowledge.[2]

The way of God includes: His timing, His methods, the necessary resources to accomplish it, who is involved, the when, where and how (but not always the why, as we are called to trust God, walking by faith and not by sight, 2 Corinthians 5:7), and continual guidance, patience and perseverance to see the job or task accomplished.

What God is directing you to do may be different than your friend. God leads people in various ways and trains them under different circumstances. Abraham had to walk across the entire land of Canaan to claim it as his inheritance (Genesis 12:7-13:1-17), but Joshua led Israel to possess the land through a series of battles and this was after Israel had been enslaved in Egypt for four hundred years (Joshua chapters 1-5). In both instances, God's will was revealed to them, but the way to fulfil it was different and so was the timing; they had to patiently endure. If you try to birth a work outside of God's will, method or timing, you could cause a lot of problems for yourself and others (see Genesis 21:5-11).

Do whatever God tells you to do in His timing and in His way. God's way is a walk of faith, we cannot depend on natural knowledge for all the answers; you must have Divine revelation of God's will (Ephesians 5:17 and James 1:5).

'Commit your works to the Lord and your thoughts will be established' (Proverbs 16:3).

Biblical Principles to Fulfil God's Direction
- To succeed, a work has to be according to God's plan (Psalm 127:1).
- Look to God and depend on Him entirely (Psalm 123:2 and Isaiah 51:1).
- Trust God and acknowledge Him in all things (Proverbs 3:5-6).
- God can see our motives (Proverbs 5:21, Proverbs 16:2 and Proverbs 21:2).
- God is in complete control of all situations, however bad they appear (Proverbs 20:24).

- God may do something different from what you have imagined (Isaiah 55:8-9).
- Have a loyal heart towards God; He is watching (2 Chronicles 16:9).
- The Lord will guide you, if the conditions have been met (Proverbs 16:9).
- God will instruct, teach and guide you (Psalm 32:8).
- Commit your work, plans and the day's affairs to God, (and dedicate all completed jobs, Deuteronomy 20:5), whilst trusting in Him (Psalm 37:4-5).

'I will instruct you and teach you the way you should go; I will guide you with My eye' (Psalm 32:8).

Missionary to China, J. Hudson Taylor, was giving advice to a group of pioneers who were under his leadership and reminded the group that there are several different ways of working for God. He said, "One is to make the best plans we can and carry them out to the best of our ability. This may be better than working without a plan, but it is by no means the best way of serving our Master. Or, having carefully laid our plans and determined to carry them through, we may ask God to help us and to prosper us in connection with them. Yet another way of working is to begin with God; to ask His plans and to offer ourselves to carry out His purposes."[3]

Words of Wisdom

In any form of work (secular or sacred) if you have the wrong motivation or use improper principles your plans will not succeed. Always check your motives (1 Chronicles 28:9 and Proverbs 5:21). If God has told you to do something (and you abide by His rules), He will give you the ability, wisdom, knowledge and resources to accomplish the task. Business people know how to succeed in a hard world but so does God, however there is often enough difference in principle and method to make them incompatible with the way of Jesus Christ (Isaiah 30:1-2).

Missionary, Alfred Ruscoe served with C.T. Studd (the founder of the Worldwide Evangelisation Crusade – WEC) in the Belgian Congo during the 1920s. He said, "The supreme test of faith is waiting and it yields the supreme reward." And, "Waiting and being content to wait, can be the most difficult thing in Christianity." In relation to his boss (the then leader of WEC), he said, "Norman [Grubb] says that 'What happens to you is incidental, but how you react is all-important.' "

Essential Issues to Think About

- God-given wisdom is needed (Exodus 28:3, Exodus 31:6 and Ezra 7:25). Ask and seek God's wisdom (Proverbs 8:12-14, 17 and James 1:5).
- Your heart needs to be stirred and motivated for the job (Exodus 35:26).
- You need God's Spirit of wisdom, understanding and knowledge (Exodus 35:31-33, Exodus 31:3 and Exodus 35:30) with the skills and expertise (Exodus 35:35).
- Teach and impart to others (Exodus 35:34).
- Materials for the job, if needed (Exodus 35:21, Nehemiah chapter 3 and Haggai 1:14).
- God-ordained plan (Exodus 25:9, 1 Chronicles 28:19, Ezekiel 43:11, Acts chapter 10 and Acts 16:6-10). God's thoughts are higher than yours (Isaiah 55:8-9).
- Pray to be strengthened by the Holy Spirit (Ephesians 3:16b and Ephesians 3:19b-20).

'...We also, since the day we heard it, do not cease to pray for you, and to ask that you may be filled with the knowledge of His will in all wisdom and spiritual understanding; that you may have a walk worthy of the Lord, fully pleasing Him, being fruitful in every good work and increasing in the knowledge of God; strengthened with all might, according to His glorious power...' (Colossians 1:9-11).

Further study: Psalm 37:4-5, Psalm 63:1, Psalm 63:3, 8a, Psalm 69:32, Psalm 127:1, Isaiah 26:9, Matthew 6:33-34, Ephesians 5:8-10 and Galatians 6:9.

Chapter Eleven

Servant-Hood

Jesus said, "If anyone desires to be first, he shall be last of all and servant of all" (Mark 9:35).

Jesus said, "Many who are first will be last, and the last first" (Mark 10:31).

As Christians, we are called to serve others and to love our neighbour as ourselves. To become a servant means that we serve other people joyfully and willingly, even in the most menial of tasks, regardless of our status or position, and that can include non-Christians. Jesus was God's Son, yet He came as a servant to serve mankind (Matthew 12:18-21). To demonstrate servant-hood Jesus washed the disciples' feet (John 13:3-17), and He was their teacher. Jesus was a meek and humble person and had God's seal of approval on Him. He spoke and moved with authority, yet willingly served mankind by giving His life as a ransom and was led as a lamb to the slaughter for the sins of mankind (Isaiah 53:7, Matthew 7:29, Mark 1:22, 27 and John 19:9-12).

'Paul, a servant of God and an apostle of Jesus Christ...' (Titus 1:1). As was Simon Peter (see 2 Peter 1:1).

Servant-hood is doing your Christian duty without expecting to be thanked or recognised for what you have done (Luke 17:7-10). Servants do not seek man's approval, but desire to honour God in all that they do (1 Corinthians 10:31 and Galatians 1:10-12). In God's eyes, the bank manager and the baker are both alike, one position is not higher than the other. Being a servant of Christ means that you do not exalt yourself, your position or title (see Proverbs 25:6-7, 27, Luke 14:7-11 and 2 Corinthians 10:18). Genuine servants want to do the will of the Father. Sometimes you have to serve upward to those in authority (1 Timothy 6:2), and at other times downward to those who are in need (Matthew 25:35-40). Servant-hood can mean many different things and can be worked out in many different ways. It may be cleaning tables (Acts 6:1-8), carrying shopping for an elderly person, preaching the Word of God (2 Timothy 2:2 and Titus 1:9), cleaning of pots and pans, chair arranging for the Sunday morning service etc., (see 1 Chronicles 9:31-32), but will always be in relation to serving others.

David was a shepherd and served under King Saul before he became king. Joseph served Potiphar's household and then his fellow prisoners before he became Prime Minister of Egypt. Elisha was the servant of Elijah for around twelve years before he became a mighty prophet. The apostles and elders served one another and their flocks.

The Apostle Paul Learnt Servant-Hood

- The apostle Paul referred to himself as the 'least of the apostles' (1 Corinthians 15:9), the 'least of all the saints' (Ephesians 3:7-8), and finally the 'chief of sinners' (1 Timothy 1:15).
- Paul was separated to the work that God had called him to (Romans 1:1 and Galatians 1:11-18).
- Paul submitted to the church at Antioch for a period of testing in whatever duties they wanted him to do (Acts 13:1). He then became a teacher (2 Timothy 1:11 and Acts 13:1-3).
- Paul's calling and anointing was recognised through his faithful serving and he ended up becoming an apostle (1 Timothy 1:12 and 2 Timothy 1:11), who wrote much of the New Testament.

A True Servant

Jesus said, "If anyone desires to be first, he shall be last of all and servant of all" (Mark 9:35). If you desire to become a real disciple and servant of God, you must abide by Jesus' rules and not those of the world. If Jesus is not Lord of all, then He is not Lord at all. Jesus was the only perfect Servant; He was not forced into that role – it was one He freely chose. Jesus knew that the cross awaited Him, but He set out resolutely towards Jerusalem (Luke 9:51-56). Jesus learnt obedience by suffering (Hebrews 5:8) and so may we.

A true servant is called and is commended by God and approved of Him to do certain works which have been pre-planned by Himself (2 Cor. 10:18 and Ephesians 2:10). That is to say, we all have good deeds to do. Not to work for our salvation (because it is a free gift), but because of our salvation. However, 'whoever has this world's goods and sees his brother in need, and shuts up his heart from him; how does the love of God abide in him? ...Let us not love in word or in tongue, but in deed and in truth' (1 John 3:17-18). These verses are directed towards the family of God, assisting the brethren in their time of need, but still reiterates the biblical principle of love in action. 'If your enemy is hungry, give him bread to eat and if he is thirsty, give him water to drink' (Prov. 25:21). See Matthew 5:44 & 19:19-21.

True servants need a deep foothold on the Rock of Christ (to stand strong amidst criticism) and must delight to do His will. Servant-hood, humility and meekness are needed to be worked out within a Christian's life in conjunction with the fruit of the Spirit (Galatians 5:22-23). Like Abraham, we have a choice to make. Abraham was a servant of God because of his obedience, sacrifice and loyal service to the Master, and was called 'the friend of God' (Isaiah 41:8). The twelve disciples of Jesus had been enrolled in Jesus' college of everyday life; they graduated from servants to friends due to their obedience (John 15:14-15). See John 14:21.

Submission to Authority

Brokenness and a contrite heart is a requirement for Christians and this is what God looks for (see Psalm 51:17, Isaiah 57:15 and 66:2). Jesus revealed that you can either be broken by your submission to Him or ground to powder by your rebellion (Matthew 21:44). If we are not with Jesus then we are against Him! (Luke 11:23). To be broken means to submit your will to the Master. The breaking process deals with submission to all authority, whether it is God's authority or delegated authority (Romans 13:1-2). It is wrong to submit only when we agree and there is a big difference between *submitting* and *delighting* as we can submit begrudgingly, which is sinful, see Ephesians 5:10 and Philippians 1:10.

Servant-Hood Can Go Wrong

Martha was *working for Jesus*, being hospitable whilst Mary was *in the presence of Jesus*, listening to His every word, (Luke 10:38-42). Your performance is not as important to Jesus as your presence. Martha was distracted by her work for Jesus and that is a danger that many can fall into. He told her that "only one thing is needed," and her sister was doing it. Servants of Christ should not fill their diaries with such schedules that they are unable to help someone in need. Sometimes, a person just needs a listening ear so that they can unburden them self or share their concerns or fears.

False servant-hood is where you do and say the right things but for the wrong motives. You can either be prideful and rebellious or live in the realm of humility and the fear of the Lord (Proverbs 22:4, Isaiah 57:15 and 66:22). As the writer, Duc de La Rochefoucauld (1613-1680) correctly noted: 'We would often be ashamed of our finest actions if the world understood all the motives which produced them.'

Solomon's son, King Rehoboam wanted to lord it over his subjects, but was advised by the elders to be a servant and serve his people. He rejected this godly counsel and lost the respect, taxes and the support of the nation of Israel (1 Kings 12:1-19), a lesson for all leaders. Self-promotion and servant-hood do not mix. Sadly, some people begin as servants but end up as celebrities and superstars because being in the spotlight can blind you!

God does not measure greatness in terms of status; but in terms of service. Not by how many serve you, but by how many people you serve. Everybody wants to lead, but not many want to serve. You may not be gifted for a particular task, but if nobody is around (at work or at church), you may have to do it. If you do not have a servant heart you may be tempted to use your spiritual gifts or talents for personal gain or to use it as an excuse to exempt yourself from areas you consider 'beneath you' (see Ecclesiastes 10:7).

Further study: Isaiah 53:7, Luke 22:24-27, John 5:30, John 15:5, Romans 12:3, 1 Corinthians 12:23, Philippians 2:1-7, Titus 2:9, James 4:6, 1 Peter 5:5 and 1 John 3:16.

Chapter Twelve

Being Faithful

Jesus said, "He who is faithful in what is least is faithful also in much; and he who is unjust in what is least is unjust also in much. Therefore if you have not been faithful in the unrighteous mammon, who will commit to your trust the true riches? And if you have not been faithful in what is another man's, who will give you what is your own?" (Luke 16:10-12).

Jesus said, "His lord said to Him, 'Well done, good and faithful servant; you have been faithful over a few things, I will make you ruler over many things. Enter into the joy of your lord' " (Matthew 25:23).

"How can I prepare for the call of God on my life?" Being faithful in whatever God has called you to do is the best preparation for today, in anticipation of tomorrow. Regardless of your occupation or family situation, do your very best in all your duties. Be faithful and trustworthy in everything; stay true to your calling, giving all the glory to God (1 Corinthians 15:58 and 1 Timothy 3:11b).

Faithfulness is a quality that is sadly lacking in many Christians' lives (Proverbs 20:6). We say one thing yet do another. We give our word, only to break it. We promise to help out, but get distracted by something of lesser importance. We rush and hurry to finish a job when our heart is elsewhere, and end up cutting corners or quitting early, this is not faithfulness and cannot be condoned.

Faithfulness involves commitment that will not casually make excuses to be exempt without hesitation or remorse for the slightest of reasons (1 Samuel 3:1-11). If you are incapable of doing the mundane and the not-so-great things you will not be qualified for anything greater (Matthew 25:23). We all have to start at the bottom and work our way up. Less-than-perfect service is always better than the best of intentions, the more we do, the more we learn and the better we will become – it is all part of our character building and training in life.

God has called us to be faithful, in both the big and the little and we must obey, and leave the results to Him. All as God wills, who wisely heeds, to give or to withhold. What is important is that you fulfil God's purpose for your life. Have you been faithful and diligent in what God has called you to?

Faithful In

Priesthood (1 Samuel 2:35), as a son-in-law (1 Samuel 22:14), in accountancy (Nehemiah 13:13), ambassadorship (Proverbs 13:17), writing and recording (Isaiah 8:1-2), stewardship (1 Corinthians 4:2), faithful to the Lord (1 Corinthians 4:17), faithful in Christ Jesus (Ephesians 1:1). Tychicus was a faithful minister (Ephesians 6:21 and Colossians 4:7). Faithful teacher of the Scriptures (2 Timothy 2:1-2 and Titus 1:9) and a faithful brother (1 Peter 5:12). The apostle Paul was placed in ministry for being faithful (1 Timothy 1:12).

'So the governors and satraps sought to find some charge against Daniel [who was one of three governors over a vast empire] concerning the kingdom; but they could find no charge or fault, because he was faithful; nor was there any error or fault found in him' (Daniel 6:4).

Use or Lose

If you fail to use your God-given talents that you have been entrusted with – you may lose them (Matthew 25:14-30). Do each task with equal determination and dedication, whether at home, at work or at church and never quit or leave the job half done. Don't run away if things become difficult; it is a learning curve and God is trying to teach you something (Ecclesiastes 10:4). If you do run away, you will only have to go through a similar experience until you have learnt what God has been trying to teach you!

Further study: 1 Chronicles 26:6-8, Proverbs 28:20a, Acts 6:1-8, Acts 16:14-15 and Colossians 1:7.

Chapter Thirteen

The Call of God for Service

'I thank my God, making mention of you always in my prayers, hearing of your love and faith which you have towards the Lord Jesus and towards all the saints. That the sharing of your faith may become effective by the acknowledgement of every good thing which is in you in Christ Jesus' (Philemon 4-6).

'Take heed to the ministry which you have received in the Lord, that you may fulfill it' (Colossians 4:17).

"I know God has called me to do a specific work for Him, but what shall I do?" The call to service is the summons of God to your spirit, for a special and specific service. This service for God may be in your normal day job (secular) or it may be a specific call (sacred) to the ministry. The terminology of 'secular and sacred' is not disparaging to one or used to uplift the other, as we are all called to do all for the glory of God. Imagine if all Christians left their secular jobs to go into Christian ministry. Where would the witness be to the vast majority of the population? The mechanic must be a good witness in his or her job (and to one's neighbours) as the teacher, checkout assistant, minister or the financial advisor. As a Christian, you should try to meet the spiritual needs of your colleagues. You are the light at work and should be the evangelist / missionary to them. Show forth the love of Christ, and use wisdom and discernment when sharing the Good News. Many believers are called into full-time Christian ministry, more are part-time whilst the majority of Christians have normal day jobs and support the others.

There is a big danger in wanting to tell the world about your calling and discussing it with anyone and everyone in your church, cell group, with friends and via social media, whilst in the process of seeking advice (or just blabbing!). When the apostle Paul heard the call of God, he 'did not immediately confer with flesh and blood' (Galatians 1:16), he did not rush out to consult with anyone else but fully trusted in God as 'He who calls you is faithful...' (1 Thessalonians 5:24). God may have given you a call for full-time Christian service, but you will have to wait until He appoints you to such a position.

> 'O Lord, I know the way of man is not in himself; it is not in man who walks to direct his own steps' (Jeremiah 10:23).

The Call of God
- The call of God is an 'upward calling' (Philippians 3:14), and is on another level from all other interests and claims of life. The higher calling to fully obey God must mean more to you than anything else (see Luke 9:57-62 and Luke 14:25-35).
- The call of God is a 'holy calling' (2 Timothy 1:9), something that is sacred and needs to be protected from compromise or defilement.
- The call of God is a 'heavenly calling' (Hebrews 3:1), a voice from heaven which calls you to Christian service, whether it comes as 'a still small voice' (as in Elijah sheltering in the rock, 1 Kings 19:9-12), or as 'the sound of many waters' (Revelation 1:15), it is the voice and calling of Almighty God.

Chosen and Commissioned to Christian Service
Jesus said, "Many are called but few are chosen" (Matthew 22:14). Many Christians are called by God into His service, some from a very young age and some later in life. Whether you choose to accept the call or reject the call is your responsibility with eternal ramifications (Joshua 24:15 and Ezekiel 3:18-20). Proverbs 1:24-32 issues a solemn warning against deferring to answer the call of God.

The commission to service is a general command, "Preach the Gospel to every creature" (Mark 16:15), but the general call is followed by an individual designation, "The fields are white unto harvest" (John 4:35). The total collection of fields is the whole world. You need to hear the order, which will tell you where your own field is and begin to break up the fallow ground (Jeremiah 4:3). Sow the correct seed, water it in prayer and watch it grow for the glory of God (1 Corinthians 3:6-7). For others, it may be a case of 'where can I go and be effective – where is the harvest?' Jesus said we should pray for more labourers to be sent out into the harvest and that the fields are white unto harvest (see Matthew 9:37-38 and John 4:35-38). You may be the answer to your prayers!

Tested by God

Between the time when a Christian is called by God into service and the time that service is actually appointed by God, there is nearly always an intervening period of testing and proving; to see if you can cope (Genesis 22:1, Exodus 15:22-25, Proverbs 24:10 and Jeremiah 12:5). Moses tried to save Egypt with his call from God, but without yet being appointed by Him; Moses ran for his life, but his wilderness experience changed him as he trusted in God and not in himself. Testing produces patience, genuine faith and godly character (James 1:2-3, 1 Peter 1:6-7 and 2 Peter 1:1-10).

God may test you if you are called to service in two main ways: By allowing things to become hard or by allowing things to become easy. You may be disappointed by one and give up, or fall into pride from the other which will trip you up (see Mark 4:1-20 and Luke 8:4-15, the parable of the sower).

Selwyn Hughes wrote: 'The Greek word for temptation is *peirasmos*. It means to test, to try or prove. The biblical use of the word (unlike the modern use of it) does not contain the idea of seduction or entrapment, but rather conveys the idea of putting a person to a test in order to deepen their personal qualities. The reason God allows temptation, then, is because it can lead to the development of the character.'[1]

Before the apostle Paul was released into the world, he had a period of training and testing. Paul was separated to the work that God had called him to (Romans 1:1). Paul is silent as to what happened in Arabia, but God was dealing with him and eventually God revealed the full Gospel to him (Galatians 1:11-18 and Galatians 2:1-2). Paul submitted to the church at Antioch for a period of testing in whatever duties they wanted him to do (Acts 13:1). Paul later wrote about the importance of testing and faithfulness (1 Cor. 4:2 and 1 Timothy 3:10). Once Paul passed the test in the ministry of 'helps' (1 Cor. 12:28), he was promoted to the office of teacher (2 Tim. 1:11 and Acts 13:1-3). Paul's calling and anointing was recognised through his faithful serving (1 Tim. 1:12). We are all called to be an example (1 Tim. 4:12).

Callings – Saved to Serve

Some callings endure 'only for a time' until 'tribulation or persecution arises.' Others get ensnared by 'the cares of the world, the deceitfulness of riches and the desires for other things [which] choke the word...' (Mark 4:17-19). Those who God accepts for His service must not be deterred by the one nor entangled by the other (Psalm 44:18). If you esteem God's Word above all else and fully trust in it (as the truth) and apply it into your life, then you will always come through trials victoriously (see Job 23:10-12, Psalm 119:15-18, 27 and Jeremiah 15:16).

Those with a Divine calling cannot live like those without one. That which God tolerates in some, He will not tolerate in those He has called into Christian ministry (the standard of leadership is far higher). Those with a Divine calling should differentiate between what I *can* do and what I am *supposed* to do. Deciding what you're not going to do is equally important. A true disciple with a Divine calling will say "no," especially to the good, in order to produce the best. The prophet Jeremiah was called from a very early age (Jeremiah 1:5-8), and described his test of loneliness as 'bearing the yoke in youth,' having to sit alone and keep silent as God had laid it on him (Lamentations 3:26-28 and Jeremiah 15:17). Jeremiah was also called not to take a wife, as a sign against Israel (Jeremiah 16:2).

If you commission yourself, you will serve yourself and your own agendas (Romans 12:3). If you go into the ministry without God's calling and appointing, you will go in your own strength and gifting. However, when God calls and appoints you, you can go in His authority and see a larger anointing with greater eternal fruit (John 15:1-11).

Further study: 1 Samuel 15:22-23, Galatians 1:10, 2 Corinthians 10:18, Ephesians 1:18 and Titus 3:1-2.

Chapter Fourteen

God-Given Vision

'Where there is no revelation the people cast off restraint [perish]...' (Proverbs 29:18).

'Delight yourself also in the Lord, and He shall give you the desires of your heart. Commit your way to the Lord, trust also in Him, and He shall bring it to pass' (Psalm 37:4-5).

"How do I go about fulfilling God's vision for my life?" In its simplest answer, it is to obey God in all that He has for you and often that is right where you are now (1 Corinthians 7:20). A general vision is to see something accomplished (which may be a revelation from God), where certain objectives or goals need to be accomplished. Another type of vision is a supernatural one that is direct from God and not everybody gets these (Joel 3:28). It can be best described as a movie screen in front of you (or sometimes within a dream), where a scene plays out before you (Isaiah 1:1, Ezekiel 40:2 and Acts 16:9-10). Sometimes supernatural visions are given to introduce (or to reinforce a more general vision for direction and action), or to show you something that God intends to do through you. The apostle Paul was not disobedient to his heavenly vision; Jesus revealed Himself and showed him that he would be a minister and witness of the things that he had seen and of the things that would be later revealed to him (Acts 26:13-16).

In the Old Testament, there were often seasons of no widespread revelation from God (1 Samuel 3:1). From Malachi in the Old Testament, to Matthew in the New Testament there were four hundred years of silence. In the twenty-first century, there is no silence from God. We have the Holy Bible to instruct and guide us (2 Timothy 3:15-17 and Hebrews 4:12), especially when it is applied to our daily lives and situations (James 1:22). We have the peace of God to confirm His Word (Colossians 3:15), the Holy Spirit will lead us into all truth (John 16:13), and we all know right from wrong, but what are our motives? (1 John 3:19-21). In any form of work or ministry, if you have the wrong motivation or use improper principles your plans will not succeed. If God has told you to do something, He will give you the ability, resources, wisdom, and knowledge to accomplish the task.

Helpers, Hinderers or Harassers

When God gives you a vision that He wants you to fulfil, then other people may be brought alongside to confirm the vision and / or assist you. It can be relatively easy to start a vision in motion to fulfil the God-given task, but hard to keep the others with you until completion. Some 'visions' are not from God – and sometimes other people cannot keep up the pace or start to march to the beat of another drummer. Those who once were helpers can end up as hinderers or even harassers! Without a vision, many 'works' would not be started or completed (Ezekiel 12:21-28), however, some works are of the flesh where a person or organisation prefers to build its own kingdom rather than God's Kingdom (Matthew 7:21-23).

Questions to Consider

Certain critical questions need to be considered, when you receive a general (or a supernatural) vision from God.

1. What does the work consist of? What does it involve and its practical application. God told Noah to build an ark and gave precise dimensions (Genesis 6:13-22).

2. Is it for now, later, or for many years away? (Habakkuk 2:2-3). Abram (later called Abraham), was promised a child and descendants as many as the stars (Genesis chapter 15).

3. What preparation can I do now in anticipation of God's timing or appointing? King David prepared all the building materials for the temple so that his son Solomon could build it (1 Chronicles chapter 17 and chapter 22).

Follow Christ

Jesus saw what His Father was doing and followed suit (John 5:19). Likewise, we are to follow in the footsteps of Jesus (John 17:18 and John 20:21). Saul (later called Paul), had a vision of Christ, who told him to go into the city of Damascus (Acts 9:1-9). Ananias also had a vision and was told to meet Saul (Acts 9:10-19). In a vision Cornelius, a Roman centurion, saw an angel of God and was told to send for Simon Peter, who was in Joppa staying at a tanner's house by the sea (Acts 10:1-8). Peter received a vision (Acts 10:9-16), which opened his heart and mind to the Holy Spirit's direction. He went with Cornelius' servants to a Gentile household where he preached the Good News and the Holy Spirit fell – revival broke out! (Acts 10:17-24).

Words of Wisdom

If God gives you a vision (a task to accomplish), then it is advisable to write it down, lest you forget over time (Habakkuk 2:2). When the going gets difficult you can refer to it (this is what God said), and be encouraged in the Lord rather than quitting. Timing is very critical to accomplish any vision (Habakkuk 2:3). The will of the Lord must always be accomplished (Ephesians 5:17). God-given wisdom is needed to work to your full potential (Exodus 28:3, Exodus 31:6 and Ezra 7:25). Pray for and seek God's wisdom (Proverbs 8:12-14, 17 and James 1:5). You will need God's Spirit of wisdom, understanding and knowledge (Exodus 35:31-33, Exodus 31:3 and Exodus 35:30-35).

Ask people to pray for you, that you may be filled with the knowledge of God's will in all wisdom and spiritual understanding (Colossians 1:9), and receive the spirit of wisdom and revelation in the knowledge of Him (Ephesians 1:15-19). A prayer to be strengthened by the Holy Spirit (Ephesians 3:16b and Ephesians 3:19b-20).

For a vision to see fulfilment, you can expect opposition. Keep your eyes on Jesus, lest you become discouraged (Hebrews 12:1-3). Keep focused on the job and abide by God's rules (Nehemiah 6:1-4 and 2 Timothy 2:3-6).

Accomplishing your Vision

- Have a plan, 'Without counsel, plans go awry, but in the multitude of counsellors they are established' (Proverbs 15:22). 'The plans of the diligent lead surely to plenty, but those of everyone who is hasty, surely to poverty' (Proverbs 21:5).

- Seek good advice, 'The first one to plead his case seems right, until his neighbour comes and examines him' (Proverbs 18:17).
- Don't overstretch yourself, 'A prudent man foresees evil [hard times] and hides himself [is prepared] but the simple pass on and are punished [quit]' (Proverbs 22:3).
- Expect difficulties, 'If you faint in the day of adversity, your strength is small' (Proverbs 24:10), see also Jeremiah 12:5, being tested in the small things.
- Be prepared to be discipled and disciplined, 'He who rebukes a man will find more favour afterward than he who flatters with the tongue' (Proverbs 28:23).

Character and Vision
- Have integrity, 'He who walks with integrity walks securely, but he who perverts his ways will become known' (Proverbs 10:9).
- Be honest, 'Wealth gained by dishonesty will be diminished, but he who gathers by labour will increase' (Proverbs 13:11).
- Work hard, 'The way of a slothful man is like a hedge of thorns, but the way of the upright is a highway' (Proverbs 15:19).
- Be dedicated, 'He who tills his land will have plenty of bread, but he who follows frivolity will have poverty enough!' (Proverbs 28:19).
- Interpersonal relationships, 'He who has knowledge spares his words, and a man of understanding is of a calm spirit. Even a fool is counted wise when he holds his peace; when he shuts his lips, he is considered perceptive' (Proverbs 17:27-28).
- Look to God and be humble, 'Pride goes before destruction and a haughty spirit before a fall. Better to be of a humble spirit with the lowly, than to divide the spoil with the proud' (Proverbs 16:18-19, see also Deuteronomy 8:6-20).

Further study: Daniel 1:17, 2 Cor. 12:1 and Eph. 5:8-10.

Chapter Fifteen

We Must Pray

Jesus said, "You have not chosen Me, but I have chosen you and ordained you that you should go and bring forth fruit, and that your fruit should remain; that whatever you shall ask of the Father in My name, He may give it to you" (John 15:16).

Jesus said, "Seek first the Kingdom of God and His righteousness, and all these things shall be added unto you. Therefore do not worry..." (Matthew 6:33-44).

"How is the best way to pray?" Prayer usually begins with "Our Father," and ends in "Jesus' name, amen." What you put in between is up to you, but we have a model prayer, The Lord's Prayer in Matthew 6:9-13 as a general guide. We should not come to God *only* to ask things from Him. We must, praise, worship and thank Him for who He is and what He has done for us. We can also thank Him for our many blessings and petition Him to do things (on behalf of others) and to help us in our daily needs – however big or small they may appear. Prayer is a two-way communication, be still before God and listen to what He has to say to you. Most Christians accept that prayer is vital for the life of the believer, and still acknowledge their inadequacy. There are numerous distractions lurking around every corner, social media, the pleasures of entertainment or socialising which can rapidly consume our time and distract us from the more important issues in life. Set aside time each day for prayer.

Scriptures on Prayer
- Jesus said, "I say to you, ask, and it will be given to you; seek and you will find; knock, and it will be opened to you" (Luke 11:9).

- 'As for me, I will call upon God...' (Psalm 55:16).
- Jesus said, "Whatever you ask in My name that will I do, that the Father may be glorified in the Son. If you ask anything in My name, I will do it" (John 14:13-14).
- Jesus said, "If you abide in Me and My Words abide in you, you will ask what you desire and it shall be done for you" (John 15:7).
- Jesus said, "...Whatever you ask the Father in My name He will give you. Until now you have asked nothing in My name. Ask and you will receive that your joy may be full" (John 16:23-24).
- Jesus said, "I say to you that if two or three of you on earth agree concerning anything that they ask it will be done for them by My Father in heaven. For where two or three are gathered together in My name, I am there in the midst of them" (Matthew 18:19-20).

Key Scriptural Principles for Answered Prayer
- Confess all known sin (Psalm 66:18).
- What is our motive in praying for ——? Is the Father glorified through your prayers? (John 16:23).
- Is it a need or a want? (Matthew 6:9-13).
- Is it God's will? (1 John 5:14).
- Ask in Jesus' name (John 16:23).
- Believe and have faith (Mark 11:24).
- Be persistent in prayer (Luke 18:1).

Seven Conditions for Answered Prayer

1. Prayers Falling on Deaf Ears Due to a Sinful Lifestyle
- 'If I regard iniquity in my heart the Lord will not hear' (Psalm 66:18). See also Psalm 18:24.
- 'He [God] also shall be my salvation, for a hypocrite could not come before Him' (Job 13:16).
- 'One who turns away his ear from hearing the law, even his prayer shall be an abomination' (Prov. 28:9).
- 'Let us search out and examine our ways, and turn back to the Lord; let us lift our hearts and hands to God in heaven. We have transgressed and rebelled; You have not pardoned. You have covered Yourself

with anger…You have covered Yourself with a cloud that prayer should not pass through' (Lam. 3:40-44).
- 'The Lord is far from the wicked, but He hears the prayer of the righteous' (Proverbs 15:29).
- 'Who may ascend into the hill of the Lord? Or who may stand in His holy place? He who has clean hands and a pure heart, who has not lifted up his soul to an idol, nor sworn deceitfully. He shall receive blessing from the Lord' (Psalm 24:3-5). C.f. Psalm 15 and Ezekiel 14:3-11.

2. Unforgiveness Hinders Prayers (2 Cor. 2:10-11)
- Jesus said, "If you forgive men their trespasses, your heavenly Father will also forgive you. But if you do not forgive men their trespasses, neither will your Father forgive your trespasses" (Matthew 6:14-15).
- Jesus said, "…Whenever you stand praying, if you have anything against your brother forgive him, that your Father in heaven may also forgive your trespasses" (Mark 11:25). C.f. Matthew 5:23-24.
- Prayers can also be hindered when your marriage is not what it should be, (see 1 Peter 3:7).

3. Continue to Seek God's Face
- 'When You said, "Seek My face," my heart said to You, "Your face, Lord, I will seek" ' (Psalm 27:8).
- 'Seek the Lord and His strength; seek His face evermore' (Psalm 105:4). In the context of our daily needs we are told not to worry (Matt. 6:9-13, 25-34).

4. Live a God-Glorifying Life
- Read Psalm 15, Psalm 24:1-6 and Galatians 5:22-35 which denotes the characteristics of the godly.
- 'As He who called you is holy, you also be holy in all your conduct, because it is written, "Be holy, for I am holy" ' (1 Peter 1:15-16).

5. Believe and Have Faith
- Jesus said, "…Whoever says to this mountain, 'Be removed and be cast into the sea,' and does not

doubt in his heart, but believes that those things he says will come to pass, he will have whatever he says. Therefore I say to you, whatever things you ask when you pray, believe that you will receive them and you will have them" (Mark 11:23-24).

- James wrote: 'Ask in faith, with no doubting, for he who doubts is like a wave of the sea driven and tossed by the wind' (James 1:6). See Hebrews 11:6.

6. Living in Unity is a Key to Blessing

- We must all 'endeavour to keep the unity of the Spirit in the bond of peace' (Ephesians 4:3).
- If there is disunity within a church or a prayer group then there will be no blessing, for God commands the blessing when there is unity (Psalm 133).
- 'A kingdom divided against itself cannot stand' (Matthew 12:25).
- Jesus said, "If you bring your gift to the altar, and there remember that your brother has something against you, leave your gift there before the altar, and go your way. First be reconciled to your brother, and then come and offer your gift" (Matthew 5:23-24).

7. Abide in God and Pray What is on His Heart

- John 15:1-11 speaks of asking in prayer, abiding in God and then bearing much fruit, (see also 1 John 2:6 and 3:24). When you pray what is on God's heart, then as the conditions are met the prayer will be answered. When you have the victory, the assurance, you know that God will intervene, then thank Him as any other prayer is a prayer of doubt.

Please note that from the time of assurance of victory that God will answer your prayer (or intercession), there may incur time-lag as in the case of Daniel's twenty-one day delay (Daniel 10:12-13). You have the victory, but the outworking of the prayer may not be instantaneous, the timing is in His hands which may differ from ours (Isaiah 55:8-9), but it is decreed in heaven (Psalm 119:89).

Further study: Psalm 73:1, Isaiah 59:1-3 & John 9:31, 14:15.

Chapter Sixteen

Intercession

'I have set watchmen on your walls, O Jerusalem, who shall never hold their peace day or night. You who make mention of the Lord, do not keep silent, and give Him no rest till He establishes and till He makes Jerusalem a praise in the earth' (Isaiah 62:6-7).

'We do not wrestle against flesh and blood, but against principalities, against powers, against the rulers of this dark age, against spiritual hosts of wickedness in the heavenly places' (Ephesians 6:12).

"What is the difference between prayer and intercession?" All genuine Christians, true disciples of the Lord Jesus Christ pray daily and have a quiet time, but intercession is Holy Spirit led prayer with Divine results. Intercession is a person interceding, one who 'stands in the gap' (Ezekiel 22:30), on behalf of another for God's will to be fulfilled. Not everyone is called to be an intercessor, though we may be called to intercede (Holy Spirit led prayer on behalf of someone or something) on many occasions in our Christian walk.

Intercession is prayer, but it's not praying for the things we want or desire, but praying the will of God as revealed by the Holy Spirit. Sometimes we want God's will, i.e. souls to be saved, but in intercession it is God who gives us the burden and shows us *what* and *how* to pray, so that the prayer will be answered. Often there is an obedience to be followed, a place of abiding and if we step outside of this abiding then the intercession will fail which can lead to dire consequences for the person or situation we were interceding for.

Andrew Murray wrote: 'Jesus Christ taught us that the answer to prayer depended on certain conditions. He spoke of faith, of perseverance, of praying in His name, of praying in the will of God. But all these conditions were summed up in one central one: "If ye abide in Me, ask whatever ye will and it shall be done unto you" (John 15:7).

'It is only by a full surrender to the life of abiding, by the yielding to the fullness of the Spirit's leading and quickening, that the prayer-life can be restored to a truly healthy state. In intercession our King upon the throne finds His highest glory; in it we shall find our highest glory too. The faith in God's Word can nowhere be so exercised and perfected as in the intercession that asks and expects and looks for an answer.'

Scriptures on Intercession

- God said, "Son of man, I have made you a watchman for the house of Israel [your country or town]; therefore hear a word from My mouth, and give them warning from Me: "When I say to the wicked, 'You shall surely die,' and you give him no warning, nor speak to warn the wicked from his wicked way, to save his life, that same wicked man shall die in his iniquity; but his blood I will require at your hand. Yet, if you warn the wicked, and he does not turn from his wickedness, nor from his wicked way, he shall die in his iniquity; but you have delivered your soul" (Ezekiel 3:17-19).

- 'I exhort first of all that supplications, prayers, intercessions and giving of thanks be made for all men, for kings and all who are in authority, that we may lead a quiet and peaceable life in all godliness and reverence. For this is good and acceptable in the sight of God our Saviour who desires all men to be saved and to come to the knowledge of the truth' (1 Timothy 2:1-4).

- 'When they cast you down and you say, 'Exaltation will come!' Then He will save the *humble person. He will even deliver one who is not innocent; yes he will be delivered by the purity of your hands' (Job 22:30). See Psalm 15, Psalm 24:1-6, *Micah 6:8, Ephesians 3:10-12 and 1 John 5:16).

- 'The Spirit also helps in our weaknesses. For we do not know what we should pray for as we ought, but the Spirit Himself makes intercession for us with groanings which cannot be uttered. Now He who searches the heart knows what the mind of the Spirit is, because He makes intercession for the saints according to the will of God' (Romans 8:26-27).

Understanding Intercession, its Framework

An intercessor is one who 'stands in the gap' (Ezekiel 22:30), and intercession can be on a local, national or international level. Unless we have proved faithful in the little (see Luke 16:10, Proverbs 24:10 and Jeremiah 12:5), a local intercession, in regard to people, our church or other situation then we will not progress onto the level of national or international intercession as revealed through the lives of the prophets / intercessors of the Holy Bible. As a general rule, intercessors in regard to national or international events are called and set apart for that particular ministry, ordained of God and will generally have a prophetic gifting. God seeks intercessors but seldom finds them (Isaiah 59:16 and Ezekiel 22:30). Maybe because the cost is too great, higher than we want to pay, so like Jonah we avoid the call – but can we run from God?

God may call us to intercede for someone to be saved, for a healing, for an addiction to be broken, for a situation to be changed or for an event to come about. We can intercede for someone without them knowing about it and without even having contact with them. At times God may permit us to let the person know that we have been called of the Lord to intercede for them and their situation as a means of encouragement for them. At other times there has to be complete silence in regard to the intercession.

Before God can really use us in intercession, He needs to deal with our flesh life, our natural carnal nature and we need to be in submission to His will. He deals with us, but we have to be willing to surrender all to the Master. He needs 'clean vessels' that are fit for the Master's use. We are meant to live for Jesus, not for ourselves. Our will needs to die and God's will should be the number one priority. John the Baptist said, "He must increase, I must decrease" (John 3:30). We, like Jesus must also be 'about our Father's business' (Luke 2:49), and let us not forget that the disciples 'Forsook all and followed Him' (Luke 5:11). This does not mean that we hand in our resignation or make rash foolish decisions, but we must be in the will of God, whatever that is for each and every one of us. We must allow the Holy Spirit to deal with us. Our love of money, personal gain, dreams, ambitions and desires, all that we want or hold dear to us. God allows situations and events to mould us and to make us into the person He wants us to be. He is the Potter and we are the clay (Jeremiah 18:6), and 'All things work together for good...' (Romans 8:28).

The more we surrender to the Holy Spirit, the more He comes in and has more of us. The Holy Spirit has no body; He comes to indwell the believer. At conversion we receive the Holy Spirit (John 20:22). Then we need to be baptised in the Holy Spirit, to have our own personal Pentecost (Luke 11:11-13, Acts chapter 2 and Acts 8:15-17), but we must be continually filled (Acts 4:31); as C. H. Spurgeon said in regards to why we must continually be filled, "Because we leak!" It is a sin not to be filled with the Spirit, 'the fullness of God,' as we are commanded to! See Acts 1:4-8, Ephesians 3:19 and Ephesians 5:18.

Through our surrender the Holy Spirit does His intercessory work on earth and we become intercessors by reason of the Intercessor within us. As crucifixion proceeds (death to self) intercessions can begin. Jesus said, "Unless a grain of wheat falls into the ground and dies, it remains alone; but if it dies, it produces much grain. He who loves his life will lose it, and he who hates his life in this world will keep it for eternal life" (John 12:24-25). The apostle Paul wrote: 'I have been crucified with Christ; it is no longer I who live, but Christ lives in me; and the life which I now live in the flesh I live by faith in the Son of God, who loved me and gave Himself for me' (Galatians 2:20).

Miss Eva Stuart Watt, Home Secretary of the Sudan United Mission wrote: 'So much of our praying gets no further than the window panes. He teaches us to pray in the Holy Ghost. We pray then because we are burdened. We pray prayers that cost. We pray until we get the thing we asked for. The Spirit Himself makes intercession for us with groanings which cannot be uttered, and sometimes He leads us to be so burdened for souls that our feelings find expression better in groans than in words. Sometimes He takes us to the mountain to speak with God in the calm of heaven and sometimes into the garden to pray and sweat the Gethsemane prayer of soul agony.'

Intercession – the Will of the Lord

Intercession is praying *in* the will of the Lord for His will to be done and there is a distinction. God's general will as revealed in the Holy Bible is for people to be saved, but He may not *call* you to intercede for souls to be saved. We can be *generally* praying the will of the Lord as revealed in Scripture, but not interceding *in* the will of the Lord as *directed* by Him and that makes all the difference. 'He who searches the hearts knows what the mind of the Spirit is, because He makes intercession for the saints according to the will of God' (Romans 8:27).

In intercession, we stand before the Lord, called of Him and plead our case before Him, often the Holy Spirit 'groaning' in us (Romans 8:26). At other times, we can approach the Lord, 'stand in the gap' and because of our position in Him we can have a prevailing place with Him as was the case with Abraham. He stood in the gap for Sodom and Gomorrah (Genesis 18:16-33), and pleaded with God that if he found forty-five righteous persons in the land, surely He would not destroy it? Abraham got bolder and bolder as he approached the throne of grace, and finally all God needed to find were ten righteous people to avoid a judgement on the two godless cities. Abraham pleaded with God, from God's decision of fifty righteous people to Abraham's ten. Abraham literally changed the mind of God, because intercession so identifies the intercessor with the sufferer that it gives him a prevailing place with God. Abraham was walking uprightly before the Lord (abiding in His general revealed will of living holy etc.) and stood in the gap on behalf of the land and negotiated for His mercy towards these two cities. However, ten righteous people were not found.

Moses went up Mount Sinai and received the Ten Commandments, but as he descended he found the Israelites unrestrained and worshipping a golden calf – their new god! Moses got very angry and threw the stone tablets to the ground. God said, "Moses stand aside, I will kill all of them and start a great nation from you." What an offer, but selfless Moses said, "No Lord, don't do it, kill me, blot my name out of the book of life. Please spare these people" (Exodus 31:18-32:33). Moses offered his soul as a ransom for a nation! He was brought up in pharaoh's household yet chose to live with his slave brothers (Exodus 2:7-11 and Hebrews 3:5), thus identifying with them as he turned his back on the privileges of pharaoh's court. The apostle Paul similarly wanted his brethren (the Jews) to know Jesus Christ as the Messiah (Saviour) and was prepared to forfeit his own salvation in order that they could be saved! (Romans 9:3 and Romans 10:1).

The Three Aspects of Intercessory Prayer

There are three aspects to intercessory prayer: 1. Identification, to identify with a person or situation. 2. Agony, to agonise over a person or a situation. 3. Authority (an assurance), to know what to do and say, because we know the will of the Lord in the situation; or that we have the assurance, the victory that what we have interceded for will come to pass.

1. Identification: Jesus Christ is the ultimate Intercessor as He identified Himself with mankind. 'Though He was a Son, yet He learnt obedience by the things which He suffered' (Hebrews 5:8). Isaiah chapter 53 speaks about the Messiah's suffering as He identified with man. Christ is our example. Jesus suffered with us and for us – 'He was wounded for our transgressions, He was bruised for our iniquities, the chastisement of our peace was upon Him, and by His stripes we are healed.' Jesus wore human flesh and lived upon earth; He came down to our level. He was crucified on the cross of Calvary. Jesus died willingly, to stand in the gap to take the sins of mankind upon Himself, to pay for our redemption. He took the punishment that we deserved and stood in the gap as the ultimate Intercessor. '...He poured out His soul unto death, and He was numbered with the transgressors, and He bore the sins of many and made intercession for the transgressors' (Isaiah 53:12). 'For He made Him who knew no sin to be sin for us, that we might become the righteousness of God in Him' (2 Corinthians 5:21). Jesus 'ever lives to make intercession' for

us, and does whilst sitting at the right hand of God (Hebrews 1:3, 4:14-16, 7:25), because by His effective pleading to the Father He is 'able to save to the uttermost them that come to God by Him' (Hebrews 7:25-27). Jesus is our representative, because He gave His life for us, He came to save us. Jesus had no self-interest, only doing the will of the Father and came to finish the work. See Zechariah 3:1-5 where the Angel of the Lord defends Joshua the high priest.

2. The second characteristic of an intercessor is agony – to agonise over a person or situation – to prevail in prayer. The writer of Hebrews says that Jesus prayed 'with vehement [loud] cries and tears...*and was heard...*' (Hebrews 5:7). Periods of intercession can be painful, if not in themselves in the identification – it will cost us something to agonise and to plead, to travail to bring to birth that which we are interceding for. '...The Spirit Himself makes intercession for us with groanings which cannot be uttered' (Romans 8:26). Paul writing to the church at Rome, wished that he 'could be accursed from Christ' so that the Jews could meet the Saviour (Romans 9:3). Like Moses, he was prepared to sacrifice his salvation for theirs.

All through the Holy Bible we can find prophets and their intercessions: Isaiah went naked for three and a half years as a sign against Israel. Jeremiah was not allowed to marry as a sign of the horrors of captivity. Ezekiel was not allowed to cry when his wife died and lived on food by weight and water by measure as a sign that Jerusalem would be under siege and of the impending slaughter. Hosea had to marry a prostitute who was unfaithful and to buy her back to demonstrate God as a faithful husband wanting to take back His unfaithful bride, Israel. These cases of intercession are on a national level and God would not call you to national intercessions unless you have been found faithful in local intercessions, in regards to people, your church or other situations.

3. The third characteristic of an intercessor is authority, an assurance of victory. It can be one of two types:

i. The ability to stand in the presence of God, being certain of your position in Christ. Your mind is soaked in prayer and your spirit in intercession that you can command things to be done as you know the Lord's mind / will in a given situation.

It gives you a prevailing place with God, an authority to speak, declare or decree – hence why intercessors have a prophetic edge.

ii. The Holy Spirit in you and through your obedience (place of abiding) gains the objective, the answer to your intercession. As when Moses stood in the gap for Israel when Joshua and Hur held up his hands in battle against Amalek (Exodus 17:8-16).

The assurance of victory may not come for weeks, months or much longer. The time taken to complete a local intercession will be shorter than an international one – but whatever the duration, stand in the gap and complete your intercession.

The process of assurance is always after a period of intercession which includes identification, agonising (which can incorporate: weeping, travail, pleading and groaning in the spirit) which results in the assurance (spiritual authority), that the victory has been won in the heavenlies and will soon be manifested physically on earth because, 'Those who sow in tears shall reap in joy' (Psalm 126:5). Intercession can even deliver one who is not innocent by the purity of one's hands (Job 22:30), but there are situations which have run their course and judgment cannot be avoided, hence Israel's and Judah's captivities (Jeremiah 11:14, Jeremiah 14:11, Jeremiah 15:1 and Ezra 14:14, 20).

Abiding in the Vine (John 15:1-11)

Within any intercession there will be a place of abiding – that is an obedience which must be meticulously followed and observed, otherwise we will no longer be abiding and the intercession will fail. This can have terrible consequences. John chapter fifteen speaks of asking, abiding and bearing fruit to the glory of God. When you pray what is on God's heart (intercede), then as the conditions are met, the prayer will be answered. You may be interceding for weeks, months or years until you have the victory, the assurance that God will act or intervene over the intercession which He has held you responsible for.

Abiding can come in many shapes and forms, but the basis for all Christians is to live holy and to obey the revealed will of God as found in the Holy Bible. Abiding is additional levels of responsibility and accountability to the Lord. God knows your life and your responsibilities that you have with your family or at work and if He calls you to intercession then He will give you a place of abiding that He knows you can cope with. As an example, more than one hundred years ago, Rees Howells was a miner from Wales who was called into a life of intercession. He was used to having four meals a day. God did not call him immediately to have one meal every three days as his place of abiding and God never called him to a two week fast whilst down the mines, as it would have been impossible without supernatural intervention. God gradually led Rees into missing one meal a day, then only having two meals a day, then fasting an entire day, then having one meal every other day until he enjoyed his one meal every third day more than his previous four meals a day.

God may not call you to fast, but God may tell you that your place of abiding is to pray in your tea break or to read certain books of the Bible. You may be called to give up certain drinks (perhaps sugary soft drinks or caffeine) or sweet foods or any combination. Often an abiding is something that has a hold over you so that during your intercession you are also helped to break an addiction, unhealthy lifestyle or to help you die to self, as in the abiding of a Nazirite (Numbers chapter 6), especially not shaving or cutting your hair! You may be called to eat only simple foods, like Daniel (Daniel 1:8-16), or to only eat certain types of food, say one bowl of rice a day as you are identifying with the person or people you are interceding for. Your abiding may mean not going to a certain place (a place which is not sinful) which you are accustomed to attend or to socialise with certain people. You may be: called to read your Bible in your lunch break, forbidden to speak of your intercession, or to weigh yourself during your fast or any combination of abiding. The Holy Spirit will show you what He wants.

Experience has taught intercessors that God starts small and gradually increases responsibility as you climb the ladder of intercession. Whatever you are led to do, be obedient. As each intercession is completed then you will have gained a position, but the mind of the Lord must always be sought in each subsequent case.

In 1907, some women from Poona and the India Village Mission led out Gospel bands (evangelistic teams) from Mukti to a very idolatrous city called Panharpur, where large numbers of Hindu pilgrims congregated at several different seasons of the year. The teams were sent off by the Lord under the leadership of Miss Parsons who had received a vision from God. She said, "I had great travail for souls, and found myself in agony during which the Lord brought before my spiritual vision a picture of the idolatrous city. I had never visited it and had no idea of its size, but when the Lord brought its need before me in prayer I could see it plainly as though I had lived in it for years." In the vision she saw the four roads leading into the city, with the pilgrims prostrating themselves before the temple idols and a terrible "immense precipice of which they were not aware until they had fallen down, lost forever." When she arrived she saw the city as revealed to her, and cartloads of dead people who had been carried off by cholera. The evangelistic bands had the opportunity of preaching to 'hundreds and hundreds' and sometimes some were 'so convicted that they seemed just bound to the spot where they stand. We pray that a spirit of repentance will fall upon them.'

A former missionary to Ethiopia writing in 1937 after the Italian invasion and expulsion of all Protestant missionaries by order of Mussolini wrote: 'How impossible it is to estimate the value of intercessory prayer. Thousands will testify that burdens have been lightened, crooked places have been made straight, and defeat has been turned into victory simply because others have prayed. Israel's victory against Amalek at Rephidim, did not depend upon the size nor the strength of her army, but upon the outstretched hand of Moses, for, when Moses held up his hands, Israel prevailed and when he let down his hands, Amalek prevailed. In proportion as hands are uplifted in prayer for the army of the Lord in Ethiopia, so will it be sustained and strengthened in battle. Would that all Christians would realise the powerful weapon they have in prayer, and that they would wield it on behalf of those who are in such sore need of help.'[1]

Further study: John 15:1-11, 1 John 2:3-6 and 1 John 3:24.

Chapter Seventeen

The Great Commission (Missions)

Jesus said, "Go therefore and make disciples of all the nations...teaching them to observe all things that I have commanded you; and lo, I am with you always, even to the end of the age" (Matthew 28:19-20).

Jesus said, "Go into all the world and preach the Gospel to every creature" (Mark 16:15).

"What is the Great Commission?" It was Jesus' last command to His followers – to go and tell the world about Him, which is revealed most clearly in the two scriptures at the start of this chapter. Jesus Christ, the Son of God was the greatest missionary who ever walked this earth, because He left His familiar surroundings of heaven and came to earth. He identified with the people He lived with and moved amongst and came to 'seek and to save the lost.' It is our job to tell people about Jesus Christ, at home or abroad, to friends, neighbours or strangers. J. Hudson Taylor, founder of the China Inland Mission said, "The Great Commission is not an option to be considered but a command to be obeyed."

The following within this chapter are Scriptures that are related to the Great Commission, missions and evangelism.

Jesus said, "For God so loved the world that He gave His only begotten Son, that whoever believes in Him should not perish but have everlasting life" (John 3:16).

The Basics of Missions
- Jesus said, "Go into all the world and preach the Gospel to every creature. He who believes and is baptised will be saved; but he who does not believe will be condemned. And these signs will follow those

who believe: In My name they will cast out demons; they will speak with new tongues; they will take up deadly serpents; and if they drink anything deadly, it will by no means hurt them; they will lay hands on the sick and they will recover" (Mark 16:15-18).

- 'As cold water to a weary soul so is good news from a far country' (Proverbs 25:25).
- 'The fruit of the righteous is a tree of life and he who wins souls is wise' (Proverbs 11:30).
- 'Those who are wise shall shine like the brightness of the firmament and those who turn many to righteousness like the stars forever and ever' (Daniel 12:3).
- 'Sanctify the Lord God in your hearts, and always be ready to give a defence to everyone who asks you a reason for the hope that is in you...' (1 Peter 3:15).

The Essential Facts

- Jesus said, "And this Gospel of the Kingdom will be preached in all the world as a witness to all nations, and then the end will come" (Matthew 24:14).
- Jesus said, "Go therefore and make disciples of all the nations..." (Matthew 28:19).
- Jesus said, "My food is to do the will of Him who sent Me and to finish His work. Do you not say, 'There are still four months and then comes the harvest?' Behold I say to you, lift up your eyes and look at the fields for they are already white for harvest!" (John 4:34-35).
- 'For "whoever calls upon the name of the Lord shall be saved." How then shall they call on Him in whom they have not believed? And how shall they believe in Him of whom they have not heard? And how shall they hear without a preacher? And how shall they preach unless they are sent? As it is written: "How beautiful are the feet of those who preach the Gospel of peace, who bring glad tidings of good things!" ' (Romans 10:13-15).
- Jesus said, "Heal the sick, cleanse the lepers, raise the dead, cast out demons, freely..." (Matthew 10:8).

- Jesus said, "...That repentance and remission of sins should be preached in His name to all nations..." (Luke 24:47).
- Jesus said, "...Tarry in the city of Jerusalem until you are endued with power..." (Luke 24:49).

Satan's Defeat

- Because of the crucifixion, Jesus 'having disarmed principalities and powers, He made a public spectacle of them, triumphing over them in it' (Colossians 2:15).
- '...The Son of God was manifested that He might destroy the works of the devil' (1 John 3:8b).
- 'They overcame him [the devil] by the blood of the Lamb [Jesus Christ] and by the word of their testimony...' (Revelation 12:11).
- 'And the devil, who deceived them [the nations], was cast into the lake of fire and brimstone where the beast and the false prophets are. And they will be tormented day and night forever and ever' (Revelation 20:10).
- 'And the God of peace will crush Satan under your feet shortly' (Romans 16:20).

Our Responsibility

- 'Deliver those who are drawn towards death, and hold back those stumbling to the slaughter. If you say, "Surely we did not know this," does not He who weighs the heart consider it? He who keeps your soul, does He not know it? And will He not render to each man according to his deeds?' (Prov. 24:11-12).
- God says, "When I say to the wicked, 'You shall surely die,' and you give him no warning, nor speak to warn the wicked from his wicked way, to save his life, that same wicked man shall die in his iniquity; but his blood I will require at your hand. Yet, if you warn the wicked and he does not turn from his wickedness, nor from his wicked ways he shall die in his iniquity; but you have delivered your soul" (Ezekiel 3:18-19). See also Ezekiel 33:8-9.

- Jesus said, "He who is not with Me is against Me and he who does not gather with Me scatters" (Luke 11:23).
- Jesus spoke about the parable of the faithful steward and said, "That servant who knew his master's will and did not prepare himself or do according to his will, shall be beaten with many stripes. But he who did not know, yet committed things worthy of stripes will be beaten with few. For everyone to whom much is given, from him much will be required and to whom much has been committed, of him they will ask more" (Luke 12:47-48).
- 'On some [mockers and sensual person, those who are not converted, verses 18-19] have compassion, making a distinction; but others save with fear, pulling them out of the fire hating even the garments defiled by the flesh' (Jude 23-24).
- 'Brethren, if anyone among you wanders from the truth and someone turns him back, let him know that he who turns a sinner from the error of his way will save a soul from death and cover a multitude of sins' (James 5:19-20). See also Galatians 6:1.

Eternity and the Judgment
- Jesus said, "For God did not send His Son into the world to condemn the world, but that the world through Him might be saved. He who believes in Him is not condemned; but he who does not believe is condemned already, because he has not believed in the name of the only begotten Son of God" (John 3:17-18).
- Jesus said, "Most assuredly, I say to you, he who hears My Word and believes in Him who sent Me has everlasting life and shall not come into judgment, but has passed from death into life" (John 5:24).
- 'It is appointed for men to die once, but after this the judgment' (Hebrews 9:27).
- Many go there! Jesus said, "... Wide is the gate and broad is the way that leads to destruction, and there are many who go in by it" (Matthew 7:13).

Chapter Eighteen

My Responsibility for The Great Commission

Jesus said, "You shall receive power when the Holy Spirit has come upon you; and you shall be witnesses to Me in Jerusalem, and in all Judea and Samaria, and to the end of the earth" (Acts 1:8).

John the Baptist said, "Bear fruits worthy of repentance" (Luke 3:8).

"Can anybody go on a mission trip as part of the Great Commission?" All Christians are called to share the Good News of Jesus Christ in whatever sphere of work or place we are in, as we interact with people. However, people may have natural limitations (a disability), a family to look after or a work commitment that may prevent them from going away on a mission trip, known as a short-term mission (STM).

God has no pleasure in the death of the wicked, but desires all people to be saved (Ezekiel 18:32 and 1 Timothy 2:1-4). Romans 10:14 asks the question, "How shall these people hear and believe without somebody telling them?" Evangelism is sharing with other people what Jesus has done for the world, at home or abroad. All Christians are called to evangelise, though they may not be evangelists. Anybody who has a testimony can speak from personal experience. If you love Jesus, you will want to obey Him and tell others about Him (John 14:12-17, 21 and John 15:14-16). If He has changed you, He can change others!

All believers have specific jobs, good works and tasks to do as part of their calling and destiny (Ephesians 2:10 and 2 Timothy 1:9). Some believers are part of the five-fold ministry of apostles, prophets, evangelists, pastors and teachers from (Ephesians 4:10-13). However, there is an open call from God to all believers to be a part of His Great Commission (at home or abroad) and that includes being fully surrendered to the Holy Spirit, so as to be able to respond to the call of God, "Who will go?" (Isaiah 6:8), or "Who will stand in the gap?" (Ezekiel 22:30), in prayer. The apostle Paul intended to visit Asia Minor but had a vision, a calling to Macedonia, where he saw a man pleading, "Come and help us" (Acts 16:6-10) and so he went. The apostle Paul was not ashamed of the Gospel of Christ, knowing its power to save people (Romans 1:16). The book of Acts is like a mission manual where the Holy Spirit fuels the disciples to proclaim the Good News in word and in act (healings, miracles and signs and wonders). Jesus told the disciples that they needed to wait for the power of the Holy Spirit to make their work effective throughout the world (Acts 1:8). See also Acts 20:27. Have you received the Holy Spirit? – He is power for service!

Every Tribe, Tongue, People and Nation
In heaven, there will be believers from every tribe, tongue, people and nation praising God (Revelation 5:9 and 7:9). Jesus revealed that the Gospel of the Kingdom will be preached in all the world as a testimony and then the end will come (Matthew 24:14). Peter revealed that Christians can 'hasten [speed up] the coming of the Lord' (2 Peter 3:12). This can be achieved only when all people groups have had an opportunity to hear the Good News about Jesus and until then, Jesus cannot return. You may be the agent God can send and the instrument He can use. If you cannot go, you can certainly pray and you may also be able to financially support those who can go.
- Go ye (Mark 16:15).
- Give ye (Luke 9:13).
- Pray ye (Matthew 9:38).

Jesus said, "The harvest truly is plentiful but the labourers are few. Pray the Lord of the harvest to send out labourers into His harvest" (Matthew 9:37-38). God may want you to be the answer to your prayers! Be willing, open and obedient.

Why Go on a Short-Term Mission
The reason people go on a short-term mission (STM) is primarily to obey the command of Jesus – the Great Commission (Matthew 28:18-20, Mark 16:15 and John 4:35).

Going on a STM implies going somewhere outside of your usual residence, generally abroad, though not necessarily so as you may live in a big country. Some people live and work in another country for years or decades (sometimes planting a church), whereas other people will go on a STM, perhaps for several weeks, a month or during a year out before university or a career break (to support the local church, or help in humanitarian aid). Let us never forget this solemn truth – the Gospel is Good News *if* it arrives in time.

Jesus said, "Go into all the world and preach the Gospel to every creature. He who believes and is baptised will be saved; but he who does not believe will be condemned" (Mark 16:15-16).

God's Desire for Mankind

- God said, "For I have no pleasure in the death of the one who dies," says the Lord. "Therefore turn and live!" (Ezekiel 18:32).
- Jesus said, "It is not the will of your Father who is in heaven that one of these little ones should perish" (Matthew 18:14).
- Jesus said, "For the Son of Man has come to seek and to save that which was lost" (Luke 19:10).
- Jesus said, "Go out into the highways and hedges and compel them to come in that My house may be filled" (Luke 14:23).
- '…God our Saviour who desires all men to be saved and to come to the knowledge of the truth' (1 Timothy 2:3-4).

Doing God's Will as Jesus Did

- Jesus said, "My food is to do the will of Him who sent Me and to finish His work" (John 4:34).
- Jesus said, "I can of Myself do nothing. As I hear, I judge and My judgment is righteous because I do not seek My own will, but the will of the Father who sent Me" (John 5:30).
- Jesus said, "Did you not know that I must be about My Father's business?" (Luke 2:49).

- Jesus said, "Abba, Father, all things are possible for You. Take this cup away from Me; nevertheless, not what I will, but what You will" (Mark 14:36).

Our Total Dependency on God

- Jesus said, I am the Vine, you are the branches. He who abides in Me, and I in him, bears much fruit; for without Me you can do nothing" (John 15:5).
- Jesus said, "...I do not seek My own will but the will of the Father who sent Me" (John 5:30b).
- Jesus said, "Your [God the Father] will be done" (Matthew 26:42 and Luke 11:2).
- Jesus said, "Unless a grain of wheat falls into the ground and dies, it remains alone; but if it dies, it produces much grain. He who loves his life will lose it, and he who hates his life in this world will keep it for eternal life" (John 12:24-25).
- '... The people who know their God shall be strong, and carry out great exploits' (Daniel 11:32b).
- 'Now when they saw the boldness of Peter and John, and perceived that they were uneducated and untrained men, they marvelled. And they realised that they had been with Jesus' (Acts 4:13).
- Jesus said, "You shall receive power when the Holy Spirit has come upon you; and you shall be witnesses to Me in Jerusalem, and in all Judea and Samaria, and to the end of the earth" (Acts 1:8).
- 'This is the Word of the Lord to Zerubbabel, "Not by might nor by power, but by My Spirit," says the Lord of hosts' (Zechariah 4:6).
- Jesus said, "The Helper, the Holy Spirit, whom the Father will send in My name, He will teach you all things, and bring to remembrance all things that I said to you" (John 14:26).

The Apostle Paul and Mission Work

The church at Antioch sent out Barnabas and Saul (also known as Paul) as directed by the Holy Spirit on a mission trip (Acts 13:1-3). Later, the apostle Paul, as a preacher and teacher of the Gospel, decided to go on another missionary journey, to visit the brethren to aid their discipleship (Acts 15:35-36). Paul also sent out fellow labourers to assist in the work (Acts 19:21-22). Paul needed to go to specific places (Acts 20:13-16), but was also flexible as doors opened (1 Corinthians 16:5-9), or closed (Acts 16:7), as other opportunities were available (Acts 16:9-10). Jesus gave the command to "preach the Good News" therefore we should use our initiative and common sense as to when and where we should proclaim the good tidings. Peter stated that we should always be ready to share our faith (1 Peter 3:15).

Paul enjoyed starting a new work; he was a pioneer, (Romans 15:18-20), and knew that a job should be done properly (Romans 15:28-33), '...Diligence is man's precious possession' (Proverbs 12:27b). Paul often had a plan to visit a certain place where the brethren could assist him on his journey (2 Corinthians 1:15-17). Paul was not a quitter, but kept persevering, choosing not to dwell on the past; pressing onwards towards the goal, of the eternal rewards (Philippians 3:12-16 and Hebrews 11:24-27).

Short-Term Missions or More

A short-term mission (STM) between jobs, a year out or during a holiday period is often easiest for the vast majority of people and is a good taster to see if the person wants to do more (if that is their calling in life). Any mission will broaden one's horizons and is educational and beneficial. Jesus never lost sight of where He came from and where He was heading and neither must you. Pray for boldness in witnessing, regardless of whether you go on a STM or not (Acts 4:13 and Acts 4:28-31). God can use anybody who is willing; it's not your ability, but your availability. Don't try to squeeze God into your plans, fit into His. Jesus did not say, "Friends, I'm leaving you all, have a great pleasure-filled life, enjoy yourselves and remember to be good." Instead, He told them to go forth and proclaim the Good News of His Kingdom, preaching repentance and the forgiveness of sins in His name. Go and make disciples of all the nations and teach the new converts how to live, cast out demons, lay your hands on the sick and raise the dead. You will speak with new tongues, *serpents will be unable to harm you (*Psalm 91:13, Mark 16:18, Luke 10:18-19 and Acts 28:5), and if you (accidentally) drink anything deadly you'll be safe (Mark 1:15, Mark 16:15-18 and Luke 12:47). You go because you are commanded to; you trust in God because He is faithful; you have the Bible as your example and the Holy Spirit to guide you.

If you found a cure for cancer, it would be inconceivable to hide it from the rest of mankind. How much more inconceivable to keep quiet when you know that Jesus is the Way, the Truth and the Life, and the cure from the eternal wages of sin, which is death (John 14:6 and Romans 6:23). Will you be willing and obedient to the call of God? Is your heart tender and open to hear God's commission for your life? Is God calling you to go on a STM? See: *Short-Term Mission, A Christian Guide to STMs* and *How to Plan, Prepare and Successfully Complete Your Short-Term Mission* both by Mathew Backholer.

> 'Preach the Word! Be ready in season and out of season...' (2 Timothy 4:2).

Geoff Green in *Has God Given you a Mission?* wrote: 'Jesus gave the Great Commission to the disciples to go into all the world and preach the Gospel, but it was still necessary for them to wait for several weeks before being empowered for the mission. Saul and Barnabas were called by the Holy Spirit at Antioch to missionary service, but those with them still continued to pray and fast for them. The commission in both cases was very clearly given and did not need to be restated, but what was necessary was their personal preparedness for the mission to which they were called. Enthusiasm is just not enough; preparation of heart is an equal necessity. We may embark on an evangelistic or missionary project with great enthusiasm in response to the Great Commission given; this is good, but unless it is accompanied by an equally enthusiastic preparation of heart, it is unlikely to succeed. Take note of Solomon's wise comments here: '...He who makes haste with his feet, misses his way' (Proverbs 19:2b).'[1]

Further study: Isaiah 28:9-10, Acts 8:14-17, Acts 13:1-5, Acts 18:1-4 and Acts 18:18-28. www.MissionsNow.co.uk.

Chapter Nineteen

Preparing for a Short-Term Mission (STM)

'The Lord gave the Word; great was the company of those who proclaimed it' (Psalm 68:11).

'As cold water to a weary soul so is good news from a far country' (Proverbs 25:25).

"How can I prepare for a short-term mission (STM)?" The best way to prepare for any STM is to be God's representative to your fellow colleagues at college, university or work, where you are now. If you are not prepared to talk about God's plan of salvation to those whom you see regularly, it is very unlikely that you will share the Good News with a complete stranger on a STM. It should be easier to share with colleagues, but it can also be an unnerving time, especially if your lifestyle is wrong. Look to God for help, open your mouth and begin to talk. Pray for Divine opportunities to share your own testimony with people; this leads to telling them the Good News. Your lifestyle can project more than your words so strive to live honourably and holy.

'For "whoever calls upon the name of the Lord shall be saved." How then shall they call on Him in whom they have not believed? And how shall they believe in Him of whom they have not heard? And how shall they hear without a preacher? And how shall they preach unless they are sent? As it is written: "How beautiful are the feet of those who preach the Gospel of peace, who bring glad tidings of good things!" ' (Romans 10:13-15).

Short-Term Missions (STMs)
Reasons for going on a STM – you may go and preach the Gospel in another country because of the command of Jesus

Christ, "Go," the Great Commission (Matthew 28:18-20, Mark 16:15-18, John 20:21-22 and Acts 1:8). There is also the Divine call of God, which will specifically direct a disciple to go somewhere. The Book of Acts has clear examples of this leading, calling and direction: 'The Holy Spirit said,' 'Showed by the Spirit,' 'The Spirit told me' etc. (Acts 8:29, 39, Acts 10:19, Acts 11:12, 28, Acts 13:2 and Acts 16:6-7).

Five False Missionary Calls

Missionary to Africa, Joe E. Church in seeking guidance to the mission field warned of the five false calls that may 'ensnare people...who are not really meant to go.' This is also true for those considering STMs.

1. The *Humanitarian* Call. Human need is made the call. We are called to evangelise not civilise. If educational, industrial or medical work have been allowed to constitute the call, or have the first place, our days will end in spiritual failure.

2. The *Adventure* Call. Going to see the world – keep on pioneering – the heroic call. (C.f. Peter leapt overboard, but later the waves nearly overcame him).

3. The *Imitation* Call. It's the done thing to be a missionary [or go on a STM] all the keen people of the Christian Union become missionaries. But remember the saying that the devil may 'send a man to the mission field to stop him being a missionary!'

4. The *Self-Denial* Call. Devoted lives, relying on works for salvation, driven to bury themselves in foreign lands, determined to give up and to sacrifice all – letting reliance on works take the place of grace. Loneliness may drive a person into this class, and the cry may go up one day, "Lord we have left all...." But the answer will be, "I know you not."

5. The *Self-Seeking* Call. In this group are those who say, "Lord may we sit the one on Thy right hand and the other on Thy left?" Those who seek earthly promotion, and find it quicker in the mission field. It must be HIM and not I if our motive is pure'[1]

Before you embark on your STM ask yourself, "Why am I doing this?" You need to have the reason straightened out in your own mind, because on your STM you may (and

- 98 -

probably will) encounter difficulties (a team member may be problematic) and you will probably not be working on a paradise beach! You could be: In freezing temperatures of Siberia's outback, mosquito infested parts of Africa, working in Europe's polluted back alleys, trying not to get caught in a sensitive nation, ministering to the multitudes in Latin America or amongst the high altitudes of the Himalayas.

Who to Go With

There are many STM organisations who give opportunities for Christians to join up with a Christian venture for short periods of time, generally from two weeks, to a year. Often these works are in the realm of social action: feeding programmes, building homes or helping underprivileged people or working with a local church, organisation or charity. Your church may organise STMs (this helps the congregation to see the 'bigger picture' of Christianity in other cultural settings). You could go independently as many churches and Christian organisations are looking for assistance from within the body of Christ and you may be able to partner with them. There is no reason why you and some friends cannot go on a STM (if it be the Lord's will). Ideally it is better to go with someone who has had previous experience, but this is not always possible.

Research your Mission Field

By using the internet or buying a travel guide you will be able to research the country's history and culture. You should find out as much as you can. To include: language, religion, politics, cost of living, currency, staple diet and types of accommodation etc. Read about missionaries (and travel journeys) as they can give you invaluable insight into what you may encounter, i.e. God's faithfulness and principles for Christian work. If you go with a mission organisation they will be able to tell you all you need to know about your particular destination, but personal research should still be done. Evangelising in some countries is illegal or a sensitive issue. Obey the laws of the land, but if they contradict God's law (which has supremacy) then God's law must be obeyed, but be very wise and prepared for the consequences of possible persecution (verbally or physically), arrest or imprisonment

(Acts 5:25-29). If you step out in faith and heed the call of the Holy Spirit you will be amazed at what can be achieved.

Words of Wisdom
Life is too short to learn all that you need to know from personal experience so it is good to meet and work with fellow labourers and glean nuggets of truth from their efforts, trials and experiences. Ideally the pastors, missionaries etc. that you work with, need to be full of the joy of the Lord, Holy Spirit filled, on fire for Jesus and willing to sacrifice personal gain and comfort to see Jesus' name lifted high, whilst giving all praise, glory and honour to the One who has done so much for them. There will be difficulties and misunderstandings on any STM, so aim to live above the mark to hit the mark; walk in unity, humility and love; have a servant heart, learn to forgive and not to take offence.

A STM must not be mistaken for a holiday, though there may be time to relax, but it will be a time when each individual will have a job to do and it will need to be done efficiently, joyfully and unto the Lord. Mundane chores like cooking and cleaning will all need to be done. Don't expect silver service, your own room, a comfortable bed or the luxury of being able to eat your own staple diet. Be prepared for hardships, frustrations, discomforts and trials.

You will be watched very closely; every characteristic, talent, hobby, social time, indulgence, failing, idiosyncrasy (a peculiar or distinctive behavioural attribute), and sin will be seen and can lead to a downfall. Be a good witness by your speech, your lifestyle and by your love. Learn to respect people's views whilst being gentle, kind and courteous. Walk in the fruit of the Spirit (Galatians 5:22-23). Cleanliness is next to godliness – the people that you may be visiting or working with, may not have the same qualities or standards as you. Do not think that you are superior to them in any way, just because you do things differently. Be wise in all that you do and say. Learn to travel light and help others.

Further study: Isaiah 55:8-9, Matthew 24:14, Acts 4:13, Acts 20:27 and 2 Peter 3:12. Recommended Reading: *How to Plan, Prepare and Successfully Complete Your Short-Term Mission* by Mathew Backholer, www.ByFaithBooks.co.uk.

Chapter Twenty

Physical, Emotional and Spiritual Preparation

'Be anxious for nothing, but in everything by prayer and supplication, with thanksgiving, let your requests be made known to God; and the peace of God, which surpasses all understanding will guard your hearts and minds through Christ Jesus' (Philippians 4:6-7).

'Ask of Me and I will give You the nations for Your inheritance and the ends of the earth for Your possession' (Psalm 2:8).

"How best can I physically, emotionally and spiritually prepare for a STM?" Any preparation for a mission is time well invested and this factor should never be under-estimated. If you are going on a STM for several months (or more) then the preparation needs to be at a much deeper level than if you were going for two weeks. If you are going with an organisation on a STM they will be able to advise you for the country, its climate or people group you will be working amongst, hopefully, everything you need to know, and what to pack. Some have orientation programmes.

Physical Preparation

The best way to physically prepare for a STM is to make sure that you are not excessively overweight or underweight. Months before you depart, it is advisable to visit your doctor and dentist for a full check-up. What you take for granted at home may not be available in your new surroundings and the methods, hygiene or workmanship may not be as good as what you are accustomed to. Naturally, it is best to get any problems cleared up as soon as possible to minimise any discomfort and dangers before you depart, as a toothache for example is hard to live with! It is important to have all the necessary medical vaccinations before you depart and where possible take a good quantity of medicines (in original packaging) etc. which you use as they may be expensive or not available where you are going to. Diarrhoea, stress and jet-lag can all affect the equilibrium of your body clock, which will take at least several days to adjust and up to a week if you have travelled through many time zones. Pack practical clothes and take a travel kettle (for hot drinks and noodles).

Do not leave things to the last minute, like vaccinations, health check-up, packing the bags etc. Where possible before you depart on your STM, make sure that you have at least a few days to relax as it is easy to run around like a headless chicken, and you do not want to be exhausted, over-stressed or nervous before you even arrive!

Emotional Preparation

The best way to emotionally prepare for a STM is to accept beforehand, that you are not going on a holiday and that things will be difficult. This is not to say that you will not have a rewarding and educational time, but to accept the fact that there will be some hardships to endure and you may encounter culture shock, especially if you go to another continent or work amongst another people group.

Culture Shock

The best way to understand a people group or another culture is to live amongst them and identify with the local population, but this does bring new and unexpected challenges. Being away from home, your familiar surround-ings and lifestyle can seriously upset your outlook on life (and cause culture shock), when all your usual references have been taken away. The unfamiliar surroundings, the new language and culture, different food, sounds, smells, environment, temperatures, humidity and especially the spiritual atmosphere can all affect your mental wellbeing and spiritual perception. The disorientation of culture shock can manifest itself in many ways. Stress and anxiety can make you feel less able to cope with your new surroundings and even minor incidents can seem like insurmountable hurdles. Stress can cause you to become irritable, angry, frustrated, tired and anxious and often leave you unable to sleep soundly (Ephesians 4:26-27). Sometimes you can start to dislike the people you are ministering to, believing that your culture is right and that theirs is deeply flawed. You may even start to resent your STM or even God Himself, you have to be careful because the devil will try to take full advantage of this, resist him (2 Corinthians 10:5).

Some of the remedies to combat culture shock are: Relax and take some time out (if that is possible), appreciate the beauty of your surroundings, catch up on lost sleep and missed meals (see 1 Kings 19:4-21). Ask God for His grace and a new challenge. If possible, talk it over with someone of your own nationality or a fellow worker and get it off your chest, as the old saying goes, 'a problem shared is a problem halved.' Get on the internet (if possible) and email some friends back home, read about news from your home country which may reignite a spark in your heart. Remember why you are on the STM (1 Timothy 1:12).

'...Whatever things are true, whatever things are noble, whatever things are just, whatever things are pure, whatever things are lovely, whatever things are of a good report, if there is any virtue and if there is anything praiseworthy – meditate on these things' (Philippians 4:8).

Spiritual Preparation

The best way to spiritually prepare for a STM is to spend time with God in prayer and in reading the Holy Bible. The better the foundations in your life before you go, the stronger you will be when you arrive. Pray for your mission organisation (or church), your team members, the area you are going to, its people, for favour, good health, protection, Divine appointments, wisdom and discernment etc.

Prayer and Action

Evangelist Gipsy Smith said, "Do you expect to see your friends and neighbours, your husband, your wife, your children converted if you do not pray? Do you talk to them about the things of God? Are you concerned, interested, infatuated with the business of bringing them to Christ? Are you grieved when you see people godless and prayer-less that you are compelled to speak to them about the things which really matter; about death and judgment and eternal life? That is the spirit of the New Testament, of Calvary, of Pentecost; and it is the spirit of the Epistles. It is the spirit which you and I have to get if we are to do anything for Christ in our own city or town. We must live in the spirit of prayer; desire to pray; love to pray – that humanity may be healed.... The church of God was born in the atmosphere of prayer. The church which loses the power of prayer has no right to call herself a church of God."[1]

Language Difficulties

Language difficulties, combined with unfamiliar social and cultural cues can make communication problematic even on a basic level. Frustration can set in when you are unable to express yourself fully. Learn to laugh at your mistakes and laugh alongside (but not at) the people you are working with and ministering to. Often when speaking via a interpreter, there will still be misunderstanding and miscommunication. Speak slowly, clearly and avoid idioms and slang. Use export English – keep it simple and speak slower!

Words of Wisdom

Accept the fact that nobody has all the answers and the way you 'do church' at home will probably be different in your new surroundings. Allow local culture to flourish inside a Christian community. Consider taking some meaningful Christian books with you, which will benefit you on your STM and possibly be a blessing to others (give them away).

Eating unfamiliar food may at first be deemed unpalatable, but with time your taste buds will get accustomed to your new source of energy, although it may take time for your stomach to adjust.

In certain cultures, how you address or interact with someone is determined by gender or age and what is permitted in your home country may not be permitted in their country. Try to analyse things through the eyes of the locals and not by your standards back home.

Further study: Psalm 127:1-2, Philippians 2:1-11, 1 Timothy 2:1-8 and 1 Peter 4:7-19. Recommended Reading: *Short-Term Missions, A Christian Guide to STMs* by M. Backholer.

Chapter Twenty-One

Warnings, Dangers and Hazards of STMs

Jesus said, "Behold, I send you out as sheep in the midst of wolves. Therefore be as wise as serpents and harmless as doves" (Matthew 10:16).

Jesus said, "...My friends, do not be afraid of those who kill the body, and after that have no more they can do. But I will show you whom you should fear. Fear Him who after He has killed, has power to cast into hell; yes, I say to you, fear Him!" (Luke 12:4-5).

"What security advice can you give me about going on a STM?" Dangers lurk everywhere, but that should not paralyse us into inaction or hold us bound by fear and in trepidation. We need to understand that God is sovereign, He is in control of all things and all things are under His control, but God's sovereignty does not relieve us of responsibility. In many respects, we can be our own worst enemy by not using our common sense and God-given wisdom. God is more than able to look after us, but we should not put Him to the test (Matthew 4:7), by our own foolishness. Therefore, let us look after ourselves and lookout for other members of the STM team.

As in your home country there are some places where it is advisable not to walk alone and not to go after dark. Unlit streets and alleyways are the norm in parts of the developing world and manhole covers may be nonexistent. Beware of potholes, raised kerbs, no sewer coverings, ditches and a thousand and one other obstacles in unlit areas.

Don't invite trouble and be sensible in what you wear and in where you go. It is always sensible not to go out alone in a foreign country, but even pairs (and groups) of foreign women will attract attention. It is always best for men to witness to men and women to witness to women, otherwise the one listening may have ulterior motives. Always let your team leader know where you are going (make sure you have their permission) and when you expect to be back.

How You Come Across

On a STM you may be the first person ever to speak of the Good News of Jesus Christ to someone. How they perceive you, is what and who you represent – the world or a loving God? If your lifestyle is not good, you go into a fit of rage, or you act inappropriately in their cultural setting etc. then this could end up as their *tainted* view of Christianity. As an ambassador you are bearing a message from the King of kings, helping reconcile people back to God (2 Cor. 5:17-21).

Eternity Has no Second Chance

In eternity there is no second chance, therefore do all you can while you can. In many countries the inhabitants have freedom of religion and therefore can seek and search for the Creator of the universe – He is not far from anybody – if they seek Him, they will find Him (Isaiah 55:6 and Acts 17:27). However, most people come to know the Saviour, Jesus Christ, through personal witness. There are countries where all religions (or the minority religions) are suppressed and others where Christians are treated as less than second-class citizens or worse. Other countries are sensitive where proselytising is illegal, so use great wisdom in these nations!

In some districts or countries, people cannot obtain Bibles. They are either prohibited or the cost is too high (from a month's to a year's average wage). Whilst many people groups, do not have a Bible or any portion of Scripture in their native language or dialect.

Jesus said, "And this Gospel of the Kingdom will be preached in all the world as a witness to all nations, and then the end will come" (Matthew 24:14).

Interpersonal Relationships and Attitudes

The lack of ability to get on with other team members can ruin a STM. Love your neighbours and fellow labourers as yourself. We are required not only to give no offence to anyone and to provide things honest in the sight of all men, but to please all men for their good. We ought to do all that is within us, to prevent the good that is in us from being spoken of as evil. Learn how to walk in love, humility and servant-hood, agree to disagree and get on with the basic living out of the Christian life and present the Gospel in a respectful and courteous manner (Proverbs 25:25 & Romans 14:1, 19).

Your own attitudes and expectations can make or break your mission experience. Don't criticise team members (especially the leader), complain, whine or moan. Beware of: Getting romantically involved with someone (it is a big distraction). Only focusing on spiritual things, "I'm here to see miracles, not wash up!" Losing touch with God, "I don't have time for prayer and Bible reading!" Being a hygiene freak; start praying grace instead of just saying it! Not wanting to be a team player, "I prefer to work alone." Not sharing what you have with team members and the local people. Not wanting to change the schedule – a chance encounter could be a Divine appointment (or a devilish appointment), beware of the devil's snares and traps.

Dishonest People

Not all people are honest and truthful and that includes those who may profess to be believers, but who are really wolves, tares or false prophets etc. (Matthew 7:15, Matthew 13:24-30 and 2 Peter 2:14-15), therefore use great wisdom and discernment. Just because someone puts a 'present' in your hand and tells you it's free does not mean that it will cost you nothing! Watch out for being short-changed or paying greatly over the odds for food and transport. Some drivers prefer to take you to their choice of hotel etc. as they get commission. Always check your change and beware of inflated bills (though allow for genuine mistakes). Beware of extra food that you did not order appearing on your table, you will be charged for it! Never accept bottled water if the seal has been broken. Pickpockets are everywhere. In some countries, complete strangers will ask you for your contact details. Don't give them out to strangers or don't be surprised if you get contacted (by letter, email or phone) asking for money. Some have even contacted a close relative, claimed to have kidnapped the foreigner, and asked for a ransom!

It is unwise to invite a relative stranger (someone whom you have been sharing the Good News with) into your room as they may be a sex worker, regardless of the fact that they are the same sex as you. Most hotels have a lobby area for visitors. People do think the worst and you do not wish to give an 'appearance of evil' (1 Thessalonians 5:22), NIV, and not even a 'hint of sexual immorality' should be found among you (Ephesians 5:3), NIV.

Partnering with Others

If you work with a church or an organisation for an extended period of time you will face additional disappointments and discouragements (especially in sickness or apparent lack of results / fruit), but God is continually trying to teach us new things. You may encounter financial pressures, differences of opinions on how money should be spent or lifestyle and conduct, or 'how to do it.' Be a good steward and use wisdom when dealing with situations and people. There will be much satanic opposition and possibly church politics, which always hinder, as well as culture. There will also be much joy and blessings. You will learn much about STMs, other people and more importantly about yourself. You will see victories and answers to prayer.

If you or your God cannot help a person in their situation, then why should they turn to Jesus and become a Christian? An alcoholic, drug addict or depressive etc. needs to know that they can be set free in Jesus' name (often deliverance is needed). This is easier if you partner with a local church that can give long-term follow up; you may only be in a town for a few weeks or a month. You cannot take something from a dependant person (alcohol or drugs etc.) unless you can give them something better. If you are passing through many towns witnessing in a sensitive nation, you have to be wise and selective with whom and where you witness. Often it is a process of sowing the seed which needs to be watered in prayer and followed up if possible by correspondence: SMS / texts, social media, emails, webcam, letters, phone calls and give their details to the local church (1 Corinthians 3:5-8).

Further study: Matthew 10:1-23, Luke 22:35, John 15:1-17 and 1 Corinthians 10:23-33.

Chapter Twenty-Two

Long-Term Missions

Jesus said, "Go into all the world and preach the Gospel to every creature. He who believes and is baptised will be saved; but he who does not believe will be condemned. And these signs will follow those who believe..." (Mark 16:15-17).

'Sing to the Lord, all the earth; proclaim the Good News of His salvation from day to day. Declare His glory among the nations, His wonders amongst all peoples' (1 Chronicles 16:23-24).

"I feel led of God to give several years of my life towards mission work; what advice can you give?" The most important thing is to make sure that this is God's will for you. People do get caught up in their emotions, especially during an appeal for Christian workers.

Find out when? Some people are called to missions (or to the Christian ministry) from an early age (or as a young Christian), but the practical outworking and appointment may not be for many years.

You need to know where? The world is a large place and you need to know where your field of labour is. Has God burdened you in prayer for any particular country or people group? Within the terminology of long-term missions, there is a vast scope to include: Bible translation, church planting, being on a pastoral team, teaching, street evangelism, children or school's work, strengthening new churches, social or medical work, humanitarian aid etc. or any combination of these. You may have particular skills in administration, finance, translating, medicine, engineering, agriculture etc. that can be utilised.

You need to know whether you are to join a mission organisation, are being sent out by your denomination or church, or has the Holy Spirit told you to go and you will be an independent worker. An independent worker is not a loose cannon who is accountable to no-one, but is one who has been called to go. They may not receive any financial support from their home church, but go with their blessing and often end up working alongside other brethren on the mission field, assisting and supporting.

Do you need some training at Bible College / Seminary or other, before you depart? Will you get a regular income or not? Bills still have to be paid. If you are married, is your spouse in full support of the call on your life? If you have children what will happen to their schooling? Do you or any members of your family have serious health issues? The medicine may not be available where you are going.

Other questions need to be asked before you depart for the mission field. What do you hope to achieve or accomplish? What are you expecting to do or find? The perception can be very different from reality. In most employment, the general hours are nine-till-five, a thirty-five to forty hour working week. On the mission field or even in any church setting you may be on call twenty-four hours a day.

Georgina A. Gollock correctly stated in *Candidates in Waiting – A Manual of Home Preparation for Foreign Missionary Work* (1892) that the fundamental principle of all true missions [is] – ' "Spiritual men for spiritual work." You must yourself be in living union with Christ, by the Holy Spirit, before you can lead others to know and love Him.'[1]

A Common Vision and Beliefs

It is important that you share the same vision as the mission organisation or church that you intend to work with – what is their mission statement? You (or they) may hold a particular theological bias which will cause contentions and some things which you believe in (and experienced) they may deny. They may not permit a woman to preach and you want to, though in some cultures, it is not permissible for a woman to preach to a mixed congregation. On the other hand, you may not want to preach or share your testimony and it may be required! Do thorough research before you decide to join any mission organisation, or commit to work with a church.

Pray for wisdom, discernment and guidance: that God will show you when and where He wants you in whatever country or district, with what organisation.

Dr. Clate A. Risley, executive secretary department of Christian Education World Evangelical Fellowship correctly noted: 'Missionary education in the local church is one of the greatest needs of our day. It is the task of the local church to produce missionary candidates. We cannot expect people to pray, give or go unless there is proper missionary education....'

'Personally, I feel many Christians accused of being indifferent did not want to be but became indifferent because they were not shown "how" to be anything else. We (the leadership), not they (the membership), are to blame.

'Inspiration is fine, but it must be accompanied by instruction and involvement or it soon turns to indifference. Involved people are not apt to be indifferent people. Our church members must become involved Christians.'[2]

Dick Pearson in *Missionary Education Helps for the Local Church* wrote: 'Prayer is *direct* missionary activity. It spells success or failure to the career of a missionary and is the key to giving and going. Jesus said this is *the* answer (Matthew 9:37-38).'[3]

Training Before Departure

When you are in training, it is usually the last opportunity in your life to hear the truth about yourself, from a person whose desire is to love and train you for the mission field (Proverbs 27:23). The onlooker can often see mistakes with a clearness, which has become impossible for the person with the problem to see (Proverbs 25:11-12, Proverbs 27:5 and Proverbs 28:17). Do not be more taken up with Divine Scripture than the Word Himself who came in the flesh. Never put doctrine before devotion. Jesus is not just seeking a personal relationship with you, but an intimate one. You are called to make disciples, not church or denominational members. Do not conform them into your image (unless you reflect the standard of Jesus Christ, see 2 Thessalonians 3:7-9, 1 Timothy 4:12, Titus 2:7, Hebrews 13:7, 1 Peter 2:21

and 3 John 11). All disciples need to be continually filled with and led by the Holy Spirit (Acts 13:52, Romans 8:14, Galatians 5:18 and Ephesians 5:18).

As an ambassador of Christ Jesus, you should use every form of courtesy among the people to whom you have been called to serve (Luke 22:24-30). Learn the language, and adapt to their culture and manner of life, without compromising the Gospel in any way, shape or form. It can take a long time to adjust to the language, environment, food, culture, people's attitudes etc. You must love the people that you are going to and feel nothing but love, compassion and pity, but at first you may struggle. Ask God to give you grace and a heart of compassion. Try to be all things to all men, that you might by all means win some (1 Corinthians 9:20-23) and if it is possible, as much as it depends on you, live peaceably with everyone (Romans 12:18).

Georgina A. Gollock wrote: 'If young missionaries go out wedded to certain methods, bent upon certain plans, fixed in certain views on minor and external matters, and not prepared to surrender everything, that does not involve a principle, they are sure to cause pain and friction.'[4]

Gollock also noted: 'Surely the missionary who would take a full Gospel to the heathen must recognise the necessity of seeking to have a whole Bible in his heart and head.'[5]

Evangelist, Gipsy Smith said, "We are church-goers – but are we spiritual? We are religious – but are we soul-winners? We bear the name of Christ – but have we His Spirit? We take the cup of communion with Him – but are we sharing His cross? Are we beneath the weight of a withered world, helping to lift sinful humanity a little nearer to God? That is the Christ spirit! Have we got that? The Christ spirit concerns itself with the suffering, the sorrowing, the dying, the blind, the sick, the lame, the lost and seeks to bring them all back to the healing hand and Father-heart of God. Are you doing that? You know – and God knows."[6]

Further study: The book of Acts and the Pastoral Epistles (1 Thessalonians to Titus).

Chapter Twenty-Three

Financing a Short-Term Mission

'As the eyes of servants look to the hand of their masters, as the eyes of a maid to the hand of her mistress, so our eyes look to the Lord our God...' (Psalm 123:2).

'My God shall supply all your need according to His riches in glory by Christ Jesus' (Philippians 4:19).

"I feel led of God to go on a short-term mission (STM); how should the trip be financed and what is the best way to budget?" There are three main ways of financing Christian work. First, use your money from your savings account. Second, your church may wish to support you (in full or in part) and this is an option to get the church more involved in the work of world missions. Thirdly, if the first two options have failed, or you have less than you need, then seek God for the remaining finances, though pray about all options.

The best way to budget is to plan well and to keep a tight account of your spending. If you are going with a mission organisation, then the costs will be calculated by them. You pay upfront before departure. Otherwise, it is essential to buy an up-to-date travel guide; a backpacker's type can save you lots of money, by showing you the cost of living, travelling, cultural tips, where to sleep, eat and the latest scams to avoid. If you are based in one location for weeks or months, then it is easier to work out the cost of living. If you will be in several locations, take the average cost based on day-to-day living expenses, plus your plane ticket and medicines etc.

Churches and Finances

Most churches will not be prepared (or may be unable) to finance a committed member to go on a STM with a mission organisation for a year, which can cost from £3,000 ($4,800) to £14,000 ($22,400) per annum (2011), especially if the person concerned is just taking a year out before university or before starting a career in secular employment. The person going for that amount of time must be seriously considering entering into Christian ministry for such a large investment, or at a minimum, know that it is God's will for them and not just an excuse to delay the inevitable – getting a job, commencing higher education or running away!

If you are a young Christian (or a new member of a church) and you have not had time to prove yourself then most churches would not financially support you. If you have not proved to be faithful in your local church, supporting the prayer meetings, local evangelism and serving others, you will not be faithful elsewhere. Some churches may consider supporting someone on a STM (of say two to four weeks), but in some countries to stay a few more weeks is not that expensive (the biggest outlay is generally a plane ticket), the cost of living is often low, even lower if you stay with native church members. However, when there is more than one church member going on the same STM, there is often not enough money to go round. If a church or group of Christians organise a STM, it can be cheaper than going with a specialised STM organisation, but the expertise, contacts and equipment could be lacking.

> 'His lord said to him, "Well done, good and faithful servant; you were faithful over a few things, I will make you ruler over many things. Enter into the joy of your lord" ' (Matt. 25:21).

The Budget

On STMs there are lots of things to budget for and you do not want to cut corners or make a financial mistake, as it will cost you in more ways than one. For those who are joining a mission organisation, all the costs will have been worked out and they will be able to inform you of any other money you may need, or what is not included in the price (day trips, local sites to visit etc.). If you have a Student Card you may be able to get a discount on your plane ticket or other items.

If you are travelling with your church, (you may be the leader who is organising the trip) or a group of friends are making up the STM team, then the smaller your budget, the more strains and tensions that will arise. In many countries it is acceptable to haggle over the price of a room, the cost of clothes and even food at markets and some shops. Always ask the price before agreeing to buy something; otherwise you may pay more than you need to. If your daily budget is tight you may find yourself haggling over pennies and cents; a fraction of the cost of a chocolate bar – and in that situation you lose sight of the purpose of the mission. The leader of a church who is estimating the cost of the STM should always add the extras just in case – from ten to twenty percent. This money can always be returned to individual STM-ers (the church or go towards the next STM), but you cannot expect individuals from the STM team to put in additional money when you are on location.

If you are financially taken advantage of and you can expect it at least once, on any independent STM exceeding a month, then it may take weeks to recover from your loss or overspend in the only overpriced hotel in town. Some towns and countries are more expensive than others and whilst you may overspend in one, you can make savings in others. An extra £4 ($6) per-person a day in a developing country can make all the difference between a flee pit of a room and one that is adequate, whilst in Europe, the difference between adequate and nice can be an additional £25 ($40) per-person. Your church may have arranged your stay with the locals (at their home, church or mission base), and whilst they may not charge you rent, you cannot be a burden to them, financially or otherwise. If you are the leader of a young inexperienced STM team, you should not take them to flee pit accommodation as they will moan constantly!

Budget for plane tickets, visa(s), vaccinations, medicine, travel insurance, accommodation, transport, food, bottled water, offerings, interpreter (if needed), any material (Bibles, tracts, CDs, etc.) and extra for the unexpected (Luke 14:28-30). Keep a record of all outgoings in a notebook and keep receipts; you may have to submit them to the church treasurer. At restaurants, beware of badly calculated bills and unscrupulous traders, especially in relation to transport (taxis and buses). In some developing countries, foreigners are often seen as an easy target, walking cash cows who only have to be asked to dispense money and goods!

Blend in – Do Not Standout

On a STM, you should not live exuberantly nor flaunt your wealth (Philippians 4:10-19 and 1 Timothy 6:6). What a Westerner earns in a month in some developing countries is an average annual wage. You may have to sacrifice a little to keep within your budget, but this is good training and discipline. Having too much or too little compared to those to whom you are ministering can have a negative effect on the message you are trying to share or the work that you are trying to do. Some ministries specialise in providing free tracts, videos, DVDs, cassettes, CDs, Bibles and other Christian literature for organisations or churches to distribute.

'Nor was there anyone among them who lacked; for all who were possessors of lands or houses sold them and brought the proceeds... and laid them at the apostles' feet and they distributed to each as anyone had need' (Acts 4:34-35).

Money Matters

Taking a pocket calculator is essential for currency conversions and budget management. Shop around for the best exchange rate and always check your money, however long it takes. Cash withdrawals are useful, but each withdrawal at the ATM machine will incur a charge, therefore it is more prudent to withdraw the maximum amount in one transaction rather than making two trips per week. Travellers cheques are a safe way of carrying 'money' but you can lose a lot on the exchange rate and commission and I personally do not recommend them. You can also buy a prepaid charge card which works likes a cash card from ATMs though standard cash cards are cheaper to use for withdrawals. Some businesses prefer a "hard" currency, such as the American dollar. A combination of two forms of money is ideal (hard cash in a money belt and a cash card), but any traveller's guidebook will give sound advice. Credit (or debit) cards are useful for expensive purchases, but only if you have the means to pay off your statement in full. Paying interest to a bank or credit card company is a false economy and we should not be in debt (Romans 13:8).

Further study: Proverbs 22:7, Matt. 6:25-34 and 25:14-30.

Chapter Twenty-Four

Supporting Christian Workers

Jesus said, "He who is faithful in what is least is faithful also in much" (Luke 16:10).

'The Lord has commanded that those who preach the Gospel should live from the Gospel' (1 Corinthians 9:14).

"If I go into the Christian ministry should I expect to get a wage?" If you work full-time within a large church or ministry organisation, as the pastor, evangelist, missionary, receptionist or administrator etc. then according to your terms of employment you will probably get a salary, though it may be basic and not as generous as secular employment. In smaller churches, often the pastor only gets a wage (or gifts). It is important to stress that going into the ministry is not a career move with good financial incentives (you should be called of God); you should not expect to be paid in the same manner or to work as few hours as if you were in traditional secular employment. Many Christian organisations or churches are small and struggle financially. When the economic climate takes a downward spiral, so does church giving. This means that there is less money in the pot to give out. It is imperative that you settle any financial concerns with the ministry concerned or with God Himself before you begin in Christian ministry.

Financially Supporting Christian Workers
In the Old Testament, the offerings went to the Levites and fellow labourers who ministered within the temple (Numbers 18:21, 2 Chronicles 31:4-10 and Hebrews 7:5). '...Those who minister the holy things eat of the things from the temple, and those who serve at the altar partake of the offering of the altar' (1 Cor. 9:13). In the New Testament, we

have the five-fold ministry from Ephesians 4:11-13 of apostles, prophets, evangelists, pastors and teachers, all of whom are working to bring the body of Christ into maturity, 'For the equipping of the saints.' If a person preaches the Gospel they should live by the Gospel (1 Corinthians 9:7-14 and Matthew 10:9-10). Many churches incorrectly believe that only the pastor should get a wage, but this is not Scriptural; based on the Old Testament system of employment, all participants in God's work were looked after – the Levites, singers, musicians, gatekeepers etc., as well as the prophets. If a person devotes all of their time towards the things of God, whether it is teaching or preaching etc. (in or outside of the church building), they should be looked after according to their needs (see Acts 6:1-8). There is a solemn warning for churches or ministries who try to take financial advantage of their workers (Jeremiah 22:13). There is also a warning for those who work with wrong motives (Ezekiel 24:1-10 and Philippians 1:15-16).

God's workers need to be fed and clothed, and many have families to support and a mortgage. Often they have to travel and need Christian materials (tracts and Bibles etc.) that incur expenses. This is not to say that all helpers in the things of the Lord get a wage (we should all be ready to do good works and there are many vital volunteers), but it is right to honour and bless people when there are the finances to do so, especially those in full-time Christian ministry.

God warned the Israelites, "Take heed to yourself that you do not forsake the Levite [God's worker] as long as you live in your land" (Deuteronomy 12:19). Nehemiah returned to Jerusalem and found that the Levites (due to God's people financially neglecting them), had returned to the fields. Nehemiah contended with the leadership for their sin as God's work was greatly hindered (Nehemiah 13:10-14).

In 1849, David Livingstone, whilst in Africa, wrote a letter to a fellow missionary, Mr Watt: 'I have a very strong desire to go and reduce the new language to writing, but I cannot perform impossibilities. I don't think it is quite fair for the churches to expect their messengers to live, as if he were the Prodigal Son, on the husks that the swine do eat, but I should be ashamed to say so to any one but yourself.'[1]

Missionary Sending Church

When a church sends someone out, it is generally their responsibility to finance them, unless they have forewarned the missionary that they are unable to do so due to financial restraints (Romans 10:15 and 1 Timothy 5:8, 18). If a church waves a missionary "goodbye" without giving serious thought to their support, then this is highly inconsistent with the words of Jesus, "Whatever you want men to do to you, do also to them, for this is the Law and the Prophets" (Matthew 7:12). Acts 18:3 reveals that the apostle Paul was a 'tentmaker' by trade and for a time supported himself and still travelled everywhere, whereas 'Peter and John were sent out by the Jerusalem Church' (Acts 8:14). Later, Paul received money from some churches to minister to others because he did not want to be a financial burden (2 Corinthians 11:7-9 and 2 Thessalonians 3:8). The Philippian Church sent aid for Paul's necessities by the hand of Epaphroditus which was 'a sweet smelling aroma, an acceptable sacrifice, well pleasing to God' (Philippians 4:15-16). On occasions, Paul asked various churches to 'help him on his way' or 'send him on his journey' (Romans 15:24, 1 Corinthians 16:6 and 2 Corinthians 1:15-16). Paul also asked the church to assist other fellow labourers (Romans 16:1-2 and 1 Corinthians 16:10-11).

'If we have sown spiritual things for you, is it a great thing if we reap your material things?' 'Do you not know that those who minister the holy things eat of the things from the temple, and those who serve at the altar partake of the offering of the altar? The Lord has commanded that those who preach the Gospel should live from the Gospel' (1 Corinthians 9:11, 13-14).

Minister with your Possessions

If you have been a receiver of spiritual things, it is your duty to help minister in material things, to continue the spread of the Good News (Romans 15:26-29, 2 Timothy 1:16-18 and 3 John 5-8). If you have more than enough, it is your duty to share (Luke 3:8-11 and 1 John 3:17-18). The disciples sent aid to the brethren living in Judea (Acts 11:29-30 and Romans 15:26-28). The phrase, 'Send them forward on their journey' (3 John 6), means to provide aid for travelling preachers. These helps can be in accommodation, money, recommendations (to other ministries or churches), food and clothing etc. Inhospitality is condemned (3 John 9-11).

German Reformation leader, Martin Luther said, "There are three conversions we must have with God. The first is of the heart; the second is of the mind; and the third is of the purse."

> Jesus said, "For God so loved the world that *He gave* His only begotten Son, that whoever believes in Him should not perish but have everlasting life" (John 3:16).

Dick Pearson wrote: 'When a church shares the heart burden of God for missions, God will show His hand of blessing in and through that church.'[2]

Own Provision
The apostle Paul worked as a tentmaker for a time (Acts 18:1-3 and 2 Thessalonians 3:7-9). Paul tried to provide for his own necessities and for those that were with him (Acts 20:34-35). Nehemiah was the governor of Jerusalem, yet he refused to tax the people or to take what was rightfully his because the people were already very poor. He even provided out of his own means for all his servants and administrators (Nehemiah 5:16-19). Today, this could be a Christian worker who declines to draw a wage because of their large savings account or generous pension.

Living By Faith
God may call you to look to Him by faith for your financial needs – simply because other options have failed or are not available to you (Hebrews 11:1). If He has, you need to be guided by Him even more meticulously (Proverbs 16:3, Proverbs 16:9, Psalm 32:8, Psalm 123:2 and Psalm 127:1). Living by faith is covered in more detail in the next chapter.

Further study: 2 Kings 12:5-15, 22:1-9, Jeremiah 17:5, 7-8, Romans 8:32, Romans 12:6-8 and 2 Corinthians 9:1-14.

Chapter Twenty-Five

Christian Workers and Finances

Jesus said, "When I sent you without money bag, sack, and sandals, did you lack anything?" So they said, "Nothing" (Luke 22:35).

Jesus said, "Seek first the Kingdom of God and His righteousness, and all these things shall be added unto you" (Matthew 6:33).

"God has called me into full-time Christian work and my home church is in agreement. However, they are unable to support me financially – what should I do?" The best thing to do is to wait on God and seek Him for further guidance. If God has called you, He will provide the resources needed and the *timing* is essential. Other options are open. You may feel at liberty to write or approach certain people and ask for financial support. This is humbling and often a dejecting experience. One man at Bible College posted one hundred appeals across the globe to friends and former associates and got zero response! For some people, asking for money is not an option as this is the way that the Lord leads some – by not asking man, nor dropping hints! For some Christian workers, looking to man to provide their monthly allowance can be a dangerous crutch; they can be so dependant on man (and on man alone to provide for their needs) that when the money runs low, they don't know what to do, and are often forced to quit. However, not having financial concerns is a blessing regardless of one's job!

Christian workers are sometimes like a puppet on a string in regards to their financial supporters being manipulated into doing certain things that are not ordained of God, or they are hindered from doing things that He has ordained! They are stuck between a rock and a hard place. Manipulation is a form of witchcraft and is condemned by God. If God is your financial supporter then as long as you abide by the rules, He will release what is needed, when it is needed.

'My God shall supply all your need [not wants or desires] according to His riches in glory by Christ Jesus' (Phil. 4:19).

God's Provision

We may tend to believe that God's provision will always come by means of a stranger handing us large sums of money. This was not the experience of Jesus, His followers or the apostle Paul. They received support from friends, supporters and churches (Luke 8:3 and Acts 20:35). Other Christians have received "blessed handshakes" (in which money appears), anonymous cheques (though they are signed!), and hand delivered envelopes with money inside posted through their letter/mailbox. Other Christians have received wads of notes, while other amounts are much smaller; just as precious as an answer to prayer and is not to be despised (Zechariah 4:10a). In God's eyes a poor widow's offering is of greater value and sacrifice than the rich who are able to give out of their abundance (Mark 12:41-44). Be thankful for the widow's mite as well as the businessman's bonus! Do not be disappointed if your parents, church, friends or work colleagues give you money, this is God's provision. To scorn them as donors is to scorn God's means of support. God is practical!

God can provide for your eternal salvation as well as your immediate and daily needs (Luke 12:22-31). J. Hudson Taylor, missionary to China said, "God's work, done God's way, will not lack God's resources."

Prayer and Work

Most Christian workers are not keen to solely pray for finances, it appears more natural to ask man for help – but what happens when man fails? If God has called you to live by faith, then you relinquish your rights to provide for yourself (which feels unnatural), but you will be at peace. You may be tempted on occasions to get a part-time job, but unless guided by God to do so, do not. You may get an offer of a job – this could either be from God as an answer to your financial needs, or a ploy of the enemy to be deviated from your primary calling, unless you are a 'tentmaker' in a sensitive country. In the rebuilding of the temple there was an offer of help, but Zerubbabel and his advisors discerned that this was not from God, and so refused it (Ezra 4:1-5).

Have Faith and Trust God

Do not speak doom and gloom over your life (cursing yourself) by saying destructive statements as, "I'll never have enough" – there is power in the tongue (Deuteronomy 30:19 and Proverbs 18:21). God wants you to have your needs met (Philippians 4:19), and He wants you to be blessed (Psalm 35:27 and 68:19). God is faithful to His Word and to what He has promised, but unless you fulfil the conditions, the promises cannot be claimed nor appropriated. If you have not honoured God with your finances in tithes and offerings (1 Corinthians 16:1-2 and 2 Corinthians 8:1-15), and have not been a good steward (Luke 16:10-12 & Hag. 1:4-9), you have given the devourer a legal right to hinder your financial needs (Malachi 3:6-11). Only when you honour God in tithes and offerings, will He rebuke the devourer for your sake.

You may have to sacrifice at first if you are called to live by faith, but very little compared to what Jesus has done for you. It is better to learn and to prove God's faithfulness now, than to struggle and fail when in the ministry. Ask God to give you a specific sum to pray for, (for yourself or someone else) and pray until you see the answer. Or pray for a specific item which someone needs. As you receive answers to your prayers your faith will grow. You may receive amounts for which you have not specifically prayed, from varying sources. If you are married pray together (1 Corinthians 7:5-6). The Lord may lead you into a specific obedience, a place of abiding (John 15:1-11, 1 John 2:3-6 and 1 John 3:24), maybe fasting to see your prayers answered. Holy living is a continual obedience. The disciples were sent on a STM where they had to prove God's faithfulness and they lacked nothing (Luke 9:3 and Luke 22:35). God, our heavenly Father likes to bless His children with good gifts (Luke 11:13).

You may wish to make your needs known only to God, or you may feel at liberty to share your prayer needs with a faithful friend, so that he or she can pray specifically and intelligently. Beware, they may feel that you are dropping hints; this can also be true of prayer letters, mailshots, newsletters, updates, social media or e-news. Only God knows the heart and the motives, but we can so easily deceive ourselves. Even living by faith can be a statement of pride. You may get a victory in finances, an assurance for a specific amount and you know you will receive it, but this does not mean that it will arrive tomorrow!

It is important not to seek God only for your daily needs, but to spend time with Him in prayer because He desires to have fellowship with you. Delight yourself in God (Psalm 27:4, 37:4-7, 84:10 and Philippians 3:10-16). There is a warning in James 4:1-3 about lusting, coveting and praying for things out of wrong pleasure-seeking motives.

God's Miraculous Provision

The Israelites clothes in the wilderness did not wear out (Deuteronomy 8:4). The widow's oil and flour multiplied to sustain her and her son (1 Kings 17:9, 14-16). Oil was miraculously multiplied to pay off a debt (2 Kings 4:1-7). Money in the mouth of a fish to pay the temple tax (Matthew 17:24-27). The feeding of the five and four thousand (Matthew 16:8-10). Jesus turned water into wine at a wedding in Cana, Galilee (John 2:1-11).

Trust God

Whatever you do, trust God to lead and guide you as He has promised to provide for your needs as long as we seek His Kingdom first (Matthew 6:33 and Philippians 4:19). We are also informed: 'Be anxious for nothing, but in everything by prayer and supplication, with thanksgiving, *let your requests be made known to God* and the peace of God, which surpasses all understanding will guard your hearts and minds through Christ Jesus' (Philippians 4:6-7).

Further study: Ecclesiastes 2:26, Acts 2:44-45, Acts 4:34-35 and Philippians 4:6-7. God's provision: Psalm 23:1, Psalm 84:11, Romans 8:32, 2 Corinthians 6:10, 9:8 and 1 Timothy 6:17. God's resources: 1 Chronicles 29:11-14, Psalm 24:1, Psalm 50:10, Haggai 2:8 and 1 Corinthians 10:26.

Chapter Twenty-Six

Practical Evangelism

Replying to the followers of John the Baptist, Jesus said, "Go and tell John the things which you hear and see: The blind receive their sight and the lame walk; the lepers are cleansed and the deaf hear; the dead are raised up and the poor have *the Gospel preached* to them" (Matthew 11:5).

The apostle Paul in a letter to a young pastor called Timothy, wrote: 'Be watchful in all things, endure afflictions, *do the work of an evangelist*, fulfill your ministry' (2 Timothy 4:5).

"How can we best evangelise?" There are three primary ways to evangelise: By your words, by your life, and by your love. The most effective is by your words, "Go into all the world and *preach the Gospel*," But when all three are combined this is most effective. Some people are hardened and blinded to the truths of the Good News, but they can see the love of Christ in you. Humanitarian work, at home or abroad is to relieve or alleviate the suffering of others and when Christians are involved, it can be the love of Christ in action, and often it is these acts of love that soften and open hardened hearts to the truths of the Gospel.

There is a fourth way of evangelism, which grabs people's attention, power evangelism. It is a demonstration of the power of God (healings, signs and wonders) that makes people more responsive to the truths and claims of the Gospel. This is covered in chapters 30, 38 and 39: Power Evangelism, Seeking Healing, and Signs and Wonders.

After the ascension of Jesus Christ, His followers 'went out and preached everywhere, the Lord working with them and *confirming the word* through the accompanying signs. Amen' (Mark 16:20).

Jesus our Example

Jesus Christ, the Son of God is the greatest Person ever to walk the face of the earth. He is our greatest example in all things and was the ultimate evangelist, as He shared the Good News and went about doing good. His love was expressed to all people and it just overflowed towards those with whom He came into contact. Jesus cared for all types of people: Children, adults, the poor, homeless, wealthy, blind, disabled, the deaf and mute, lepers and even the dead. He raised them from the dead! Jesus touched the untouchables. Children were very important to Jesus and parents wanted Him to bless them. Jesus was just as concerned over individuals as He was with the crowds. Jesus mingled with all classes and social groups of people. Jesus did not hold any prejudices. He ate with sinners, immoral people and tax collectors yet never lowered His standard of godliness, but He met the people where they were. Jesus did not condemn those with whom He came into contact, (except the hypocrites), but loved them. Jesus missed meals and went without rest, just so that He could minister to people's needs. He travelled through Samaria, just to meet one woman – the woman at the well. Jesus taught, instructed and preached wherever He went, with whomever He came into contact.

Personal Evangelism

No two encounters are the same, though there may be similarities. We may not be an evangelist, but we are all called to evangelise. For many Christians, their first step in evangelism is by sharing their testimony, individually (or collectively amongst a group), at home, amongst friends or at work. Included within your testimony you may be able to share some passages of Scripture from the Holy Bible. As a Christian you will let your life shine in holiness and godliness and don't be surprised if work colleagues come and ask you about your faith, as they will see an evident change in you. Not everyone will appreciate your testimony or views, but your actions will speak louder than your words. Look for opportunities to share the Good News and pray for Divine appointments. Most people have many encounters with the Gospel before they acknowledge their sins and put their faith in Jesus Christ, whilst others totally reject it. It is the Holy

Spirit's job to bring conviction of sin and bring people into a saving knowledge of Jesus Christ, when they repent of their sins and put their faith in Jesus Christ. We are not called to 'Bible-bash' as people can become hardened (Acts 19:8-9).

Hard Truths

Such a comment as, "All religions lead to God" is wrong and removes the need to make a rational and sometimes hard choice that involves becoming committed to a certain path and often a change of lifestyle. It allows people to believe everything and nothing, without real responsibility. World religions in many 'key areas' often say contradictory things. They cannot all be right. To throw away these 'key areas,' you are saying they must all be wrong. If you throw away all the disagreeable parts, then there is no substance left. Most religions put the emphasis on man working towards God's (or gods') approval. Jesus Christ put the emphasis on a personal, loving God, who has made the ultimate sacrifice to reach out towards mankind. Jesus Christ is 'the Way, the Truth and the Life' (John 14:6), and 'there is no other name under heaven given among men by which we must be saved' (Acts 4:12). He died so that we may live. There is a heaven to embrace and a hell to shun. The wages of sin is death, but the gift of God is eternal life in Christ.

People can be sincere in what they believe, but they also can be sincerely wrong. The Holy Spirit can convict people of their sins, illuminate them with the truth and remind you of things to say. The first disciples of Jesus were 'uneducated and untrained men' but they had been with Jesus (Acts 4:13). This reveals that if you spend time with God, in prayer and reading of the Holy Bible, you too can be like the disciples 'who turned the world upside down' (Acts 17:6b), who were empowered by the Holy Spirit (Acts 1:8 & 2:1-13).

'I exhort first of all that supplications, prayers, intercessions and giving of thanks be made for all men, for kings and all who are in authority, that we may lead a quiet and peaceable life in all godliness and reverence. For this is good and acceptable in the sight of *God our Saviour who desires all men to be saved* and to come to the knowledge of the truth' (1 Timothy 2:1-4).

Tact, Wisdom and Timing

In 1892, Georgina A. Gollock wrote *Candidates in Waiting – A Manual of Home Preparation for Foreign Missionary Work*. In relation to one-on-one evangelism, she wrote about the need for tact and wisdom and how the promise in James 1:5 answers the need. She wrote: 'It is easy, unless we are guided by wisdom from above, to do a right thing in a very wrong way. It is quite possible for zeal to outrun discretion, and many a young worker has overstepped the boundaries of social reserve in an honest desire to help another soul. Here is a serious danger for Christians... [whom must] avoid 'every form of evil' and to do all things for the glory of God. Integrity of motive is not enough; there should be wisdom in action as well. It is also quite possible to put a right truth in the wrong way. The Gospel message is many sided [you can approach from different angles] and so is human nature. The same side will not fit every one at first. You will find a wonderful variety in the aspects of the Gospel presented by our Lord in His interviews, and it is evidently clear that these aspects fitted in each case the one to whom He spoke. Further, it is possible to speak in the right way but at the wrong time. Have you noticed that our blessed Lord met St. Peter more than once after the denial, but it was not until that morning by the lake that He saw it was the time for the tender, solemn questioning which melted the disciples soul?

On the other hand, it is possible to get so enamoured of tact as to lose *directness*. We may talk of Christian work, yet never of Christ; we may discuss conventions, but not the truths taught at them; we may witness, with great tact, perhaps to the fact that we are Christians, and yet fail to *win souls*. That, after all, is the paramount aim of individual work. Anglers are sent to catch, not to play with fish.'[1]

Practical Evangelism Tips

- What is it? It's not a religion, but a relationship with Jesus Christ the Son of God.
- What will it do for you? By accepting Him you will find forgiveness of your sins and new life in Jesus Christ.
- Who says so? Jesus Christ says so through His Word, the Holy Bible. God does not lie.

- How can you get it? By repenting of your sins and turning to Jesus Christ, faith in His atoning work.
- Never argue or raise your voice in evangelism, it is better to reason things out. Always show the utmost respect towards people and their opinions, however absurd they may be. Do not get rattled or angry.
- Try to stick to one subject at a time, don't move on until your point has been made, don't be intimidated by multiple questions. Beware of trick questions, red herrings and time-wasters!
- If they tell you that the Bible is full of contradictions, ask them how they reached such conclusions, ask them to show you the proof.
- Ask them what they believe about sin, salvation, heaven and hell etc., then they will be more willing to listen to your views. If possible, quote Scripture to back up your point of view.
- If you have the truth, it will set others free, you may not have all the answers, but a fact remains a fact, if Jesus has changed you, He can change others.
- Persevere and don't be discouraged if you apparently do not see any progress, it is God who ultimately saves people, just continually plant the seeds and pray. You may be just one link in a long chain.
- Ask the Holy Spirit for a word of knowledge that will open their heart so that they will listen.

'We are called to evangelise, not civilise' – Joe E. Church, missionary to Africa in the 1930s. After evangelisation comes regeneration (conversion) and then civilisation!

Scriptures to Pray and Consider
- Pray for the people you meet. It can move mountains and especially people's hearts and minds. "If you have faith…nothing will be impossible" (Matt. 7:20).
- There will be more joy in heaven over one sinner who repents than over ninety-nine just persons who did not need to repent (Luke 15:7).
- All are called to evangelise; to preach the Good News. Jesus came to "Seek and to save that which

was lost" (Luke 19:10). "Compel them to come in" (Luke 14:23). Invite people to hear the Gospel.

- God enlightens the mind and soul, the Holy Spirit "Will convict the world of sin, and of righteousness and of judgment" (John 16:8).
- '...Whatever you do, do all for the glory of God' (1 Corinthians 10:31). If we do our part and sow the seed of the Gospel and pray, then God will not fail to do His part (see 1 Corinthians 3:5-9).
- 'I can do all things through Christ who gives me strength' (Philippians 4:13).
- '...He who is in you is greater than he who is in the world' (1 John 4:4).

A. W. Tozer said, "The most effective argument for Christianity is still the good lives of those who profess it."[2]

Leading Doctrines of the Bible

Georgina A. Gollock in *Candidates in Waiting* noted the leading doctrines of the Christian faith, alongside essential truths and those preparing to do mission work (practical evangelism at home or abroad), should know them. They are: 'The inspiration of the Bible; the fall of man, and the consequent depravity of the whole human race; the nature of sin; the power of idolatry; the need of atonement; the principles of substitution; the glorious fullness of Redemption, shadowed in types, brought to light under the Gospel; justification by faith; sanctification; the doctrine of the Trinity; the Divinity of the Lord Jesus Christ; the personality and work of the Holy Spirit; the second coming of Christ, especially in its practical bearing upon daily life; the eternal separation from God of those who 'obey not the Gospel,' these and many other cardinal truths, and the whole of God's teaching about them should be known.'[3]

'The heart of the righteous studies how to answer...' (Proverbs 15:28a).

Further study: Proverbs 11:30, Romans 10:9-14, 2 Timothy 4:5, 1 Peter 3:15 and 1 John 4:18. Read the Holy Bible.

Chapter Twenty-Seven

Personal Evangelism

'Sanctify the Lord God in your hearts, and always be ready to give a defence to everyone who asks you a reason for the hope that is in you...' (1 Peter 3:15).

'The fruit of the righteous is a tree of life and he who wins souls is wise' (Proverbs 11:30).

"I want to share my faith with others, but often don't know how to begin." You have to begin somewhere and conversations with friends, family, work colleagues or even complete strangers at the bus stop or in a queue, can drift onto various subjects or can be turned and focussed onto religion in general and Christianity as a specific. As the old saying goes, 'practice makes perfect.' Sometimes you might not say that much, often a poignant word or sentence here or there, which a person can walk away with and think over. Memorise some key salvation Scriptures (at the end of this chapter). Pray for opportunities (Divine appointments, word of knowledge) and ask the Holy Spirit to guide you.

Useful evangelistic tools are Christian tracts or pamphlets, which explains the Gospel message in a clear and concise manner. There are hundreds of types with varying themes, though the central message is the same. After a conversation, give them a tract, "Here is something for you to read." For those who are interested, consider offering them a Gospel booklet (Mark or John).

Remember: Mankind is guilty of sin and subject to God's wrath and condemnation. Jesus Christ the incarnate Son of God, gave His life as a substitute for sinful man, so that man could be set free. Jesus can redeem anyone from the power of sin and its consequences. Man can be justified solely by the grace of God, (His free gift), through repentance (Mark

1:15 and Mark 6:12) and faith in Christ's death on the cross and His resurrection from the dead. Jesus said, "You must be born again" (John 3:3, 7). All must look by faith to Jesus Christ for their salvation and turn away from their sin.

Approaches to Evangelism

- With your testimony, '...Always be ready to give a defence to everyone who asks you a reason for the hope that is in you...' (1 Peter 3:15).
- Compel the downcast and despised to come to church (or an invite to a cell group etc.), 'Go out into the highways and hedges and compel them to come in, that My house may be full' (Luke 14:23).
- Strike up a conversation with a stranger and gradually (or be direct) and talk about the Good News, like the apostle Paul at the riverside (Acts 16:13-15).
- General chitchat, talking about God and the Bible, 'Faith comes by hearing and hearing by the Word of God' (Romans 10:17).
- Reasoning with individuals or small groups; the apostle Paul was on trial, 'As he reasoned about righteousness, self-control and the judgment to come...' (Acts 24:25).
- Live honourably as Christ's ambassadors, 'We are ambassadors for Christ as though God were pleading through us...be reconciled to God' (2 Corinthians 5:20). While Paul and Silas were singing in prison, an earthquake opened the jail doors and the jailer and his household were converted (Acts 16:25-34).
- Reason with people from the Scriptures, as was the apostle Paul's custom when he went to the Synagogue (Acts 17:2).
- Discussions or debates in public places leading to Divine appointments. The apostle Paul, 'reasoned in the Synagogue with the Jews and with the Gentile worshipers, and in the marketplace daily with those who happened to be there' (Acts 17:17).
- Using local knowledge or an issue to bridge the gap, to talk about Christ Jesus. The apostle Paul spoke to the men of Athens at Areopagus (Acts 17:22-34).

- Preach Christ crucified and glory in the Lord as the apostle Paul frequently did and he did not use eloquent words of wisdom (1 Corinthians 1:18-31).
- We persuade men, reminding them of the judgment to come, 'Knowing therefore the terror of the Lord we persuade men' (2 Corinthians 5:11).
- Present the ministry of reconciliation, talk about man's disobedience, how Jesus bridged the gap; and that man can become a new creation in Christ (2 Corinthians 5:17-18).
- Be ready at all times, preaching the Gospel message on all occasions, 'Preach the Word! Be ready in season and out of season' (2 Timothy 4:2).
- Whosoever wants to, can come to God; those who are seeking God need to be pointed in the right direction. 'The Spirit and the Bride [the Church] say, "Come!" And let him who hears say, "Come!" And let him who thirsts come. And whosoever desires, let him take the water of life freely' (Revelation 22:17). 'Whoever calls upon the name of the Lord will be saved' (Joel 2:32, Acts 2:21 and Romans 10:13).

'...If you confess with your mouth the Lord Jesus and believe in your heart that God has raised Him from the dead, you will be saved. For with the heart one believes unto righteousness, and with the mouth confession is made unto salvation' (Romans 10:9-10).

Salvation Scriptures
- 'All we like sheep have gone astray; we have turned every one to his own way and the Lord had laid on Him [Jesus] the iniquity of us all' (Isaiah 53:6).
- '...That they are all under sin. As it is written: "There is none righteous, no, not one...there is none who does good, no, not one" ' (Romans 3:9-10).
- 'All have sinned and fall short of the glory of God, being justified freely by His grace through the redemption that is in Christ Jesus, whom God set forth to be a propitiation by His blood, through faith...' (Romans 3:23-25).

- 'But God demonstrates His own love toward us, in that while we were still sinners, Christ died for us' (Romans 5:8).
- 'Just as through one man sin entered the world, and death through sin, and thus death spread to all men, because all sinned' (Romans 5:12).
- 'As through one man's [Adam's] offences judgment came to all men, resulting in condemnation, even so through one Man's [Jesus'] righteous act the free gift came to all men resulting in justification of life' (Romans 5:18).
- 'For the wages of sin is death, but the gift of God is eternal life in Christ Jesus our Lord' (Romans 6:23).
- 'For God so loved the world that He gave His one and only Son that whoever believes in Him shall not perish but have everlasting life' (John 3:16).
- '...Christ died for our sins' (1 Corinthians 15:3).
- 'For by grace you have been saved through faith and that not of yourselves; it is the gift of God, not of works, lest anyone should boast' (Ephesians 2:8-9).
- 'For there is one God and one Mediator between God and men, the Man Christ Jesus, who gave Himself a ransom for all, to be testified in due time' (1 Timothy 2:5-6).
- 'He who has the Son has life; he who does not have the Son of God does not have life' (1 John 5:12).
- 'He who believes in Him [Jesus] is not condemned; but he who does not believe is condemned already, because he has not believed in the name of the only begotten Son of God' (John 3:18).
- 'Repent therefore and be converted that your sins may be blotted out, so that times of refreshing may come from the presence of the Lord' (Acts 3:19).
- 'If we confess our sins, He [God] is faithful and just to forgive us our sins and to cleanse us from all unrighteousness' (1 John 1:9).

Further study: Proverbs 15:28, Isaiah 60:1-2, Matthew 4:19, Luke 2:49, John 4:34, 1 Corinthians 5:14 and 9:6.

Chapter Twenty-Eight

Evangelism Tips

'There is one who scatters yet, increases more; and there is one who withholds more than is right, but it leads to poverty. The generous soul will be made rich and he who waters will also be watered himself' (Proverbs 11:24-25).

'I planted, Apollos watered, but God gave the increase. So neither he who plants is anything, nor he who waters, but God who gives the increase. Now he who plants and he who waters are one, and each one will receive his own reward according to his own labour' (1 Corinthians 3:6-8).

This chapter consists of evangelism tips. More than a century ago, Rev. B. Fay Mills wrote: 'The very best way to learn how to bring souls to Christ is to be earnestly engaged in endeavouring to do it. There is nothing in which practice makes perfect more than this.' Rev. Mills went on to state many points in relation to evangelism which included: know that you yourself are converted, be gentle in your dealings with people and do not pray with them until they are ready to submit their wills to God. He wrote: 'There are four things to which he must be led if his salvation shall be complete. The first is the renunciation of every known sin. Never speak one word of peace to an inquirer until you are sure he is willing to give up every known sin. The second is the consecration of the neutral things and the good things to God. He must be willing to put at the disposal of God his time, money, influence, ambition, pleasures, friends etc. In the third place, he must see that he must depend entirely upon Christ for the cleansing of his heart and his preservation in the path of life. In the fourth place he must be willingly open to confess Christ as his master. Never call the work done until these four things have been accomplished.'[1]

In the famous psalm of confession and forgiveness of sin, King David wrote: 'Restore to me the joy of Your salvation and uphold me with Your generous Spirit, then I will teach transgressors Your ways, and sinners shall be converted to You' (Psalm 51:12-13). An anonymous author wrote: 'It is the duty of believers to teach transgressors their ways. Common humanity should prompt us to do this. Saved ourselves, we are under obligation to try and save others. This responsibility never ceases till we have done all we can to rescue the lost. There may not appear to be much hope of success, we may feel there is no use in trying, but our responsibility has not ceased till we have tried and exhausted every known means.'[2]

Sharing Our Faith

The Bible states that we should 'always be ready to give a defence as to the hope that is in us' (1 Peter 3:15), and that 'now is the day of Salvation' (2 Corinthians 6:2). We should not harden our heart in the day that He speaks (Hebrews 3:14-15 and Hebrews 4:7-11), which relates to being under conviction of sin and entering the rest of God through Jesus Christ. There is no assurance that we will be alive tomorrow (Proverbs 27:1, Luke 12:16-20 and James 4:13-15), and hence the urgency to share the Good News. D. L. Moody, a great American evangelist preached a Gospel message on 8 October 1871, and gave his audience one week to consider the claims of Christ. The Chicago fire broke out that night and consumed four miles of buildings with the loss of 250 lives. D. L. Moody was cut to the heart and vowed that he would never end a service without giving an invitation for people to accept Jesus Christ (as their Lord and Saviour).

But, the danger lies in *cajoling* or encouraging people to make a profession of faith when they have not come under conviction of sin; they have not been drawn by the Father (John 6:44 and John 15:16a), nor convicted by the Holy Spirit (John 16:8). The seed on rocky ground springs up quickly but withers just as quick! The Spirit of God blows where He wills (John 3:5-8). Before we can be saved, we MUST know we are sinners and feel it. We must truly repent, renounce the devil and his works, thus turning from our sinful ways, look to Jesus Christ, accept the gift of salvation and live for God. You can do great damage in trying to console a person who is under conviction of sin when they need to go deeper into the valley of mourning, until they see their total depravity, the cross in all its fullness, and the price that Jesus has paid for them. Too many 'premature' births have resulted from people interfering when a person is under conviction; they offer peace, when there is no peace. Some have not passed from death to life, from the power of Satan to God and because the work was shallow, merely emotional or a quick prayer, they quickly fall away (Matthew 13:1-43). In times of revival, people can be under conviction of sin for days, weeks or months, until the Light of Christ shines into their hearts. The work of God in conversion is deep.

We can witness at any time, but God's timing is perfect. Philip was led of the Holy Spirit to go and walk alongside the chariot in which the Ethiopian treasurer was riding. When the time was right, Philip asked a question and began to share truths from the Scriptures. Philip explained the passage from Isaiah 53 and preached Jesus Christ to Him. The Scripture referred to, spoke of the Messiah, who is Jesus Christ (Acts 8:26-38). The apostle Paul was in prison, where an earthquake and its consequences, permitted him to share the Gospel with the jailer (Acts 16:25-31), as well as on a sinking ship in the midst of a hurricane! (Acts 27:20-27).

Sowers, Builders and Reapers

Dr. Robert Morrison of China, Robert Moffat of Kuruman, South Africa, and Adoniram Judson of Burma, all pioneering missionaries in the early nineteenth century saw their first converts in their unevangelised fields after seven years of hard labour. Often it is a case that the grain of wheat has to fall into the ground and die – and if it has died, it can sprout and produce much fruit (John 12:24). However, in the twenty-first century a large proportion of the world's population have some knowledge, understanding or concept of Christianity. The Good News has been proclaimed (or at least the name of Jesus Christ has been heard); so the fields have been ploughed to some degree or other. There are many links that make up a chain of grace, and often our evangelism / personal witnessing is part of a spiritual chain that leads to a person's conversion to Jesus Christ.

The Bible speaks of Sowers, Reapers and Builders, and in the Kingdom of God we all have our part to play (see Matthew 13:3-9, John 4:37-38 and 1 Corinthians 3:3-17). David Hill, missionary to China in the nineteenth century, noted that the Sowers field of labour 'is the most extensive,' those who sow the good seed of the Gospel. Reapers, he wrote: 'Seek to gather into one visible body, one elect community' (the new converts becoming the local church), whilst the Builders are 'elders ordained out of every city, whose province is to build up those gathered into the Church' (to make strong and healthy disciples).[3]

The apostle Paul wrote: 'I planted, Apollos watered, but God gave the increase.... Now he who plants and he who waters are one, and each one will receive his own reward according to his own labour' (1 Corinthians 3:6-8). Thus with different talents, callings and giftings, we work together for the common good to build the Kingdom of God, and let us be faithful to serve our generation (see Acts 13:36).

Quick Reference Scriptures

For Backsliders (Jeremiah 2:19, 3:13, 14, Hosea 14:4 and 1 John 1:9). For those slightly convicted (Romans 3:10-23, 8:24, 1 John 1:10, Ecclesiastes 7:20, Isaiah 53:6, Psalm 143:2, Acts 13:39, Galatians 2:10 and Eph. 2:8-9). I am too evil to be saved (Isaiah 1:18, 43:25, 44:22, Romans 5:6-8, 1 Peter 2:24 and Rev. 22:17). For those who are afraid that they may not be able to hold out (John 10:28, 1 Peter 1:5, 4:19, Psalm 121:1-8, Isaiah 43:2, 1 Corinthians 10:13, 2 Corinthians 12:9 and Romans 8:38-39). For those who wait for a more convenient time (Proverbs 27:1, 2 Corinthians 6:2, James 4:13-14, and Hebrews 3:13). For those who have too many things to give up (Mark 8:35-37 and Philippians 3:7-8). For sceptical inquirers (John 6:40, 7:17 and Psalm 25:14). For those who want to know how to believe (John 5:24), it is to *receive* (John 1:11-12), it is to *trust* (Isaiah 26:3-4), it is to *take* (Revelation 22:17). Results of believing: You become a child of God (John 1:12), and receive forgiveness of sins (Acts 2:38 and Acts 3:19). You will experience: Joy (John 15:11), rest (Matthew 11:28-29), and peace (John 14:27). Inquirers are sometimes in darkness because they have not confessed with their mouth (Romans 10:10).

Chapter Twenty-Nine

How to Evangelise

Jesus said, "...Lift up your eyes and look at the fields, for they are already white for harvest! And he who reaps receives wages and gathers fruit for eternal life that both he who sows and he who reaps may rejoice together. For in this the saying is true: 'One sows and another reaps.' I sent you to reap that for which you have not laboured and you have entered into their labours" (John 4:35-38).

Jesus saw Simon and Andrew, brothers who were fishing and said, "Come after Me and I will make you fishers of men" and they left their nets and followed Him (Mark 1:17-18).

This chapter concerns the 'how to' of evangelism. Jesus said, "Go into all the world, and preach the Gospel to every creature" (Mark 16:15). The apostle Paul wrote: 'For whosoever shall call upon the name of the Lord shall be saved. How then shall they call on Him in whom they have not believed? And how shall they believe in Him of whom they have not heard? And how shall they hear without a preacher? ... As it is written, 'How beautiful are the feet of them that preach the Gospel of peace, and bring glad tidings of good things!' So then faith comes by hearing, and hearing by the Word of God' (Romans 10:13-15, 17).

The apostle Paul became like all things to men to save some (1 Corinthians 9:19-22). As we are called to be fishers of men then like fishermen, we need to use different types of bait (methods, approaches and / or various type of Christian literature), to hook and catch different types of people.

How to Share Our Faith
- We must be sure that we are born again ourselves, truly converted (John 3:3, 7).

- We must be clean vessels, leading holy lives (Isaiah 52:11, Matthew 14:15 and 1 Peter 1:16).
- We must be able to clearly present the Gospel (1 Peter 3:15), without getting bogged down with complex theological words and profound concepts. Keep it simple and concise.
- We must stick to the main point of the Gospel. 'Christ died for our sins according to the Scriptures' (1 Corinthians 15:3). Don't argue, get angry or allow yourself to be sidetracked by irrelevant questions. Other questions can be answered later.
- Use the Word of God – quote it. The Bible says, 'The wages of sin is death...' (Romans 6:23).
- Allow the Holy Spirit to guide you and be led of Him (John 16:7-14, Acts 6:10 and 1 Corinthians 2:4).

How to Save Souls

More than a century ago, Rev. F. G. Dickey wrote: 'There is much discussion of methods to be used in winning souls to Christ, but after all has been said, there remains the modicum of difficulty – "How?" The need of the hour is not so much *new* methods as the better use of biblical methods....

'The *how*, God explains in the most excellent textbook on "personal work" – the Bible. Whoever becomes practically acquainted with Jesus' rules for saving souls, will not enter heaven empty handed. Christ said, "I will make you fishers of men" – a promise of *how* and success.

'He [Jesus] lays down as a fundamental rule – love. "God so loved the world that He gave His only begotten Son, that whosoever believeth in Him should not perish, but have everlasting life" (John 3:16). The passion of Christ for a lost world must become the passion of the Christian, if he converts men. He must love men, as men, for Jesus' sake.... A Christ-like love will begot the apostle's state of heart, "I have great heaviness and continual sorrow in my heart, for I could wish that myself were accursed from Christ for my brethren, my kinsmen according to the flesh; who are Israelites" (Acts 9:3). This love will urge a person to study that he may 'show himself approved unto God, a workman that needeth not be ashamed' (2 Timothy 2:15).

'Study men...and human nature. Jesus 'knew what was in man' and so recognised the difference between a Pharisee and a publican, and acted accordingly. His treatment of Nicodemus and of the Samaritan woman differed greatly in the one from the other. A physician who attempts to heal all manner of diseases with physic [a purging medicine] and plasters will have many funerals.... Everyone has an approachable side. The Christian worker should know which side that is of each unsaved person he seeks.

'Then study to know your man – what he believes, what he loves, his modes of thought, his associations – in brief, make a mental biography of the man. Find some point of personal contact....'

'Another important study is the Bible...Jesus' counsel for it is, "Search the Scriptures." ...Skimming [it] will not secure the cream. Faithful work, only avails. It will open 'hidden things' in one's own soul; it will also supply knowledge of the 'hidden things' in every soul. Faces may differ in form and colour, but how similar are hearts in their deceitfulness and wickedness. The depth and kind of depravity is learned from the revelations of God. If this study has been what it should be, the attention will have been fixed upon the work of the Holy Spirit in the heart. Right acquaintance with this is crucial. Shortcoming here is wrongful, as it is dangerous.

'...The Spirit was as definite in His instructions to Philip as He was distinct in His voice, "Go join thyself to this chariot." Philip went and the [Ethiopian] eunuch was converted and baptised. Peter heard the voice of the Spirit, after God had cleansed his mind of a good bit of rubbish. Peter obeyed that voice, nothing doubting, Cornelius and his household were converted and baptised.'

'... The Holy Spirit works simultaneously in the heart of the soul seeker and in the heart of the unsaved. He has instructed the disciple to preach of sin and of righteousness and of judgment to come, and at the same time is convincing the unsaved of the same truths.

'...Doctrines of the Bible may be essential, yet well selected passages *stored away in memory* will become in the lips of the consecrated worker the needlepoint of the Spirit.'

'...The whole – and a whole – counsel of God, must be declared, in order to succeed. [See Acts 20:25-28].

'The last and always requisite in "how to save souls" is prayer. However successfully one may prosecute other branches of Christian work without prayer, in this, he must if he wins, pray without ceasing.... The prayer of faith will save the sick and the lost. Persistent prayer, and that which springs from a soul in travail, will avail to the salvation of the lost.

'...Why and how prayer touches the sources of Divine will, and causes it to cooperate with our weak strength, God has not revealed, but the Bible is replete with instances of its effectiveness. When we comprehend the scope of Christianity in its effect in man here, how it changes him into a 'new creation,' when the insistence of God is that this change is necessary here and now to salvation, and the lack of it dooms a man to eternal torment; when the sufferings of the Son of God in the garden and upon the cross are the Divine illustration of the awfulness of that torment, shall we not, ought we not, must we not go out into the highways and hedges and compel them to come 'that their blood will not be required at our hands?' (See Ezekiel 3:18-19).'[1]

Don't be in a Hurry

R. A. Torrey, in his book, *How to Bring Men to Christ* (1903) noted: Don't be in a hurry. One of the great faults of Christian work today is haste. We are too anxious for immediate results and do superficial work. It is very noticeable how many of those with whom Christ dealt came out slowly. Nicodemus, Joseph [of Arimathaea], Peter and even Paul, though the final step in his case seems very sudden – are cases in point. It was three days after the personal appearance of Jesus to Paul on the way to Damascus before the latter came out into the light and openly confessed Christ (Acts 22:16). One man with whom slow but thorough work has been done and who at last has been brought out clearly for Christ, is better than a dozen with whom hasty work has been done, who think they have accepted Christ when in reality they have not. It is often a wise policy to plant a truth in a man's heart and leave it to work. The seed on rocky ground springs up quickly, but withers as quickly.' See the Parable of the Sower (Matthew 13:3-30, Mark 4:1-20 and Luke 8:4-15).[2]

Four Classes of Inquirers

Evangelist D. L. Moody from the nineteenth century, stated that there were four classes of inquirers:

1. *Christians who are still in bondage* – who have no liberty. The first Epistle of John [1 John] was written on purpose to help this class.
2. The next class are *backsliders* – (Jeremiah 2:5 and Jeremiah 13:12-13 – how the Lord pleads with backslider to return to Him).
3. The third class are those *slightly convicted*. They must not be dealt with like those bowed down under the burden of sin. Don't offer healing until the wound has been made (Romans 3:10, Isaiah 1:6, Jeremiah 17:9 and 1 John 1:10).
4. The fourth class are *deeply convicted*. The devil has two ways of dealing with people. He tries as long as he can to keep their eyes of their own heart, chiefly by setting them to watch their neighbour. If in that he fails, he says, "O, you are so bad the Lord won't have you anyway" (Isaiah 1:18, Isaiah 43:25 and Isaiah 44:22). In John 1:11-12 we learn the way to peace with God is to receive Jesus Christ... "How can I be sure these promises are mine?" (John 3:16-17 and John 5:24).'[3]

Dealing with Seekers in an After-Meeting

An after-meeting is where people are invited to stay behind after a church or Gospel service, where they are presented with further claims of the Good News. They are often invited into another room and given an opportunity to respond. There will be other Christians on-hand available to talk to the enquirers one-on-one, to answer questions, show them various passages of Scripture, to personally show them that they are a sinner in need of a Saviour. Dr. Reuben A. Torrey in *How to Bring Men to Christ* (1903) gives fifteen general suggestions for an after-meeting. They are:

1. As a rule choose persons [people] to deal with of your own sex and about your own age.
2. Whenever it is possible, get the person with whom you are dealing alone. [Individuals within groups will often not talk honestly and openly].

3. Let your reliance be wholly in the Spirit of God and the Word of God.

4. Do not content yourself with merely reading passages from the Bible – much less in merely quoting them, but have the one with whom you are dealing read them himself that the truth may find entrance into the heart through the eye as well as the ear.

5. It is oftentimes well [best] to use but a single passage of Scripture, drive that home and clinch to it so that the one with whom you have been dealing cannot forget it.

6. Always hold [direct] the person with whom you are dealing to the main point of accepting Christ.

7. Be courteous. [You can be well meaning but rude. Your words and questioning can be searching but your manner should be gentle and full of concern].

8. Be in dead earnest. [Truly believe what you're talking about! Be firm in your points and not distracted].

9. Never lose your temper when trying to lead a soul to Christ.

10. Never have a heated argument with one whom you would lead to Christ. [Don't argue and witness].

11. Never interrupt any one else who is dealing with a soul.

12. Don't be in a hurry. One of the great faults of Christian work is haste. We are too anxious for immediate results and do a superficial work.... It is often a wise policy to plant a truth in a man's heart and leave it to work. The seed on rocky ground springs up quickly but withers as quickly.

13. Whenever it is possible and wise, get the person with whom you are dealing on his knees before God. [Ask them to kneel with you].

14. Whenever you seem to fail in any given case go home and pray over it and study it to see why you failed.

15. Before parting from the one who has accepted Christ, be sure to give him definite instructions as to how to succeed in the Christian life.[4] That is, read the Bible, pray, be joined with a church and be baptised.

Chapter Thirty

Power Evangelism

After the ascension of Jesus Christ, His followers 'went out and preached everywhere, the Lord working with them and *confirming the word through the accompanying signs.* Amen' (Mark 16:20).

'My speech and my preaching were not with persuasive words of human wisdom, but *in demonstration of the Spirit and power,* that your faith should not be in the wisdom of men but in the power of God' (1 Corinthians 2:4-5).

"How did the early Christians evangelise?" Before Jesus ascended into heaven, He told the disciples that they had to be endued with power from on high (Luke 24:49 and Acts 1:1-8). This was fulfilled at Pentecost, when the Holy Spirit came down upon them (Acts 2:1-4), though this was not a one-off experience (see Acts 4:31). With this new found freedom and anointing, whilst daily walking in holiness and the fear of the Lord, they were able to preach with a new boldness and authority (which cut to the heart), and this is why so many people became followers of Jesus in the early days (Acts 2:14-41). The Christians were in one accord and lived for the will of God (Acts 2:42-47 and Acts 4:32-37). All of the apostles moved in signs and wonders, and miracles were performed in Jesus' name (Mark 16:15-18). Demons were cast out and people were healed, this naturally got the people's attention. The apostles then pointed the inquirers to Christ Jesus (Acts 3:1-21, 4:29-33, 8:4-8 and 19:11-12).

Jesus told His disciples to go forth and proclaim the Good News of His Kingdom, preaching repentance and the forgiveness of sins in His name, making disciples of all the nations; teaching the believers how to live so that they too could become disciples, casting out demons, laying hands on the sick and raising the dead. You will speak with new tongues He stated and serpents will be unable to harm you (Mark 1:15, 16:15-18, Luke 10:18-19, 12:47 and Acts 28:5).

Jesus and Miracles

Jesus' first miracle was at a wedding where He turned water into wine. The Scriptures record: 'This *beginning of signs* Jesus did in Cana of Galilee, and manifested His glory; and His disciples *believed in Him*' (John 2:11). The Jews said to Jesus, "How long do you keep us in doubt? If you are the Christ, tell us plainly." Jesus replied, "I told you and you do not believe. The *works* that I do in My Father's name *bear witness of Me*" (John 10:24-25).

'For the Kingdom of God is not in Word but in power' (1 Corinthians 4:20).

Sharing the Good News is sometimes not enough; there may need to be a demonstration of power to make the work more effective, so that people stand up and take notice (Acts 14:3, Romans 15:19 and 1 Thessalonians 1:5). This is not a party trick, nor should we put the Lord our God to the test. However we are called to '...Make known His deeds among the people' (Psalm 105:1b), "You are My witnesses," says the Lord (Isaiah 43:10), and 'Jesus Christ is the same yesterday, today, and forever' (Hebrews 13:8).

'Now when He [Jesus] was in Jerusalem at the Passover, during the feast, *many believed* in His name *when they saw the signs* which He did' (John 2:23).

Words of Wisdom

Offer your bodies as living sacrifices, by surrendering your will to God. Do not be conformed to this world. Renew your mind. Be holy. Do not think too highly of yourself, be humble. You are part of the body of Christ and have your part to play. Use your gifts for God's glory. Love sincerely. Hate what is evil and cling to what is good. Have brotherly love towards all. Honour each other. Don't get discouraged, have great zeal. Keep up the enthusiasm. Bless those who persecute you and do not repay evil with evil. Do not be proud. Try to live at peace with all people. Do not take revenge. Live honourably before God and have a clear conscience. Serve one another in meekness and humility, giving all honour and glory to God. Abide in God and see eternal fruit. With God nothing is impossible; have faith (Mark 9:23 and Luke 1:37). Do I trust more in my own intellect when evangelising or in the Holy Spirit's power to convict of sin, revealing the judgment to come and righteousness? (John 16:7-11). In your own strength you may fail, but in Jesus Christ you can have victory and receive strength to succeed (1 Corinthians 15:57 and Philippians 4:13), but you *must* be baptised in the Holy Spirit and be led of the Spirit (Romans 8:1, 14).

> Philip the evangelist preached in the city of Samaria 'and the multitude with one accord *heeded the things spoken by Philip, hearing and seeing the miracles* which he did. For unclean spirits, crying with a loud voice, came out of many who were possessed; and many who were paralyzed and lame were healed' (Acts 8:5-7).

Evangelism and Miracles

T. L. Osborn was a preacher for seven years before he saw his first miracle, as a missionary in India, in 1947. He went on to hold evangelistic and healing campaigns around the world in nearly forty countries. In relation to Matthew 13:44 'The Kingdom of heaven is like unto *treasure hid* in a field...' he wrote: 'The responsibility to invade these enormous frontiers and possess this treasure [of souls] demands unselfish and sacrificial devotion to the cause for which Jesus died – the evangelisation of the world.'

In *Frontier Evangelism – God's Indispensable Method for World Evangelism* (1955), T. L. Osborn wrote: 'The ministry of faith and miracles is indispensable to the evangelisation of the world.... At this momentous hour in Church history, evangelists, pastors and laymen are beginning to realise that the supreme task of the Church is the evangelisation of the world... They see that they must begin to take the initiative and act accordingly in doing what they can to take the Gospel to the heathen [unevangelised].... The book of Acts is our example. It is our pattern for worldwide missionary enterprise. It is our standard for publishing the Gospel. *It is a combination of evangelism and miracles.*'

'...I tell you, the demand for the heathen today is for 'mighty men' (Joel 3:9-14), men of faith (Acts 6:8), men of courage, men whose ministries are confirmed by miracles. A return to the order of the Acts of the Apostles is imperative. Otherwise, millions will be lost who would believe and be saved if given a chance to hear – even once. "His blood will I require at thine hand" (Ezekiel 3:18). Preachers abroad [on the mission field] without miracles are almost wasting their time and the people's money who support them. And miracles at home without the objective of world evangelisation are missing their God-ordained purpose.'

'...The baptism of the Holy Ghost which the disciples received on the day of Pentecost is the key to world evangelisation. All that followed in the book of Acts was the outcome of that experience. The outpouring of the Holy Ghost in anyone's life is the only authority which will enable him to command the attention and respect of the unsaved, the unregenerate, the heathen.... I am talking about an enduement of Divine energy, of supernatural power in one's life which makes him master of the situation when it comes to winning souls. I am speaking of the kind of experience the disciples received on the day of Pentecost in Jerusalem' (Acts 1:8, chapter 2, 19:2, 20:24 and Mark 16:17-18).

'There is only one way to evangelise the world before Jesus comes; that is not with hospitals nor with schools and colleges; not with leporsariums, nor with manual and social training; *the only way is to proclaim this Gospel with evidence in the power of the Holy Spirit.*'[1]

The apostle Paul and Barnabas were at Iconium where they preached the Good News and saw opposition. 'Therefore they stayed there a long time, speaking boldly in the Lord, who was *bearing witness to the word of His grace, granting signs and wonders to be done* by their hands' (Acts 14:1-4).

Further study: Proverbs 15:28, Matthew 10:8, Mark 6:2, Mark 16:15-18, Luke 4:14, Acts 4:33, Acts 5:12, Acts 9:34-35, Romans 1:16, Romans 10:14, 17 and 2 Timothy 4:5. See chapters 38-39, Seeking Healing, and Signs and Wonders.

Chapter Thirty-One

Teaching Others Knowledge

The apostle Paul wrote to his spiritual 'son' Timothy: '...My son...the things that you have heard from me among many witnesses, commit these to faithful men who will be able to teach others also' (2 Timothy 2:1-2).

'Grow in the grace and knowledge of our Lord and Saviour Jesus Christ. To Him be the glory, both now and forever. Amen' (2 Peter 3:18).

"How can I help train a Christian to become a disciple?" To lead a person, you only need to be one-step ahead, though it helps if you have had many more years in the Christian faith, studying the Holy Bible and fellowshipping with the brethren. Churches should have Bible study groups / meetings, discipleship, baptism and church membership courses all of which teach basic biblical truths in a systematic format. The church fellowship is responsible for providing an environment in which spiritual growth can be encouraged and stimulated (Acts 20:7-11, 27 and Colossians 1:28).

Teaching others is the best way to find out how much you have learnt yourself. The best place to begin with teaching others knowledge in the process of discipleship is to start where you are, with what you have and build upon that (see Isaiah 28:9-10, Acts 20:20, 1 Corinthians 3:1-17, Hebrews 5:12-14, Hebrews 6:1-2 and 1 Peter 2:2). Whatever you have been taught (assuming it lines up with Scripture) then begin to teach and share what you have learnt with other Christians, often in an informal way. If you get asked a question, you and the questioner will soon find out whether you have the answer or not! If you don't know, that's OK, search the Scriptures for an answer, and ask the same question to someone who is older in the faith than you.

Christians need to be taught the whole counsel of God (Acts 20:27-28) and must also read the Bible prayerfully for themselves. The Holy Spirit is able to sustain and guide us into all truth (John 16:13 and Acts 20:32), though part of discipleship is drawing alongside other Christians and helping them along in the 'most holy faith' (Jude 20).

Jesus Training the Disciples

Jesus saw Simon and Andrew, two brothers who were fishing and said, "Come after Me [follow Me] and I will make you fishers of men" – and they immediately left their nets and followed Him. A little further on, Jesus saw James and John, the sons of Zebedee. He called them and they too followed Him (Mark 1:14-18). Jesus saw Levi (Matthew), the son of Alphaeus sitting in his tax office and said to him, "Follow Me," and he arose and followed Him (Mark 2:12-13).

The primary designation of the twelve disciples was to extend the Kingdom of God and they were trained by Jesus. 'Then He appointed twelve, that they might be with Him and that He might send them out to preach, and to have power to heal sicknesses and to cast out demons' (Mark 3:13-19). Just before Jesus' ascension (into heaven), He told His followers to go into all the world and make disciples of all nations (Matthew 28:18-20 and Mark 16:15-20). They were to repeat the cycle of preaching, teaching with signs following, to the next generation of Christians.

Jesus, on occasions openly rebuked the disciples (Mark 8:33 and Mark 16:14). At other times He told parables to address certain issues, but to teach humility He washed their feet, leading by example (John 13:1-17).

Study the Scriptures

The best way to learn how things should be done is by reading and studying the Scriptures, as it was 'written for our learning' (Romans 15:4). We should judge all things with Scripture (Romans 4:3a, Isaiah 8:20, Acts 17:10-11, 1 Thessalonians 5:21 and 2 Timothy 3:16-17). The early disciples turned the world upside down (Acts 17:6b). As they travelled, they planted churches, baptised new converts in water and laid hands on them, so that they could receive the baptism of the Holy Spirit; elders were appointed to oversee the flock. They kept in touch by correspondence and went back and visited the brethren for fellowship, to further disciple, correct, encourage, nurture, discipline, rebuke, to inform and to deal with any errors or questions.

The Pharisees and religious rulers of Jesus' day were experts in the Law of Moses, but knew nothing about the heart of God (Luke 11:37-52). They taught man-made rules (Matthew 15:7-14), and were quick to condemn people, whereas they should have been quick to help (Matthew 23:4-8, 13). People are always more important than rules or structures, and mercy is better than sacrifice (Psalm 51:17 and Hosea 6:6).

People look for role models to aspire to; do not be hypocritical (Matthew 23:3). A real teacher will talk the talk and walk the walk (Acts 1:1-2). A living sermon is better than a verbal one (Luke 6:12, 40, 9:18, 28 and 11:1). Teaching others should not be mechanical, rigid or forced, but a responsible time of praying, sharing and fellowship; being open, frank and honest (Matthew 16:13-27). Discuss problems and issues, instill discipline and have a process of accountability. When King David committed adultery and murder (2 Samuel chapter 11), it was Nathan the prophet who had to tell David his sin (2 Samuel 12:1-7). Nobody is beyond accountability and every disciple should be accountable to another. Regularly talk about and discuss the things of God (Deuteronomy 6:4-7 and 11:18-19). Talk about your experiences, especially the mistakes and struggles, be honest and open, as your testimony and experiences will speak volumes (2 Corinthians 6:11-13 and 2 Timothy 3:10-11). Challenge those under your care, "How is your walk with God?" (Proverbs 27:17, 23). God desires truth in the inward parts (Psalm 51:6). Often we confess our minor issues to God, (and to others) in the hope that it will distract from any larger problems – this is self-deception. Confess all sin to God. There is also a time and place to confess sins one to another (James 5:16). See also Proverbs 28:13.

Investing into Others

A faithful teacher will have a vision of investing his or her life in and through the lives of their students (Matthew 5:19 and 2 Timothy 3:10-11). It is a sin not to invest and entrust biblical truths into other people's lives. "For everyone to whom much is given, from him much will be required..." (Luke 12:48). We make a deposit into people's lives, so that it will incur interest in the form of spiritual fruit for God's Kingdom (Matthew 9:36-38, John 4:34-38 and John 15:1-11). Time invested wisely into others can produce results that will endure for a lifetime (Mark 4:30-34).

Moses, the leader of Israel, imparted his life into Joshua, who led the nation into the Promised Land (Deuteronomy 31:7-14). Paul taught Timothy, a young pastor, how to look after converts (see 1 and 2 Timothy). When Paul travelled, he took people with him for on-the-job training (Acts 12:25 and Acts 20:1-4), and there were disagreements (Acts 15:36-41 and 2 Timothy 4:11).

Words of Wisdom

We all need the spirit of wisdom and knowledge (Ephesians 1:17-18). Being taught by the Holy Spirit is very important (Romans 7:6, 2 Corinthians 3:6 and 1 John 2:26-27). Subjective knowledge is better than objective knowledge. Objective knowledge is something you acquire from a distance. Subjective knowledge is more than head knowledge; it is knowledge that is gained by experience. Teaching is communicating truths that people need to know. Training is seeing that they apply these truths to daily living. Believers are united by their faith in Jesus Christ (not doctrine, see Ephesians 4:11-13). There is no need to major on the minors. There will be disagreements amongst most groups of believers (Mark 9:33-34), but godly leaders will emerge (1 Corinthians 11:18-19). Relationships seldom grow without facing difficulties that need to be resolved; do not run away from them. Paul wrote a rebuke to the Corinthian church with tears and sorrow (2 Corinthians 2:1-8). Disciple thoroughly and your student will be like you (Luke 6:40).

Further study: Deuteronomy 31:22-30, Matthew 10:7-8, John 13:34-35, John 24:45-47, Acts 2:42, Acts 15:36, 41, Acts 18:23-26, Acts 20:7-12, Romans 15:4, 1 Corinthians 3:5-10, 9:18, 10:11, 12:27-28, Ephesians 4:10-16, Colossians 4:7-9, 1 Thessalonians 3:1-10 and Titus 1:5. A free 55 subject, discipleship course: www.byfaith.co.uk/paulni5.htm.

Chapter Thirty-Two

Christian Teachers

'All Scripture is given by inspiration of God and is profitable for doctrine, for reproof, for correction, for instruction in righteousness, that the man of God may be complete, thoroughly equipped for every good work' (2 Tim. 3:16-17).

'Be diligent to present yourself approved to God, a worker who does not need to be ashamed, rightly dividing the Word of truth' (2 Timothy 2:15).

"How can I best train and disciple Christians more effectively?" After a period of time every Christian should be able to teach basic truths to others (Hebrews 5:12-14 and Hebrews 6:1-2). What they have learnt they should be able to pass on to others. A teacher can and should lay firm biblical foundations for a believer (1 Corinthians 3:5-10), but all Christians must dig into the Word of God for biblical truths. Teachers need to systematically teach and it is foolish to teach deep truths to one who is still a babe in Christ (Isaiah 28:9-10 and 1 Corinthians 3:1-2). Jesus called and appointed the twelve disciples (and the seventy, Luke 10:1-2), with whom He lived, and imparted His very life to them (Mark 3:13-14, John 13:1 and John 13:13-17). Jesus told them to make disciples also, "Teaching them to obey everything I have commanded you..." (Matthew 28:20).

You may not have the gift of teaching (1 Corinthians 12:27-28), but that does not mean that you cannot teach. A person with a gift of ministry (service, Romans 12:7), may take the role of a teacher (in church, cell / youth group or Sunday school etc.), simply because no one else has come forward to fill that gap. If you have the gift of teaching, then teach according to the grace that has been given you (Romans 12:6-7). Faithfully teach others (1 Corinthians 4:1-2).

How Jesus Taught the Twelve Disciples

1. Jesus ministered and the disciples watched – they heard and saw. Jesus preached, spoke into people's lives, cast out demons, and healed people (Matthew 11:5, Matthew 12:15 and Luke 7:22).

2. Jesus ministered and the disciples participated – feeding of the five and four thousand. The disciples collected a small amount of food, they brought it to Jesus (He did the miracle) and they collected the remains (Matthew 14:13-21 and Matthew 15:32-39). Jesus walked on water and Peter partook of the same experience (Matthew 14:25-32).

3. The disciples ministered and Jesus helped – Jesus sent out the twelve and the seventy on a STM (Matthew 10:1-16, Matthew 11:1 and Luke 10:1). The Passover was prepared and celebrated, Jesus told them what to do and the disciples organised it (Matthew 26:17-31). The disciples could not cast out a mute spirit, so Jesus did it for them saying, "This kind can come out only by prayer and fasting" (Mark 9:17-29).

4. The disciples ministered and Jesus left – the Great Commission (Matthew 28:18-20 and Mark 16:15-20). Peter preached at Pentecost and three thousand people were converted (Acts 2:14-41). Peter and John performed a miracle on the way to the temple, when the lame man asked for money (Acts 3:1-11). Jesus ascended into heaven, but the disciples carried on the work, even under persecution and saw great fruit for their labours, unto the glory of God (Luke 24:49-53 and Acts 4:23-27).

'Your Word is a lamp to my feet and a light to my path' (Psalm 119:105).

Study the Holy Bible

All believers should desire the pure milk of the Word (1 Peter 2:2-3), and those in charge of a congregation should feed them (1 Peter 5:2). However, it is wrong for a Christian to keep saying, "Feed me, feed me" (Job 23:12), when they are not trying to feed themselves! As you read the Holy Bible, ask God to speak to you and reveal to you His truth (Psalm 119:18). As you read the Word try to find out: What is the subject of this passage about? Who is speaking and to whom and about what? What can I learn from the passage?

Does the passage show me any sin I have to confess and forsake? Are there any instructions I have to follow and obey? Are there any promises or a blessing to consider? Is there a spiritual principle to be noted and applied?

We should all study to be approved by God, correctly dividing the Word of truth (2 Timothy 2:15). Psalm 1:1-3 states that if you study the Word of God you will be blessed (see also Revelation 1:3). By meditating on it day and night, you will be like a well watered tree, which brings forth fruit in its season.

'The law of the Lord is perfect, converting the soul; the testimony of the Lord is sure, making wise the simple; the statutes of the Lord are right, rejoicing the heart; the commandment of the Lord is pure, enlightening the eyes; the fear of the Lord is clean, enduring forever; the judgments of the Lord are true and righteous altogether. More to be desired than gold...by them your servant is warned and in keeping them there is great reward' (Psalm 19:7-11).

To Grow Daily all Disciples Need to Be
- Nourished in the Word of God, man cannot live on bread alone (Matthew 4:4).
- Drink deeply from the living water of the Holy Spirit (John 7:37-39).
- Abide in God and be pruned regularly to produce more fruit (John 15:1-4, 7-8).

Read Christian Books
Disciples who have no desire to read Christian books and say, "I only read the Bible" (as commendable as this is), sadly, miss out on nearly two thousand years of Church history (plus biographies, testimonies, the advance of missions, accounts of revivals as well as spiritual principles applied and lived etc.), in which they could have learnt from those who have gone before us. Do not be more taken up with Divine Scripture than the Word Himself (Jesus Christ). Read the history of the past and discover its lessons (Romans 15:4 and 1 Corinthians 10:11-12). The apostle Paul wanted his parchments (portions of Scripture) and books (2

Timothy 4:13-14). He told Timothy to give attention to reading etc., (1 Timothy 4:13) and wished to present every man perfect in Christ (Colossians 1:28). Whilst study is good, too much is bad (Ecclesiastes 12:11-12). Beware – 'Knowledge puffs up, but love edifies' (1 Corinthians 8:1).

The Attitude and Character of a Teacher

A teacher serves and should not abuse his or her authority in the Gospel (Mark 10:43-45 and 1 Corinthians 9:18). Teachers should be self-controlled, reverent, diligent, consistent, patient, humble, gentle, longsuffering and bearing with one another in love (Ephesians 4:1-2). The true love of God passes all knowledge and is filled with the fullness of God (Ephesians 3:17-20). Speak words that build up and which bring grace to the hearers (Ephesians 4:29). Be tender, kind and humble, bearing with one another and forgiving; let the Word of Christ dwell in you richly, teaching and admonishing one another in psalms, hymns and spiritual songs with grace (Colossians 3:12-17). It is better to rebuke, than to sing the songs of fools (Eccl. 7:5). Open rebuke is better than love carefully concealed (Proverbs 27:5). A teacher who is pressed for time will willingly endure, so as to be able to continually impart truth to others (Acts 20:7-12).

In Rome, Italy, the apostle Paul who was under arrest 'dwelt two whole years in his own rented house, and *received all who came to him,* preaching the Kingdom of God and *teaching the things which concern the Lord Jesus Christ* with all confidence, no one forbidding him' (Acts 28:30-31).

Role Models in the Christian Faith

People look for role models to aspire to, therefore set a high example. The leaders in Ezra and Nehemiah's day did not do so and the people went astray (Ezra 9:1-2. See also Galatians 2:11-13). Jesus gave a solemn warning for anybody who makes a child (of God) stumble (Matthew 18:5-7). Jesus told the people to obey those who sit in Moses' seat (the scribes and Pharisees), but not to follow their hypocritical example (Matthew 23:1-8). This is why we must have godly examples who not only talk the talk, but walk the walk. Let us not be hypocrites, as a teacher or as a disciple.

- 156 -

The Apostle Paul's Godly Example

- Paul's teaching demonstrated to the Ephesians how they should live, 'I commend you to God...I have shown you in every way' (Acts 20:31-35).
- Paul wrote to the church at Philippi, 'The things which you learned and received and heard and saw in me, these do' (Philippians 4:9).
- Paul wrote to the church at Thessalonica, 'For you yourselves know how you ought to follow us, for we were not disorderly among you' (2 Thess. 3:7-9).
- Paul warned of the coming apostasy (rejection of God's principles), 'But you have carefully followed my doctrine and manner of life etc.' (2 Timothy 3:1-10).

Godly Examples

- Consider the outcome of their conduct [those who are over you], (Hebrews 13:7).
- '...Do not imitate what is evil, but what is good...' (3 John 11).
- Mould them into Christ's image (1 Peter 2:21-23).

'The entrance of Your Words gives light; it gives understanding to the simple' (Psalm 119:130).

Fellow Labourers

Tychicus and Onesimus were sent to the city of Colosse to inform and comfort the hearts of the brethren (Colossians 4:7-9). Timothy was sent to Thessalonica to help establish and encourage the believers in their faith (1 Thessalonians 3:1-10). Elders, (those who were mature in the faith) were appointed in every city where the Good News had been proclaimed and a Church had been formed (Titus 1:5-9). Testimonies encourage the brethren (Acts 15:12). The apostle Paul and his team revisited the Churches to help strengthen them (Acts 15:36, 40-41 and Acts 19:22).

Words of Wisdom

Every teacher is called to make disciples, not denominational members or churchgoers with the nickname Christian. Teachers will soon realise that not everybody learns or understands at the same pace. Many disciples will slip up and make mistakes. The object for each individual is to learn from experience (yourself or others) and not make the same mistake twice. As the years pass, your understanding of lesser doctrines may change (not orthodox teachings of the virgin birth, salvation, atonement, Jesus' deity and the resurrection etc.), as more truth is revealed to you. You may hold to one particular doctrine or viewpoint until more light is revealed from other verses of the Holy Bible, and then you get to see the bigger picture. If you seek the Lord you will understand all (Proverbs 28:5).

An anointing (or gifting to teach) should be more important than your qualifications (Acts 4:13). Just because a person is highly educated does not mean that they make wise decisions, are good communicators or lead a godly lifestyle. A disciple cannot be above his teacher, but can be like him or her (Matthew 10:24-25). Even mature disciples need to be strengthened (1 Samuel 30:6 and Acts 18:23).

Teachers must be aware of being so minute in their drawn-out teaching, that the hearer may miss the message. Also, beware of confusion, what you thought you taught you didn't teach, and what you didn't mean to teach you taught! All preachers and teachers must be able to explain, what their teaching means today, in the twenty-first century; how can this truth be applied to my life? Or why is this doctrine so important? A genuine teacher will be happy to answer questions. If they do not know, they will admit it (not fobbing you off with highfaluting language), find the answer and get back to you.

By reading about the seven churches in the Roman province of Asia (Revelation chapters 2-3), the Pastoral Epistles (1 and 2 Thessalonians, 1 and 2 Timothy and Titus) and the letters to the churches (1 and 2 Corinthians, Ephesians, Philippians, Colossians, James and 1 and 2 Peter), you can understand the difficulties there are in trying to teach people. Many of these letters were not only to inform, but also to correct and exhort.

Further study: Psalm 119:113b-114, Hosea 6:3, John 4:34, John 13:34-35, John 14:15, Acts 20:32 and 3 John 12-14.

Chapter Thirty-Three

Pure Doctrine

'Holding fast the faithful Word as he has been taught, that he may be able, by sound doctrine, both to exhort and convict those who contradict' (Titus 1:9).

'For whatever things were written before were written for our learning... and comfort of the Scriptures' (Romans 15:4).

Doctrine is important and must be kept pure, but sadly, all too often doctrine can become polluted or corrupted because we drift from the anchor of truth – the Holy Bible. There is also a grave danger in over-emphasising some doctrines whilst ignoring other essential truths (this is covered in detail in the next chapter). The Bible also warns of false teachers, charlatans and those who teach (or preach) for financial gain, that is, with wrong motives. Therefore, a wise person will sift everything they hear or read to see whether it lines up with Scripture. Jesus said, "My doctrine is not Mine but His who sent Me" (John 7:16). If something is taught as 'truth' then it must line up with what the Scriptures say (Isaiah 8:20 and Acts 18:28). Fellow believers who teach truth are known 'by their fruits' (Matthew 7:15-23). We should judge all things with Scripture which is the final measuring line and absolute (Acts 17:10-11, Galatians 4:30a and 1 Thess. 5:21). Our opinions and culture can change, the laws of the land can change but the Bible and the truths contained within it do not (Psalm 119:89-91 and 1 Peter 1:24-25).

Doctrine
1. Jesus said, "If anyone wants to do His will, he shall know concerning the doctrine, whether it is from God or whether I speak on My own authority. He who speaks from himself seeks his own glory; but He who seeks the glory of the One

who sent Him is true, and no unrighteousness is in Him" (John 7:17-18). Jesus said, "Do not judge according to appearances but judge with righteous judgment" (John 7:24).

2. 'And they [the disciples and new believers] continued in the apostles' doctrine and fellowship, in the breaking of bread, and in prayers' (Acts 2:42).

3. 'For whatever things were written before were written for our learning, that we through the patience and comfort of the Scriptures might have hope' (Romans 15:4).

4. 'That we [Christians] should no longer be children tossed to and fro and carried about with every wind of doctrine, by the trickery of men, in the cunning craftiness by which they lie in wait to deceive' (Ephesians 4:14).

5. Paul writing to Timothy, '...My son, be strong in the grace that is in Christ Jesus. And the things that you have heard from me among many witnesses, commit these to faithful men who will be able to teach others also. You therefore must endure hardship as a good soldier of Jesus Christ' (2 Timothy 2:1-3).

'Do not remove the ancient landmark [boundary of truth]...' (Proverbs 22:28a).

Is it Correct?

The apostle Paul explained and demonstrated from the Scriptures (Acts 17:2-4). The Bereans, on hearing Paul's new teaching, checked the Scriptures to see if what had been said was correct, "We will hear you again on this matter," they said (Acts 17:16-32). Paul working in Ephesus served the Lord in humility, he taught all he knew, publicly and from house to house and with tears and trials he taught the whole counsel of God (Acts 20:17-27). The elders of Judah did not like the prophecies of Jeremiah, but it did confirm what had already been spoken by Micah of Moresheth, which had been written down in Scripture (Jeremiah 26:4-18). If the foundations of truth are moved, what can the righteous do? (Psalm 11:3). See also 1 Corinthians 3:9-17.

Christians cannot say, "Jesus is Lord of my life" and then denounce the Holy Bible and the teaching contained within it. It is also wrong to read the Bible and not apply its teachings

(John 14:21 and James 1:22). Believers should have a good working knowledge of the Bible, though this happens over many years, reading portions of it daily (2 Timothy 3:14-16).

Worldviews and Christian Viewpoints
There are different types of worldviews (materialistic, pagan, Christian, Buddhist etc.), but when people come to Jesus Christ, their worldview will need to be conformed into the image of Christ, as their mind is renewed (Romans 12:1-2). This will take time and much patience will be needed.

When missionaries first took the Gospel into different countries and saw their first converts (Christians) they had to sift through the local culture to see what was compatible with Christianity, what was not, what could be retained, and what had to go upon profession of conversion. (We are not called to enforce Christian standards upon a non-believing community, 1 Corinthians 5:12). Various cultural ways can be compatible with the Bible, but also at odds with it:
1. It is compatible, if it is a biblical principle.
2. It is incompatible, if it is unbiblical.
3. It is neutral and can be retained.

'But God forbid that I should glory except in the cross of our Lord Jesus Christ, by whom the world has been crucified to me, and I to the world' (Galatians 6:14).

Culture and Tradition
Jesus said, "Go and make disciples of all the nations," not denominational members or churchgoers with the nickname Christian. Do not confuse people by allowing them to believe that basic church principles such as baptism, church membership, tithing or good works are paramount to eternal salvation (as we are saved by grace, Ephesians 2:8-9).

Beware of preconceived ideas, interpretations, opinions or prejudice (denominational, nationalistic, personal, racial and theological), which can distort biblical doctrine. The Bible reveals that the Lord's Supper (the Breaking of Bread / Communion) was a meal, which began as part of the Passover Feast (Matthew 26:26-29, Luke 22:14-20, Acts 2:46, 20:11 and 1 Corinthians 11:17-34). Yet most churches use a small wafer, cracker or a piece of bread and a drop of wine (or red juice), which is what we now participate of, (not a meal), but the principle of Jesus' words, "Do this in remembrance of Me" is still functional and is retained.

Christians often think that what they do on a Sunday morning within church is Christian culture whereas it may only be the culture of your country, (denomination or leader), it is the way we do things and our interpretation of certain Scriptures coupled with Christian tradition. If you were to travel to different fellowships or denominations, but especially churches in other countries, these differences are more noticeable. Often our opinion is formed more by our country or our denomination's traditions rather than what is laid down in the Holy Bible. Are our Christian practices biblical or cultural? To answer this we each need to read the Holy Bible and see if what we do is in line with Scripture; if not then we have drifted from the biblical anchorage of truth.[1]

We are called to come together in the 'unity of the faith' (Ephesians 4:11-13), not the unity of *our* doctrine as non-orthodox doctrines vary whilst the fundamentals of orthodox Christianity are unchanging. Therefore, we should not stand aloof because of denominational nonessentials. Some truths are fundamental whilst others are not as central as we might believe. We should have love one for another so that all men will know that *we are His disciples* (John 13:34-35).

Mistakes will be Made

Even the best teachers will at times make mistakes. Sometimes we all say things that we did not mean to say (because of confusion, tiredness, slip of the tongue) or did not say what we intended to say (Luke 9:33 and James 3:2). Do not disregard or dismiss a person's teaching because you disagree with one sentence – take the best and leave the rest; maturity is being able to sift the wheat from the chaff. It is possible for the same event (or portion of Scripture) to be seen or interpreted differently than our own. When the Lord appeared to Saul, his companions all saw the light, they were all afraid, but only Saul heard Him speak (Acts 22:16-19).

Liberal teachers, (those who deny the Bible as God's final authority and absolute truth) are the devil's friends; being godless and faithless and should be avoided (2 Timothy 3:5).

Chapter Thirty-Four

Combating Error

'Examine yourselves as to whether you are in the faith. Prove yourselves. Do you not know yourselves that Jesus Christ is in you? – Unless indeed you are disqualified' (2 Corinthians 13:5).

'Brethren, if anyone among you wanders from the truth, and someone turns him back, let him know that he who turns a sinner from the error of his way will save a soul from death and cover a multitude of sins' (James 5:19-20).

"In relation to Christian doctrine how can I best combat error?" The best way to combat error is to teach truth. All believers need to be discipled, having firm, solid foundations in the Word of God, the Holy Bible which is our measuring line. When a Christian hears various preachers and their teaching they should be able to discern whether it is correct or incorrect – does it line up with Scripture? (Hebrews 5:14). The five-fold ministry is to equip the saints for maturity and ministry, so that we are no longer tossed to and fro and carried with every wind of doctrine. Some people are knowledgeable in certain areas of biblical doctrine, but completely ignorant of other important truths (Acts 18:24-28 and 19:1-6), whereas some over-emphasise one doctrine to the neglect of other important truths. Christians need to be taught biblical doctrines; Jesus taught His followers and then 'explained all things to His disciples' (Mark 4:33-34). Those with incorrect doctrines need to be lovingly corrected (Eph. 4:11-16). In Acts eighteen there was a certain Jew named Apollos, a preacher of Jesus Christ who knew the Scriptures well, the Old Testament. He was fervent in his proclamation of the Good News and 'taught accurately the things of the Lord though he knew only the baptism of John.' When Aquila and Priscilla heard him, 'they took him aside and explained to him the way of God more accurately' (Acts 18:24-26).

How Jesus used Scripture to Teach or Combat Error

1. When the Sadducees asked Jesus a question about the resurrection (a doctrine they did not believe), He countered their wrong doctrine by Scripture (Mark 12:18-27).

2. Jesus pointed to the Scriptures and confronted the blind teachers of His day (Luke 6:39 and John 5:39-47). Jesus often denounced hypocrites (Matthew 16:1-4).

3. Jesus rebuked the Pharisees because their man-made doctrines were more important than their devotion to God and to obeying His laws (Matthew 23:13-28 and Mark 7:1-13). Do not add to God's Word (Proverbs 30:6), because it is timeless (Psalm 119:89), and transcends cultures.

4. Concerning John the Baptist, Jesus asked a leading question, to get the people to think (Luke 20:1-8).

5. To combat the misperception of the coming Messiah, Jesus posed a question to the scribes, asking them to explain a particular portion of Scripture (Luke 20:41-44).

6. On the road to Emmaus, Jesus talked to two dejected disciples and used the Scriptures to expound the doctrines concerning Himself (Luke 24:13-27).

Truth out of Balance

We should not build our biblical knowledge or faith on one truth only to neglect other truths which are equally important. We can over-emphasise or give more prominence to some issues and neglect or under-emphasise others. If you take just one part of truth and do not consider the other parts then you will reach a wrong conclusion. A Scripture text out of context can become a pretext! There is a danger in building a lot on a little, especially when the little happens to be a preconceived idea. Church historian, J. Edwin Orr wrote: 'Half the heresies are due to an over-emphasis of real truth without the balance of other doctrines in proportion.'[1]

Truth out of balance becomes error. There is truth, half truth and error. Truth is found in having firm grounding in the Word of God. Half-truths or error can be because of ignorance (Acts 18:24-26), deception (2 Timothy 3:13), or being under the influence of deceiving spirits (1 Tim. 4:1-2).

The question arose in the early church, do the brethren need to be circumcised and follow the Law of Moses? (Acts 15:1-21). The church elders discussed this question over a period of time and James replied with the answer, "No" – "It seemed good to us and to the Holy Spirit..." (Acts 15:28).

Leaders must be sensitive as to know when to address an issue and when to keep quiet to allow the Holy Spirit to point out the error. Some people hold allegiance to a particular leader, whilst rejecting others (1 Corinthians 1:12-13, 30-31), yet our allegiance should always be to Jesus Christ and His doctrine. James aptly pointed out: 'We all stumble in many things' (James 3:2), so none of us are perfect. Jesus warned about judging and with the measure we use it will be measured back to us (Matthew 7:1-6).

False Teaching

If a person or an organisation teaches contrary to the Scriptures, this is false teaching (which corrupts) and is taught by those in error, or false teachers especially leaders of cults. A heretic is one who teaches heresy, being opposed to *orthodox teaching (*holding the commonly accepted faith and established doctrines). A distinction between teachers and followers does need to be made (Jude 17-22). One may be ignorant of biblical truths (Acts 8:1-3 and Acts 8:8-24). Some deliberately distort or twist the Word of God to fit their doctrine or to make their doctrine fit! (Galatians 1:6-7, 3:1 and 2 Peter 3:16-17). When Jesus was in the wilderness, the devil tried to tempt Him and even quoted Scripture (which was out of context). Jesus refuted the devil with Scripture (Matthew 4:1-11). When Jesus was on trial, perjurers tried to twist His Words (Matthew 26:59-60 and Mark 14:55-59). When the apostle Paul was in Thessalonica, people who were not persuaded by his evangelism, preaching and use of Scripture, being envious, twisted his words, hired scoundrels and caused a riot (Acts 17:5-8). Other teachers take away, or add to biblical truth (Deuteronomy 4:2, Galatians 1:8-9 and Revelation 22:18-19). These teachers often appeal for financial gain (2 Corinthians 12:17-18, 1 Timothy 6:3-10 and Jude 10-13). Some are giving heed to deceiving spirits and doctrines of demons (1 Timothy 4:1 and James 3:14-16).

Whilst others walk according to their own ungodly lusts, being fleshly division makers (Jude 16-19).

False Teachers with Incorrect Doctrine

- The apostle Paul warned the elders at Ephesus that after he departed, savage wolves would come; men who would rise up to draw disciples to themselves (Acts 20:28-31).
- People will try to deceive you with persuasive words, vain philosophy, empty deceit, tradition and worldliness; we are complete in Christ (Col. 2:4-10).
- In Christ there is freedom from the deceptive, self-imposed religion of the doctrines of men, valueless false humility and bodily neglect (Colossians 2:20-23).
- Various events that will happen preceding Jesus' second coming; false signs, the falling away etc. (2 Thessalonians 2:1-12), 'Let no one deceive you by any means...' (2 Thessalonians 2:3). See Matt. 24:23-25.
- During the apostasy (falling away), religious people will resist the truth, having a form of godliness but denying its power, having corrupt minds (2 Timothy 3:1-9, 13).
- Many believers will not endure sound doctrine, having itching ears and wanting to hear what they want to hear, they will find such teachers (2 Timothy 4:3-4).
- False teachers (who practice for dishonest gain) need to be resisted and rebuked; they profess to know God, but by their works deny Him (Titus 1:10-16).
- God's eternal doctrine is unchanging, Jesus Christ is the same yesterday, today and forever. Do not be carried about with strange doctrines (Hebrews 13:7-9).
- False teachers will bring in destructive heresies, even denying the Lord; by covetousness they will financially exploit believers by deception (2 Peter 2:1-3).

Be humble and have a teachable spirit. The Holy Spirit can guide us into all truth (John 16:13-15), and bring to remembrance God's Word (John 14:26), but only if we have read it!

Further study: Nehemiah 9:1-3, Joshua 1:8, 1 Cor. 13:5-8, 2 Cor. 2:4, James 2:13, 2 Peter 1:20-21 and Jude 10.

Chapter Thirty-Five

Calvary and the Blood of Jesus Christ

'According to the law almost all things are purged with blood, and without the shedding of blood there is no remission [forgiveness]' (Hebrews 9:22).

'In Him [Jesus] we have redemption through His blood, the forgiveness of sins, according to the riches of His grace' (Ephesians 1:7).

"Why is Calvary (the cross) and the blood of Jesus Christ so important?" Under the old covenant, animal sacrifice was a ritual through which the Israelites made atonement (payment) for their sins (Exodus 24:6-8, Leviticus chapters 1, 3, 4 and 7 and Leviticus 17:11). This included consecration, expiation (covering of sin), and propitiation (satisfaction of Divine anger), and emphasised the importance of blood and its covering. Jesus was (and is) the sacrificial 'Lamb of God who takes away the sin of the world' (John 1:29). Jesus said, "For even the Son of Man did not come to be served, but to serve, and to give His life a ransom for many" (Mark 10:45).

Jesus Christ was sinless, without fault, yet He was mocked, whipped, beaten and a crown of thorns was pressed onto His head. Jesus was then led to a place called Calvary (Luke 23:33), Golgotha in the Hebrew language (John 19:17), nailed to a cross to die whilst crowds were mocking. Jesus came to seek and to save that which was lost. He conquered sin and defeated death. Jesus shed His blood so that we could be redeemed and be reconciled back to God (Revelation 5:9). Jesus' death (and resurrection) ushered in the new covenant with its better promises (Matthew 26:28, Galatians 3:10-29, Ephesians 1:7-9, Colossians 1:14, Hebrews 9:6-28 and Hebrews 10:19-20). He died, so that we may live. Because of Jesus' sacrificial death and His shed blood there are other promises and declarations which can be appropriated and outworked in and through our lives on a day-to-day basis. This includes: our position in Christ (Romans 5:9 and Hebrews 13:12), healing (Isaiah 53:5, 10, Matthew 8:17 and 1 Peter 2:24), and Divine protection (Exodus chapter 12).

> 'To Jesus the Mediator of the new covenant, and to the blood of sprinkling that speaks better things than that of Abel' (Hebrews 12:24).

The Passover

Exodus chapter 12 speaks of the Passover, when the Israelite slaves were delivered from Egypt. The angel of death passed over the households who had applied the blood (of a lamb without blemish) to their doorposts and lintels (Exodus 12:1-51 and Exodus 13:1-16). The Passover was a shadow of the things to come, which pointed the way to the Lamb of God who took away the sin of the world.

If the blood of Jesus Christ had not been shed, mankind would not have been able to enter into a relationship with the living God. The blood is precious. We need Jesus, the sacrificial Lamb of God, and His shed blood to cleanse and protect us from the destroyer, the devil, so that we too may have eternal life. For the Egyptians who were not covered by the blood, the firstborn in every household died. Pharaoh then let God's people, the nation of Israel go. Likewise, when we plead the blood over our lives (and we are not living in wilful unrepentant sin 1 John 1:5-10), then the devil has to let us go as he has no legal right or hold over us (1 John 5:18-19). The Advocate our dear Lord Jesus Christ, pleads our case and is Himself the propitiation for our sins (1 John 2:1-3, see also Zechariah 3:1-5).

Three Effects of the Atonement

1. The atonement gives us redemption from past sin. 'Add to your faith, virtue...knowledge...self-control... perseverance...to godliness brotherly kindness...and love. For if these things are yours and abound, you will neither be barren or unfruitful...[Do not forget that] he was purged from his old sins' (2 Peter 1:5-9).

There is no need to feel condemned or guilty over past sins that you have repented of. 'If we confess our sins, He is faithful and just to forgive us and to cleanse us from all unrighteousness' (1 John 1:9).

2. The atonement gives us the ability to live differently from the world. 'Pure and undefiled religion before God and the Father is this: to visit orphans and widows in trouble and to keep oneself unspotted from the world' (James 1:27).

3. The atonement gives us a reason to live, other than for self. 'And He [Jesus] died for all, that those who live should live no longer for themselves, but for Him who died for them and rose again' (2 Corinthians 5:15). 'I have been crucified with Christ; it is no longer I who live, but Christ lives in me...' (Galatians 2:20).

Eight Blood-Bought Privileges

1. We are at peace with God having been reconciled. 'By Him to reconcile all things to Himself, by Him, whether things on earth or things in heaven, having made peace through the blood of the cross' (Colossians 1:20).

2. We are brought near to God. 'In Christ Jesus you who were once far off have been made near by the blood of Christ' (Ephesians 2:13).

3. We can receive forgiveness of our sins. 'In Him we have redemption through His blood, the forgiveness of sins, according to the riches of His grace' (Ephesians 1:7).

4. We are sanctified (made holy). 'Jesus also, that He might sanctify the people with His own blood, suffered outside the gate' (Hebrews 13:12). '... The blood of Jesus Christ His Son cleanses us from all sin' (1 John 1:7).

5. We are justified (declared not guilty). '... Having now been justified by His blood, we shall be saved from wrath through Him' (Romans 5:9).

6. In prayer we have access to the Holy Place, the throne room of God and access to the Father through Jesus the Mediator. 'Brethren, having boldness to enter the Holiest by the blood of Jesus' (Heb. 10:19).

7. We are righteous. 'For if by the one man's [Adam's] offence death reigned through the one, much more those who receive abundance of grace and of the gift of righteousness will reign in life through the One, Jesus Christ' (Romans 5:17).
8. Healing (for body, mind and soul). 'He [Jesus] was wounded for our transgression...by His stripes we are healed...It pleased the Lord to bruise Him...He bore the sins of many...' (Isaiah 53:5, 10, 12). 'He Himself took our infirmities and bore our sicknesses' (Matthew 8:17). 'Who Himself bore our sins in His own body on the tree...by whose stripes you were healed' (1 Peter 2:24). See also 1 Peter 3:18 and chapters 37 and 38 which deals with healing.

Jesus – Man's Substitute

Evangelist T. L. Osborn wrote: 'Three years of Jesus' life were occupied in healing the sick and forgiving the sinful. Then came the crucial time during which He was to become man's Substitute. He would become sinful with our sins (2 Corinthians 5:21) and He would become sick with our sicknesses (Isaiah 53:10). Both sin and sickness had to be put away, but before they could be justly put away, the penalty for both had to be paid. Jesus Christ, the sinless, sickless One, was the only one who could do this; but He did it because of His great love, and He did it for us (Isaiah 53).'

'...Jesus our Lamb suffered in two ways. He shed His blood on the cross for our salvation from sin, and He bore the stripes on His body for our healing from sickness.'[1]

The Cross and its Benefits

* The cross gives us freedom, knowing that in Christ Jesus all confessed sin has been put under the blood and we are forgiven. 'There is therefore now no condemnation to those who are in Christ Jesus, who do not walk according to the flesh, but according to the Spirit' (Romans 8:1, see also 1 John 1:9).
* The cross gives us an understanding of a covenant. The sins of the world were placed upon Jesus at the cross of Calvary. Jesus took the punishment that we deserved so that we could go free and enter into a

covenant relationship with Him. 'He [God] made Him [Jesus] who knew no sin to be sin for us, that we might become the righteousness of God in Him' (2 Corinthians 5:21). Read Isaiah ch. 53 and Heb. 9-10.

- The cross gives us peace. Jesus is a peacemaker and in Christ we can be at peace and reconciled back to God. 'By Him [God] to reconcile all things to Himself, by Him [Jesus], whether things on earth or things in heaven, having made peace through the blood of His cross' (Colossians 1:20).

- The cross gives us a positional standing in Christ Jesus. I am a new creation, justified, sanctified, made righteous, a child of God, a son and a co-heir in Christ and part of a holy priesthood (John 1:12, Romans 3:24, 5:19, 8:17, 2 Corinthians 5:17, Hebrews 10:10, 1 Peter 2:9 and Revelation 1:5-6).

- The cross outworked in our own lives aids development of character. True character is only inwardly changed by embracing the cross; knowing Jesus better and living for Him will produce outward fruit. Jesus said to the woman caught in adultery, "...Go and *sin no more*" (John 8:11). The apostle Paul stated, 'I count all things loss for the excellence of the knowledge of Christ Jesus my Lord, for whom I have suffered the loss of all things, and count them as rubbish that I might gain Christ [be more like Him]' (Philippians 3:8).

- The cross gives us victory. There is victory in Christ Jesus over death and Hades (1 Corinthians 15:55-56). 'Thanks be to God, who gives us the victory through our Lord Jesus Christ' (1 Corinthians 15:57). 'They [the believers] overcame him [the devil] by the blood of the Lamb [Jesus Christ] and by the word of their testimony, and they did not love their lives to the death' (Revelation 12:11). All believers have a testimony that they have been forgiven and cleansed by the blood of Jesus. God forgives all confessed sin.

- The cross when embraced assures us of eternal life in heaven. '...God has given us eternal life, and this life is in His Son. He who has the Son has life; he who does not have the Son of God does not have life' (1 John 5:11-12). 'We know that the Son of God has come and has given us an understanding, that we may know Him who is true; and we are in Him who is true, in His Son Jesus Christ. This is the true God and eternal life' (1 John 5:20).

> Jesus said, "Whoever does not bear his cross and come after Me, cannot be My disciple.... So likewise whoever of you does not forsake all that he has cannot be My disciple" (Luke 14:27, 33).

Message of the Cross
David E. Carr wrote: 'Without the message of the cross, Christianity is only a good idea, another set of religious beliefs or a high moral code.... Unless you preach the cross, Jesus has done nothing – but He has in fact done everything! Why do so many ministers avoid preaching this?'[2]

A Christ-less, cross-less, blood-less Gospel message will result in spine-less, defence-less and power-less church-goers with the nickname Christian, because a fast-food Gospel message will result in biodegradable believers.

Effective Blood
For the blood to be effective, it must be applied to the sin or the situation in our lives. If we live in unrepentant sin, we have no forgiveness. But if we repent, the devil has no legal right over us because the Advocate pleads our case (Colossians 1:21-22 and 1 John 5:18-19). Forgiven sins are vanquished (Psalm 103:12 and Micah 7:19). Jesus' blood is imperative for atonement and is a powerful weapon of victory. This was achieved on the victorious cross of Calvary. Jesus' blood is still as powerful now, as it was two thousand years ago.

Further study: Isaiah 1:18, Romans 3:23-25, 1 Corinthians 1:18, Ephesians 2:13, Hebrews 10:19, 1 Peter 1:18-21, 1 John 5:18 and Revelation 13:8.

Chapter Thirty-Six

Sin, Sickness and Decay

The Lord God commanded Adam, saying, "Of every tree of the garden you may freely eat; but of the tree of the knowledge of good and evil you shall not eat, for in the day that you eat of it you shall surely die" (Genesis 2:16-17).

'Why do I take my flesh in my teeth, and put my life in my hands? Though He [God] slay me, yet will I trust Him…He also shall be my salvation' (Job 13:14-16).

"Does sin cause illness or sickness?" God created a perfect world and created man to live forever without pain or decay. However, sin entered into the world through Adam and Eve when they disobeyed God (Genesis chapter 3). Due to a direct result of their sin, sickness and diseases started to appear and man began to decay – that is, we all degenerate over the years and will eventually die. The Holy Bible does reveal that an individual's sin can cause sickness (Psalm 38:3-5, Matthew 9:2-6 and John 5:13-14). Though we can be unwell or catch a disease through natural causes such as poor sanitation, polluted water (1 Timothy 5:23), alongside infections and hereditary genes etc., which can cause disability (John 9:1-3). A balanced diet with moderate daily exercise is a way to try and stay healthy (1 Timothy 4:8).

John Woolmer in *Healing and Deliverance* (1999) wrote: 'It is too simple to say that sickness is caused by the devil, or by sin. Sickness is part of life's tapestry. Our bodies have been given an amazing programme which involves natural healing – blood clotting to stop a wound is a simple example, but they also have an inevitable tendency to decay and death.'[1]

Scripture reveals that some serious physical conditions are associated with demonic and emotional problems (Matthew

8:28, 12:22, Mark 1:26, 5:2-7, Luke 4:35, 8:29 and 11:14). John Wimber in *Power Healing* (1986) wrote: 'The origin of physical illness may be demonic, emotional, spiritual (from sin), psychological or chemical.'[2]

Sickness From...

- Should not this woman, a daughter of Abraham, whom Satan has bound, be set free? (Luke 13:16).
- Disobedience can lead to disease and other problems (Deuteronomy ch. 28), Miriam's misplaced words against her brother's marriage to an Ethiopian woman caused leprosy (Numbers 12:10). She was healed after Moses' intervention in prayer.
- The writer to the Hebrews wrote of the Lord's discipline (Hebrews 12:4-11).
- The book of Job shows God's permissive will – that the devil can afflict suffering, death, destruction and illness (Job 1-3), but God is ultimately in control (see Deuteronomy 32:39 and Isaiah 45:7).
- REMEMBER, Jesus 'came to destroy the works of the devil' (1 John 3:8).

Sin and Problems

- Sickness and disease can come from a direct result of disobedience to the Word of God (Exodus 15:26, Deuteronomy 28:15, 18, 27-28, 34-35 and 59-60).
- Demons can take advantage of a person and cause sickness (Mark 9:17-25 and Luke 13:11-16).
- If we take communion (the Lord's Supper) whilst not being in a right relationship with God or a fellow believer, we can become ill (1 Corinthians 11:23-29, 1 John 1:5-9 and 1 John 2:9-11).
- Unforgiveness can lead to resentment and bitterness. This can result in various illnesses and diseases such as stomach ulcers, arthritis, anxiety and high blood pressure. We must forgive because God commands us to (Matthew 6:14-15 and Matthew 18:35).
- God can allow situations, so that He can be glorified (through the healing) or to bring a person where He wants them to be (John 9:1-3 and Hebrews 5:8). God

is also glorified through a person's endurance and godly fortitude in difficult situations (see 1 Peter 1:3-7 and 1 Peter 4:12-13). C.f. John 17:1-5.

- After Jesus healed the man at the Pool of Bethesda, He found him in the temple and said, "See you have been made well. *Sin no more less a worse thing come upon you*" (John 5:1-14). To the woman caught in adultery, Jesus said, "Neither do I condemn you; go and *sin no more*" (John 8:3-11).
- God can take away sickness through obedience to the Word of God (Deuteronomy 7:11-15). God is the Creator and He can make people whole and He allows infirmities (Exodus 4:11, Deuteronomy 32:39, Psalm 146:8, Jeremiah 32:27 and Matthew 11:5-6).

God is Sovereign

The disciples once asked Jesus, "Who sinned, this man or his parents that he was born blind?" Jesus responded, "Neither this man nor his parents sinned, but that the works of God should be revealed in him." Jesus put clay on the blind man's eyes and told him to wash in the pool of Siloam. He 'went and washed and came back seeing' (John 9:1-7).

Jesus spoke about the Galileans whose blood Pilate had mingled with the Jewish sacrifices and the eighteen people who were killed when the tower of Siloam in Jerusalem fell. He noted that the victims "were no worse sinners than all other men...." But, "Unless you repent, you will all likewise perish" (Luke 13:4). Bad things can happen to good people.

God can and does heal, but not everybody is healed. Only the sovereign God has all the answers. Ahijah's eyesight deteriorated as he got older until he was blind (1 Kings 14:4), yet Moses never lost his sight or his strength (Deut. 34:7).

Christians and Infirmities

The body wears out and is eventually 'destroyed' (2 Corinthians 5:1), and we should take obvious precautions to prevent us from becoming ill. Godly people can become ill, and this includes Christian workers: Elisha died of an illness, yet even his bones had power in them to raise a dead man (2 Kings 13:14, 21), so it cannot be claimed he died in a sinful state! The apostle Paul told Timothy to drink a little wine and not just water, because the impure water was upsetting his stomach, and Timothy had 'frequent infirmities' (1 Timothy 5:23). Paul also wrote of 'Luke the beloved physician' and so evidently had no qualms with doctors or their medicines (Colossians 4:14). Epaphroditus, Paul's fellow labourer was sick 'almost unto death; but God had mercy on him' (Philippians 2:25-30). Paul left Trophimus in Miletus because he was sick and moved on to other fields of ministry (2 Timothy 4:20).

Paul speaks of his 'physical infirmity' which allowed him to preach the Gospel to the Galatians which was 'a trial in the flesh' (Galatians 4:12-15). He may have had problems with his eyes (or some other infirmity) or the reference to 'eyes' (v15), was a term of affection in the same way we talk of, "cut off our right arm for..." Paul in a rebuttal about his apostleship alludes to some issue (2 Corinthians 11). Paul wrote that he was 'not at all inferior to the most eminent apostles' (v5), and that he was 'a burden to no one' (v9), which may allude to a sickness. However, the chapter may simply be a rebuttal to his appearance, which made some in Corinth doubt his apostleship. Tradition records that Paul was of short stature with squinty eyes. (C.f. 2 Cor. 10:10).

Natural Healing and Curative Methods

Healing evangelist, George Jeffreys wrote: 'It is a huge mistake on the part of the many devout believers in the truth of Divine healing to ignore natural healing. Some earnest saints have regarded the work of physicians and nurses who minister in the natural realm as being distinctly evil carnal. A few have gone so far as to disregard the essential laws of hygiene, to ignore natural curative means and even refuse the absolute necessities of the body, in case they should manifest unbelief and dishonour God. Such indiscretion has hindered many from taking a stand for the truth, and often resulted in the work of God being brought into disrepute. It is most necessary that the truth of bodily healing should be viewed from the right perspective, and that its presentation be sane, sound, and balanced.'[3]

Further study: Psalm 34:19, 146:8-9, 147:3-4, John 11:4, Romans 15:13, 1 Cor. 10:31, Heb. 12:1-3 and 1 Peter 2:24.

Chapter Thirty-Seven

Hindrances to Healing

'Is anyone among you sick? Let him call for the elders of the church, and let them pray over him, anointing him with oil in the name of the Lord. And the prayer of faith will save the sick, and the Lord will raise him up. And if he has committed sins, he will be forgiven. Confess your trespasses to one another, and pray for one another, that you may be healed. The effective, fervent prayer of a righteous man avails much' (James 5:14-16).

'Let a man examine himself, and so let him eat of that bread and drink of that cup [Lord's Supper]. For he who eats and drinks in an unworthy manner eats and drinks judgment to himself, not discerning the Lord's body' (1 Cor. 11:28-29).

There are many hindrances to Christian healing and this chapter aims to answer the many reasons as to why some people are not healed (instantly or progressively). However, in many cases, a non-healing is a complete mystery and we can only trust God in His full sovereignty and infinite wisdom.

Hindrances to Healing
- Unforgiveness (including bitterness and deep-rooted anger) – if you don't forgive others, God will not forgive you (Matthew 6:14-15), coupled with the elders prayer for the sick and confession of sin (James 5:14-16). Jesus said, "...Forgive us our debts as we forgive our debtors" (Matthew 6:12).
- Being guilty of personal sin (Psalm 66:18).
- Unconfessed sin – elders praying for the sick and anointing with oil is interlinked with confession of sin (James 5:14-16). Confess and forsake sin (Leviticus 5:5 and Proverbs 28:13).

- Disunity with another brother or sister in the Lord – be reconciled and then offer your gift to God (Matt. 5:23-24). Unity is key to spiritual blessing (Ps. 133).
- Lack of faith – numerous cases of people healed because of their faith. The woman with the issue of blood (Matthew 9:21), two blind men (Matthew 9:29), and Jesus said, "If you have faith..." (Matthew 17:20 and 21:21). Unbelief (Mark 5:4-6 and Romans 14:23).
- Poor spiritual atmosphere – at Nazareth, Jesus 'could do no mighty works there' and 'marvelled at their unbelief' (Mark 6:1-6 and Matt. 13:54-58). The two men of Gadarene were delivered as the demons were cast into the herd of pigs. But the whole city asked Jesus to depart from the area! (Matt. 8:28-34).
- Lack of prayer or persistence – Jesus said, "Men always ought to pray and not lose heart" (Luke 18:1), and the story of the persistent friend (Luke 11:5-13).
- Occult involvement – renounce the devil and all his works. Even Jesus, after His forty days in the wilderness said, "Away with you, Satan!" (Matt. 4:10).
- Generational problems (see Exodus 20:3-6).
- Misuse of the Lord's Supper – brings judgment on yourself, resulting in weaknesses, sickness or even death (1 Corinthians 11:27-32).
- Some sins can cause sickness – 'The prayer of faith will save the sick and if he has committed sins, he will be forgiven' (James 5:15). See also James 5:20 and Jude 22-23, making a distinction between people in error. Some sins lead to death and we may not necessarily pray about that (see 1 John 5:14-17).
- Seeking healing for self-gratification or wrong motives (James 4:3). God knows the heart – why should He heal someone if they will only live for his or her self? Jesus and the ten lepers, all ten were cleansed but only one returned to give thanks. Jesus said that his faith had made him well and the text implies that the others were not fully healed (Luke 17:11-19).
- Sometimes an act of obedience is needed – the ten lepers as mentioned above, 'as they went' on their way to show themselves to the priests 'they were

cleansed' (Luke 17:14). Healing is not always instantaneous. Naaman the commander of the Syrian army was a leper who had to dip himself seven times in the river before he was healed (2 Kings 5:1-16). A blind man saw people walking like trees; so *Jesus prayed for him a second time* (Mark 8:22-26).

Possible Reasons for a Non-healing

Sometimes we just don't know why people are not healed. Jesus healed the man at the pool of Bethesda, but there were evidently multitudes whom He did not pray for and who did not receive healing (John 5:1-9). On occasions, power emanated from Jesus Christ so that everyone was healed (Luke 6:19), or just *one person* amidst a crowd (Luke 8:46).

There is nothing wrong in using medicine, seeing a doctor or going to hospital, it makes sense to use the skills of those who have been medically trained. In the Old Testament we have prophetic allusion to those skilled in binding up wounds, setting bones and use of the balm of Gilead (Isaiah 1:6, Jeremiah 8:22 and Ezekiel 30:21). Herbs and plants were used in medicine (2 Kings 20:7 and Isaiah 38:21) and it is highly probable that King Solomon knew how to make medicine from plants (1 Kings 4:29-34). The New Testament states: 'Luke the *beloved physician'* (Colossians 4:14).

God can allow sickness to get us to a place where He wants us to be. A time of recuperation or a time to hear what He wants from us. Elijah rested at the brook after he fled from Jezebel (1 Kings 19:1-18). Whilst Job, the wealthiest man in his day was attacked by Satan with painful boils (Job 2:7-10), it was in the permissive will of God and Job was ultimately more blessed in the latter days of his life than at the beginning (Job 42:12 and James 5:11). The apostle Paul was given a thorn in the flesh to keep him humble because of his majestic revelations (2 Corinthians 12:7-10).

God may allow self-afflicted illness to heal over its natural course so that we learn a valuable lesson, not to abuse ourselves in the future. Neglect of the body is sin (overeating, under-eating, lack of exercise or sleep. Our body is the temple of God (1 Corinthians 6:19); look after it!

The body naturally wears out and deteriorates and we all have to die someday (2 Corinthians 4:7-5:5). Is prayer for healing for a Christian in their eighties (who has poor quality of life) selfish on our part? Should they not depart and be with the Lord, which is far better? 'Absent from the body and to be present with the Lord' (2 Corinthians 5:8). Even Paul was torn between the two – 'Having a desire to depart and be with Christ which is far better,' but he knew the church at Philippi needed his help (Philippians 1:23-24). Others have sustained injuries, disabilities or terminal illness that give them no quality of life. There is a danger in giving false hope that does not allow the person concerned to make their peace with God, especially after continued prayer with no visible results, should they not be allowed to face death, to settle their affairs and die with dignity, a holy death in Christ Jesus? Healing may only be a temporary reprieve from death, or may give them extra time to make their peace. An untimely death can happen for a variety of reasons, good or bad (see 1 Kings 14:12-13, 2 Kings 22:19-20, 2 Samuel 12:14-15, Job 34:10-11 and Isaiah 57:1-2).

For some people it has 'been granted on behalf of Christ, not only to believe in Him, but also to suffer for His sake' (Philippians 1:29). Jesus 'learned obedience by the things which He suffered and having been perfected...' (Hebrews 5:8-9). The New Testament writers related the word 'suffering' with 'persecution' (Romans 8:17, 2 Corinthians 1:5, Philippians 3:10, Hebrews 2:10, 1 Peter 4:1 and 12-13).

Words of Wisdom

Now Jesus 'could do no mighty works there, except that He laid His hands on a few sick people and healed them. And He marvelled because of their unbelief...' (Mark 6:5-6a).

Faith is needed in healing, but it is wrong to point the finger and say that someone has not been healed due to *their* lack of faith (Mark 9:23-24, 10:52, 11:22, Luke 17:15, Acts 3:16 Romans 1:11-12 and 3:3). Be persistent in prayer and don't get discouraged, perhaps the timing is wrong (Ecclesiastes 3:3 and Luke 18:1-14). Seek God's will (Acts 21:14). Jesus has identified with our humanity (Hebrews 4:15-16), and in heaven, there is no sickness, pain or suffering (Rev. 21:1-7).

Jesus went down from the mountain 'and the whole multitude sought to touch Him, for power went out from Him and healed them all' (Luke 6:19).

Chapter Thirty-Eight

Seeking Healing

'He was wounded for our transgressions, He was bruised for our iniquities...by His stripes we are healed' (Isaiah 53:5).

'Who Himself bore our sins in His own body on the tree, that we, having died to sins, might live for righteousness – by whose stripes you were healed' (1 Peter 2:24).

God is a God who heals; some Christians say healing is *a right*, others state it is *a sign*, whilst some sadly deny the power of God by stating that healing is not for today, and / or attribute *all* healings as from the evil one (and some is Matthew 24:24). Praise God that He is unchanging and we can receive healing in and through Jesus Christ. However not everybody who seeks healing finds it. To many this is a complete mystery. In addition, there is no point in praying for healing when a person needs deliverance. Demons may have brought about the affliction; as in the woman bent over double for eighteen years who was bound by Satan (Luke 13:11-16). Therefore, they do not need prayer for healing, but deliverance from demons (this is covered in chapter 48).

Any Christian can pray for healing (for themselves or others), whilst some have 'gifts of healings,' or 'the working of miracles' as part of the nine gifts of the Spirit (1 Corinthians 12:4-11, 28, 30). Another gift is 'faith' (v9), and whilst a Christian may not have the other two previously mentioned gifts, faith may rise up in them and they may see the person healed instantly or progressively. On other occasions, a word of 'wisdom' or 'knowledge' (v8), may be spoken which is the key to the person's healing. It may reveal why the person is sick (underlying issues) or how they can receive their healing. Some issues are demonic in nature or a person needs inner healing of their soul or spirit to receive an outer healing, as mind and body are interconnected, see chapter 44, Receiving Inner Healing. We can also ask the elders within our church to pray for us and anoint us with oil as a step of faith, as we confess our sins (James 5:14-16). Partaking of the Lord's Supper (communion) in an unworthy manner can lead to sickness – conversely, if we eat it in a *worthy manner* we can ask God for our healing or to keep us in good health. The bread and the wine (or whatever elements used) is symbolic of the body and blood of Jesus Christ (1 Corinthians 11:23-31), which was broken and poured out for us (see Isaiah 53:5, Matt. 8:17 & 1 Pet. 2:24).

Scriptures on Healing to Pray and Believe

- "If you diligently heed the voice of the Lord your God and do what is right in His sight…I will put none of the diseases of which I have brought on the Egyptians. For I am the Lord who heals you" (Exodus 15:26).
- "The Lord will take away from you all sickness, and will afflict you with none of the terrible diseases of Egypt which you have known…" (Deuteronomy 7:15).
- 'Bless the Lord, O my soul, and forget not all His benefits, who forgives all your iniquities, who heals all your diseases' (Psalm 103:2-3).
- 'He sent His Word and healed them, and delivered them from their destruction' (Psalm 107:20).
- 'Fear the Lord and depart from evil. It will be health to your flesh and strength to your bones' (Prov. 3:7b-8).
- 'He was wounded for our transgressions…by His stripes we are healed…. It pleased the Lord to bruise Him…He bore the sins of many…' (Isa. 53:5, 10, 12).
- 'He Himself took our infirmities and bore our sicknesses' (Matthew 8:17).
- 'Who Himself bore our sins in His own body on the tree…by whose stripes you were healed' (1 Pt. 2:24).

Saved and Healed

In Romans 10:9 (if you confess with your mouth…the Lord Jesus…and believe…you will be saved), the English word 'saved' comes from the Greek word 'Sozo,' meaning 'healed' – healed spiritually and healed physically. Healing evangelist

T. L. Osborn wrote: 'Healed in body and healed in soul, or saved from sin and saved from sickness. It is translated, 'heal, preserve, save, and make whole.' ... 'Healing in the Bible is spiritual as well as physical. Disease manifests itself in the physical, but its roots are in the spiritual.'[1]

English plumber turned preacher, Smith Wigglesworth was used mightily in signs and wonders and saw more than a dozen people raised from the dead! His theology on healing was: "There is healing through the blood of Christ and deliverance for every captive. God never intended His children to live in misery because of some affliction that comes directly from the devil. A perfect atonement was made at Calvary. I believe that Jesus bore my sins, and I am free from them all. I am justified from all things if I dare to believe. He Himself took our infirmities and bore our sickness; and if I dare believe, I can be healed."[2]

Two Redemptive Names of God

Jehovah-Tsidkenu is the redemptive name of God that reveals God's redemptive provision for the soul (conversion). 'The Lord our Righteousness' (Jeremiah 23:6).

Jehovah-Rapha is the redemptive name of God that reveals God's redemptive provision for the body (healing). 'I am the Lord that heals you' (Exodus 15:26).

Why Jesus Healed People

- To demonstrate that the Kingdom of God had arrived (Matthew 4:23-25, 12:28, Mark 1:14, Luke 4:17-22 and Luke 11:20), and to reveal the glory of God as a sign and testimony (John 2:1-11).
- To demonstrate His compassion and mercy (Matthew 14:13-14, 20:29-34 and Mark 1:41).
- To declare that Jesus was the One promised by the Father (Matthew 8:14-17 and Matthew 11:1-6).
- It bore witness to the Truth of Jesus Christ and the claims He made about Himself (Matthew 8:14-17 and Luke 5:18-25).
- To bring people to repentance (Luke 10:8-12).
- To demonstrate that the Gospel is for all nations, Jews as well as Gentiles (Luke 7:1-10).[3]

Proclamation and Demonstration

John Wimber wrote: 'Jesus' public ministry had two elements: *proclamation* of the Good News of the Kingdom of God and *demonstration* of its power through casting out demons, healing the sick, and raising the dead.'[4]

An unnamed author wrote: 'Jesus by His preaching, by His manner of life in associating with the marginalised people (Matthew 9:12-13 and Luke 15:1-2), and by His healing and exorcism manifested the fact that "The Kingdom of God has come!" (Mark 1:14 par.).' In applying the promise of Isaiah 61:1-2 to Himself, 'Jesus was announcing that in His person the Kingdom of God was breaking in (Luke 4:17-21). By healing from disease and casting out demons, Jesus inaugurated the Kingdom of God and embodied it (Matthew 12:28 and Luke 11:20).'[5]

Things to Remember when Seeking Healing

Healing evangelist, George Jeffreys wrote: 'The state of your spiritual life can easily affect the condition of your body.'

- Therefore see that your spiritual life is nourished by prayer, and the reading of God's Word. 'Is anyone among you suffering? Let him pray' (James 5:13). 'This is my comfort in my affliction, for Your Word has given me life' (Psalm 119:50).
- Healing, like salvation, is all of grace; therefore do not consider your own unworthiness: 'He who did not spare His own Son, but delivered Him up for us all, how shall He not with Him also freely give us all good things?' (Romans 8:32).
- Do not worry over your little faith, but consider the greatness of the Divine Physician: Jesus said, "If you have faith as a mustard seed, you can say to this mulberry tree, 'be pulled up by the roots and planted in the sea' and it would obey you" (Luke 17:6).
- You must not be overburdened about your long-standing disease. Cases like yours have been healed before: 'There was a woman who had a spirit of infirmity eighteen years and was bent over and could no way raise herself.... He [Jesus] laid His hands on her, and immediately she was made straight, and glorified God' (Luke 13:11, 13).

- 184 -

- You must not be discouraged if not immediately healed. Yours might be a gradual recovery: 'Then he inquired of them the hour when he got better. And they said to him "Yesterday at the seventh hour the fever left him" ' (John 4:52).
- Due attention must be given to the laws of health as to food, hygiene, bodily exercise and rest: 'If you diligently heed the voice of the Lord God and do what is right in His sight, give ear to His commandments and keep all His statutes, I will put none of the diseases on you which I have brought on the Egyptians. For I am the Lord who heals you" (Exodus 15:26).
- A cheerful heart is a tonic to yourself and to others, therefore cultivate a happy disposition: 'A merry heart does good like medicine...' (Proverbs 17:22a).
- God is glorified and His works made manifest when the supernatural is in evidence: 'The disciples asked Jesus, "Who sinned, this man or his parents that he was born blind?" Jesus responded, "Neither this man nor his parents sinned, but *that the works of God should be revealed in him*" (John 9:2-3). 'This beginning of signs Jesus did in Cana of Galilee, and *manifested His glory*; and His disciples believed in Him' (John 2:11).[6]

Instant and Progressive Healing

George Jeffreys wrote: 'The gifts of healing are amongst the nine miraculous gifts that are distributed to the Church by the Holy Spirit. The word *healing* suggests a gradual recovery, and many are restored in this way. Another among the nine gifts is the working of miracles, which suggests an immediate Divine interposition, so that a person is instantly healed. In our Lord's ministry there were these two kinds of healing.'[7]

- The nobleman's son was healed, the same hour in which Jesus had said, "Go your way, your son lives" (John 4:50-53).
- Jesus touched a man who was full of leprosy and he was instantly healed (Luke 5:12-13).
- The paralysed man was instantly healed (Jn. 5-1-9).

- Nahaam dipped himself seven times in the river before he was healed of his leprosy (2 Kings 5:1-16).
- Hezekiah had a boil and was near death. Isaiah spoke the Word of the Lord that he would live 15 extra years and that on the *third day* he would go up to the house of the Lord. A lump of figs was applied as a poultice on the boil, 'and he shall recover' (2 Kings 20:1-11 and Isaiah 38:1-21).
- Jesus prayed for a blind man twice. The first time the man saw people walking like trees (Mark 8:22-26).
- Jesus told the ten lepers to go on their way and as they did they were cleansed (Luke 17:11-19).

Medicine and Prayer Combined

George Jeffreys wrote: 'Some of the most spiritual saints who pray for healing feel quite free to cooperate with the natural law of healing in the use of natural curative means. This attitude is sanctioned in Scripture, for Paul prescribed means for Timothy's "often infirmities" [1 Timothy 5:23]. Prayer and coordination with the natural law of healing, which is inherent in human nature, often results in acceleration, and healing has come with astonishing speed. We have frequently come into contact with saints who have testified to marvellous healing results in this way. Others have felt definitely led of God to abandon all natural curative means, and they too have testified to astounding miracles of healing in answer to prayer. We do not presume to dictate to saints in this matter, for it is one that must be decided by themselves. But we do advise to act wisely concerning the law of cleansing against contagion, and the law of isolation against infection, which were undoubtedly embodied in the "statutes" mentioned in the great Healing Covenant of Exodus 24.'[8] See also Exodus 23:25-26.

Steps That Lead to Healing

George Jeffreys noted some steps that lead to healing:
- Be sure you are in line with God's will (1 John 5:14).
- If you are a backslider, get restored (Hosea 14:1, 4 and 2 Chronicles 7:14).
- If unsaved you should be saved (1 Timothy 2:3-4).

- Obey the commandments of God (John 14:15).
- If you are saved you should remember the Lord's death [communion] (1 Corinthians 11:24-26).
- If you are saved you should bring your tithes into the storehouse (Malachi 3:10-11).
- Be sure you confess any wrongdoing to those you have injured (James 5:16).
- You should manifest love to other Christians (1 Peter 1:22).[9]

Modes of Healing

George Jeffreys noted some modes of healing. They are:
- The direct appeal on the part of an individual. A leper appealed directly to Jesus and received healing (Matthew 8:2).
- The cooperation and fellowship of practical sympathisers. The friends who lowered the paralytic man through a hole in a roof. Jesus saw their faith and the man took up his bed and walked away (Mark 2:4-5).
- The cooperation and mutual fellowship of prayer warriors. If two agree on earth in Jesus' name (Matthew 18:19).
- The laying on of hands (Mark 16:18).
- The anointing with oil (James 5:14).
- The going forth of God's Word. 'He sent His Word and healed them...' (Psalm 107:20).
- The ministry of prayer in the church. 'By stretching forth Your hand to heal and that signs and wonders may be done by the name of Your holy Servant Jesus' (Acts 4:30).[10]

Healing Scriptures

- Jesus gave the disciples 'power and authority over all demons and to cure diseases' (Luke 9:1).
- Jesus said, "Heal the sick, cleanse the lepers, raise the dead, cast out demons..." (Matthew 10:8).
- Some people can *only* be delivered / healed by *prayer and fasting* (Matthew 17:14-21). It is the anointing that breaks the yoke (Isaiah 10:27). Often those who are used in healings or move in signs and

wonders maintain a lifestyle of prayer and fasting, or they are called to fast for a period of time for a specific case or time of ministry.

Not All who Seek Healing Find It

George Jeffreys wrote: 'Although bodily healing is one of the present benefits of the atoning work of Christ on the cross, the Scripture definitely shews [establish the validity] that all who truly seek bodily healing do not find it. It is possible for a person to be suffering from some physical infirmity, and yet be in the will of God.' Job received painful boils directly from Satan who had received permission from God (Job 2:1-10). Jesus said to the apostle Paul, "My grace is sufficient for you, for My strength is made perfect in weakness," and Paul boasted in his 'infirmities that the power of Christ may rest upon me' (2 Corinthians 12:9-10).

Jeffreys continued: 'One cannot be dogmatic concerning the nature of Paul's thorn in the flesh. Taking for granted that the messenger of Satan which buffeted him was some physical infirmity, Paul under the circumstances set a fine example of importunate prayer and faith for Divine healing. He manifested implicit faith in his claim to deliverance by presenting it until the revelation came that he was to suffer. Paul's attitude towards his thorn in the flesh, instead of being an argument against Divine healing, is a weighty one in its favour. We maintain that every child of God, provided he complies with relative conditions, can rightly seek healing, unless he is assured that it is God's will for him to suffer' (2 Corinthians 12:7-9).'

'...All were not healed in the days of our Lord (Mark 6:5-6). ...We do not attribute all failures to the lack of faith. There might be other reasons why people are not healed. Hindrances in the lives of seekers, and unwillingness to obey the commandments of the Lord, can hinder the work of healing. Again, some are allowed to suffer for disciplinary and other purposes.'[11]

Further study: (Old and New Testament healing atonement: Lev. 14-15, Num. 21:9, Job 33:24-25, Gal. 3:13, Heb. 7-11). Prov. 4:20-22, Isaiah 53, Luke 4:14, Acts 3:1-8, 16, 6:8, 9:36-42, 14:3, 9-10, 19:11-12, Rom. 15:13 & Heb. 10:35-36.

Chapter Thirty-Nine

Signs and Wonders

The apostle Paul wrote: 'Truly the signs of an apostle were accomplished among you with all perseverance, in signs and wonders and mighty deeds' (2 Corinthians 12:12).

'For our Gospel did not come to you in word only, but also in power, and in the Holy Spirit...' (1 Thessalonians 1:5).

Healings, miracles and signs and wonders attested and attracted people to Jesus Christ, and this chapter is a compilation of many of these Scriptures. George Jeffreys wrote: 'It is evident to the careful reader of the Gospels that miracles and healings served more than one purpose. They were not only given to attest the ministry of our Lord and those He had appointed, but they were instrumental in attracting people to Christ and in encouraging faith.'[1]

- Jesus turned water into wine at a wedding. 'This beginning of signs Jesus did in Cana of Galilee, and manifested His glory and His disciples believed in Him' (John 2:11).
- 'Now when He was in Jerusalem at the Passover, during the feast, many believed in His name when they saw the signs which He did' (John 2:23).
- After Jesus Christ fed the five thousand men beside women and children, 'a great multitude followed Him, because they saw His signs which He performed on those who were diseased' (John 6:2).
- At Jerusalem during the feast 'many of the people believed in Him and said, "When Christ comes, will He do more signs than these which this Man has done?" ' (John 7:31).
- The Jews said to Jesus, "How long do you keep us in doubt? If you are the Christ, tell us plainly." Jesus

replied, "I told you and you do not believe. The works that I do in My Father's name bear witness of Me" (John 10:24-25).

- The raising of Lazarus from the dead caused many of the Jews to believe in Jesus (John 11:45 and John 12:11, 18). It glorified God (John 11:4), c.f. John 17:4.

Philip preached in the city of Samaria 'and the multitude with one accord heeded the things spoken…hearing and seeing the miracles which he did. For unclean spirits…with a loud voice, came out of many who were possessed; and many who were paralyzed and lame were healed' (Acts 8:5-7).

Signs and Wonders Confirm the Gospel Message

- After Jesus' forty days in the wilderness He 'returned in the power of the Spirit to Galilee and news of Him went out through all the surrounding region' (Luke 4:14). In a synagogue in Nazareth, Jesus read from Isaiah 61 verses 1-2 and said, "Today this Scripture is fulfilled in your hearing" (Luke 4:21) because Jesus preached the Gospel, healed the broken-hearted and moved in signs and wonders.
- Jesus sent the twelve disciples out saying, "Heal the sick, cleanse the lepers, raise the dead, cast out demons…freely give" (Matthew 10:8).
- Before Jesus' ascension (return of Jesus to heaven), He said, "Behold, I send the Promise of My Father upon you, but tarry in the city of Jerusalem until you are endued with power…" (Luke 24:49).
- Jesus said, "Go into all the world and preach the Gospel…. And these signs will follow those who believe: In My name they will cast out demons; they will speak with new tongues…they will lay hands on the sick and they will recover" (Mark 16:15-18).
- After Peter preached at Pentecost, 'Then fear came upon every soul, and many wonders and signs were done through the apostles' (Acts 2:43).
- 'And with great power the apostles gave witness to the resurrection of the Lord Jesus. And great grace was upon them all' (Acts 4:33).

- 'Through the hands of the apostles many signs and wonders were done among the people' (Acts 5:12).
- 'So that they brought the sick out into the streets and laid them on beds and couches, that at least the shadow of Peter passing by might fall on some of them. Also a multitude gathered...bringing sick people and those who were tormented by unclean spirits, and they were all healed' (Acts 5:15-16).
- 'And Stephen, full of faith and power did great wonders and signs among the people' (Acts 6:8).
- Philip preached in the city of Samaria 'and the multitude with one accord heeded the things spoken by Philip, hearing and seeing the miracles which he did. For unclean spirits...came out of many who were possessed; and many who were paralyzed and lame were healed' (Acts 8:5-7).
- At Lydda, Peter prayed for a man who had been bedridden, paralysed for eight years and he was healed. 'So all who dwelt at Lydda and Sharon saw him and turned to the Lord' (Acts 9:34-35).
- At Joppa, a follower of Christ, a godly woman called Tabitha (also known as Dorcas), had died. Peter prayed for her and she was raised from the dead! 'And it became known throughout all Joppa, and many believed on the Lord' (Acts 9:40-42).
- The apostle Paul and Barnabas were at Iconium where they preached the Good News and saw much opposition. 'Therefore they stayed there a long time, speaking boldly in the Lord, who was bearing witness to the word of His grace, granting signs and wonders to be done by their hands' (Acts 14:1-4).
- At Ephesus 'God worked unusual miracles by the hands of Paul, so that even handkerchiefs or aprons were brought from his body to the sick, and the disease left them and the evil spirit went out of them' (Acts 19:11-12).
- The apostle Paul wrote: 'For the Kingdom of God is not in word but in power' (1 Corinthians 4:20).
- The 'signs of an apostle were accomplished...signs and wonders and mighty deeds' (2 Cor. 12:12).

- Paul wrote: 'My speech and my preaching were not with persuasive words of human wisdom, but in demonstration of the Spirit and power, that your faith should not be in the wisdom of men, but in the power of God' (1 Corinthians 2:4-5).

> '...While healing is the sign of the Kingdom [of God], the cross is the gateway to it' – John Woolmer.

- "You are My witnesses," says the Lord (Isaiah 43:10).
- 'Give thanks to the Lord! Call upon His name; make known His deeds among the people' (Psalm 105:1b).
- 'Jesus Christ is the same yesterday, today, and forever' (Hebrews 13:8).

The Good News is Foremost

Preaching the Gospel must always be the priority of believers. Healing, deliverance and signs and wonders as important as they are (and were to Jesus, Luke 4:18-19), are subservient to the Good News. Salvation is the greatest miracle. It would be a tragedy if a person was healed in Jesus' mighty name but was not given the Gospel (see Mark 8:36 and Luke 9:25). After Peter's mother-in-law was healed, 'the whole city gathered at the door' and Jesus 'healed many who were sick with various diseases, and cast out many demons' (Mark 1:21-34). The following day, when everybody was looking for Jesus, He said to His disciples, "Let us go into the next towns, *that I may preach there also*, because for this purpose I have come forth" (Mark 1:38). The signs attracted people to Jesus (John 6:2), and occasionally the food (John 6:26), but the teaching was central which some followers could not handle and so fell away (John 6:47-66).

Elymas the sorcerer withstood the preaching of Barnabas, and Saul (Paul) who commanded him to be blind for a time! This led the proconsul to believe in the Lord (Acts 13:6-12).

David Holden wrote: 'We don't need a new approach to evangelism. We need to receive a greater anointing of the Spirit so that we can become more effective in sharing our faith.'[2]

Chapter Forty

Ministering to People

Jesus said, "The Kingdom of heaven is at hand. Heal the sick, cleanse the lepers, raise the dead, cast out demons. Freely you have received freely give" (Matthew 10:7-8).

'Having then gifts differing according to the grace that is given to us, let us use them: if prophecy, let us prophesy in proportion to our faith; or ministry, let us use it in ministering; he who teaches, in teaching' (Romans 12:6-7).

"Why and how do we minister to people?" We minister to people because Jesus set the benchmark and we follow His example (Luke 4:18-19), as did the disciples and subsequent followers of Jesus Christ. When you come to faith in Christ Jesus, He accepts you as you are, including all your problems and excess baggage, scars from the past. As you walk the path of being a disciple of Jesus Christ, you will realise that you will have areas of your life that are not under the lordship of Jesus Christ. These areas need to be surrendered, but there can be other spiritual forces that are in opposition to this. We speak in the context of ministering to people; often by the laying on of hands, so that excess baggage etc. can be dealt with or demons / evil spirits can be cast out (or off) from a believer so that they can be set free (delivered from demons). A fellow Spirit-filled Christian can pray with you, to help you be released and set free from any demonic baggage, soul ties, spiritual bondages and help with regards to inner healing (released from past hurts and memories), and physical healing of the body or mind in the name of Jesus Christ. Subsequent chapters deal with these individual areas in specific detail.

Ministering can be as simple as the laying on of hands and praying for God to heal someone in the name of Jesus;

anointing with oil, or can involve casting out demons, praying for the Holy Spirit to set a person free from inner wounds. Have tissues and a bin at hand. John Wimber said, "Ministry is meeting the needs of others with the resources of God."[1]

The Holy Spirit

We all need to be endued with power from on high and baptised in the Holy Spirit (Acts 1:8), our own personal Pentecost. Even Jesus, the Son of God received the Holy Spirit at His baptism (Luke 3:21-22). Then He was 'filled with the Spirit' and was 'led by the Spirit into the wilderness' where He fasted for forty days (Luke 4:1-13). After this He returned 'in the power of the Spirit' (Luke 4:14), and His ministry began. Jesus, in the synagogue of Nazareth read from the book of Isaiah, "The Spirit of the Lord is upon Me, because He has anointed me to preach the Gospel to the poor. He has sent Me to heal the broken-hearted, to preach deliverance to the captives and recovery of sight to the blind, to set at liberty those who are oppressed, to preach the acceptable year of the Lord" (Luke 4:18-19).

Benny Hinn in *Good Morning Holy Spirit* (1990) wrote: 'If the Spirit was necessary for Christ, He should be every bit as important to you. Jesus was born of the Spirit, anointed by the Spirit, cast out devils by the Spirit, received His fullness by the Spirit, and performed miracles by the Spirit. And it was by the Holy Ghost [Spirit] that He taught, gave commands, empowered and governed the church, offered Himself on the cross, and was resurrected... (Hebrews 9:14). The same Spirit that was essential for the earthly work of Christ is necessary for you. He is indispensible.'[2]

Ministry and Submission

If a person needs ministry and comes to you for help then wisdom dictates that it is best to tell them to see their pastor, first. The pastor will (or may) know his flock better than you, their lifestyle and whether they are truly committed to the cause of Christ or not. However, if the pastor does not know what to do or may be unable to deal with the situation, he or she may recommend or refer the believer to someone else within the church, or a Christian ministry that specialises in these areas. Where possible, get your pastor's permission if you are going to minister to people from within the congregation. It is biblical to be subject to those who are in authority over you (Romans 13:1-2, Titus 3:1, Hebrews 13:7 and 1 Peter 2:13-16). Sometimes people in need go from one person to the next seeking help, but refuse to do their part. Some are time-wasters and attention seekers. Many churches have a time of ministry after the service where people can come forward for prayer. Other churches have ministry teams available for harder cases, because ministry can take hours and often involves meeting weekly.

I do not recommend ministering to non-Christians, as they are not in a covenant relationship with Jesus Christ (Matthew 7:6, 12:43-45, 15:21-28 and Luke 10:17-20). Conversion is more important than being healed or delivered from demons, however sometimes people do surrender their lives to Jesus Christ, once they have been touched by God.

> 'Now may the God of peace sanctify you completely; and may your whole spirit, soul and body be preserved blameless at the coming of our Lord Jesus Christ' (1 Thessalonians 5:23).

Words of Wisdom

Only God can heal people and set them free, we are just vessels He uses to work through (Luke 17:10). If possible work in pairs (or more) when ministering to someone as Jesus sent the disciples out in pairs (Mark 6:7), ideally one person having had some previous experience in these areas; if not, it's on-the-job training! It is best to pray with people of your own gender. If this is not possible and a man is praying for a woman then another woman needs to be present. It is unwise for men to pray for a Christian woman to be delivered without the consent and, or presence of her Christian husband. Ideally, it is still better to have another woman present even when the husband is around. Allow no room for misunderstandings or reproach and give no appearance of evil (Romans 14:6, 2 Corinthians 6:3, Ephesians 4:27, Colossians 3:18, 1 Thessalonians 5:22 and 1 Timothy 4:12).

If there is any unforgiveness, (towards God, themselves or others), bitterness or unconfessed sin in the person's life, they will not be able to be fully delivered or set free (Matthew

5:23-24, 6:14-15, 9:2-6, John 5:14 and 1 John 1:5-7). These sins will give any demonic being(s) or a curse, a legal right to stay and torment or afflict. The person needs to renounce the devil and all his works, confess their sin, repent and turn from the sin (Psalm 32:5, 139:23-24, James 4:6-7, 5:16 and 1 John 1:9). God's forgiveness is freely available.

> Ministering in pairs releases us from both the spiritual burden of 'failure' and the awful spiritual pride of 'success' – John Woolmer, author of *Thinking Clearly About Prayer*.

Counselling and Hands on Ministry

When you visit your doctor, you explain your problem or symptoms and allow a diagnosis to be made. The doctor will ask you some questions, examine you and give you a prescription or practical advice to aid recovery. Ministering to a person takes the same sort of lines. You may need to give a spiritual prescription (or feel prompted by the Holy Spirit), i.e. read this portion of Scripture daily, make amends for that sin, e.g. theft, be reconciled to that person. If they truly want to be made well they will take the spiritual prescription.

It is futile to verbally counsel or listen to a person without getting to the root of their problem and dealing with it. All talk and no ministry will not set a person free. There is a time and a place for chatting to discover the root of a problem and the ultimate Counsellor is the Holy Spirit, so allow Him to guide you. He may want to give you a word of wisdom or knowledge (1 Corinthians 12:1-12), in relation to the person you are ministering to; even before the time of ministry has begun. The Holy Spirit reveals all truth (John 16:13). Listen to His still small voice and act on what He says (Acts 8:29 and Acts 10:19). He may show you specific things that the person who is being ministered to has done (which needs repentance), or that which has been done to them (they may need to forgive the offender). Sometimes when praying for someone, especially in healing or for a fresh touch of the Holy Spirit, you may feel what can best be described as energy, electricity, warmth, heat or a presence on or inside your body. Sometimes the area in question relates to the person you are praying for. At other times it is a sign of the anointing on you or them. Remember – there is no point praying for a person to be healed if they need deliverance. Cast out or off the demon(s) and the person can be healed.

When ministering to people, do not just hear, but listen to what they have to say; do you need to read between the lines? (Matthew 13:9-10). Watch their body language, are they agitated when you mention certain words or sins? Walk in love, do not judge or condemn them (John 8:7-11). Remind them that you are there to help. When ministering it is best to explain what you will do (and are doing) as you go along to help put the person at ease, it is also a good teaching aid. Remind them that you are on their side.

Sometimes people only want to tell you their problems and do not wish to be set free (John 5:6). They may enjoy feeling sorry for themselves (self-pity is sin) and seek attention, also you are cheaper than a counsellor or psychiatrist, as ministry is given freely (Matthew 10:8). Sometimes the person seeking help will try to control the situation, e.g. "I can't see you on Friday evening as the football match is on." If they are serious about being set free and healed from whatever bondages, they will make every effort to be available at an appointed time (Mark 10:47-52). You may need to minister to a person (for hours) several times or more over weeks or months until they are completely free. After each prayer session ask for the cleansing of the blood of Jesus (on all present and their families) and then ask the Holy Spirit to come and fill the person who has been ministered to afresh (Luke 11:13 and Acts 8:14-16). Give God all the glory and acknowledge without Him we can do nothing.

Spiritual Weapons for Ministry
- Spiritual armour, wear it (Ephesians 6:10-18).
- The Word of God, the Holy Bible, know it, verses of Scripture (Isaiah 55:11 and Hebrews 4:12).
- Jesus' name (Matthew 28:18-20 and Acts 4:10).
- Plead the precious blood of Jesus Christ (Ephesians 1:7 and Ephesians 2:13).
- Know and use your authority in Christ Jesus (Romans 8:17 and Galatians 4:7).
- You can partake of the sacrament of communion, the Lord's Supper during ministry (1 Cor. 11:23-31).

- Anointing with oil (Mark 6:13 and James 5:14-16).
- Holy water (water that has been prayed over and blessed in the same fashion as the anointing oil). It can be drunk or lightly sprinkled over the person.
- Praying in tongues (1 Corinthians 14:2, 14-15).
- Angels can help you (Daniel 6:22, 10:12-13, 20 and Hebrews 1:14).
- Praise and worship, as gentle background music (Psalm 149:6).
- Look to the Holy Spirit to lead you, and by the use of His gifts (1 Corinthians 12:1-11).

Bodily Healing

George Jeffreys in *Healing Rays* (1932) wrote: 'The subject of bodily healing is evidently claiming the attention of Christendom.... The one great reason why it is dominating the mind of the public is the fact that thousands...claim to have been miraculously healed in answer to prayer under the ministry of the laying on of hands or the anointing with oil, as people were in Bible days. These manifestations are not confined to the British Isles, they are being experienced over the whole world. Everywhere deliverances from deadly diseases are avowed, and miracles are being wrought, the replicas of which can only be found in the Bible. Neither are they exclusively experienced by any one particular sect or community that holds bodily healing as one of its tenets of belief, but by spiritual ministers, evangelists and church workers of all denominations....

'The method of procedure in ministering to the sick is not always the same. Some evangelists are called upon to lay hands publicly, and vast congregations have witnessed astounding miracles, others anoint the sick with oil in the quiet bedroom, and have rejoiced in healing as a result of their obedience. Again there are the many prayer circles where written requests for healing are remembered before the throne. The source of all healing virtue is in the Lord Jesus Christ, and although methods differ, the all-important matter is to get the sick into touch with Him.'[3]

Further study: Jeremiah 23:29, Matthew 25:40, John 14:14, 1 Corinthians 12:1-11, 25-27 and 1 Corinthians 13:4-7.

Chapter Forty-One

Anointing With Oil

'They went out and preached that people should repent. And they cast out many demons, and anointed with oil many who were sick, and healed them' (Mark 6:12-13).

'Is anyone among you sick? Let him call for the elders of the church, and let them pray over him, anointing him with oil in the name of the Lord. And the prayer of faith will save the sick...' (James 5:14-15).

"Why do some people get anointed with oil?" Oil is symbolic of the Holy Spirit and of consecration, being set apart for the service of God. Anointing, or the pouring of oil was common practice in biblical times and is also used metaphorically in such passages as Psalm 23:5 and Psalm 92:10.

In the Old Testament, objects were anointed and consecrated for the service of God (Exodus 30:25-30). Oil was used for the consecration and sanctification of the tabernacle, its utensils and the priests who were to minister before the Lord (Exodus 40:9-15, Leviticus 8:1-5 and chapters 10-13). Priests were set apart and ordained into office by anointing (Ex. 28:41), as were prophets, when Elijah commissioned Elisha as his successor (1 Kings 19:16). Kings were inducted into office by oil being poured over their heads (1 Samuel 10:1), and the Holy Spirit came upon David when this function was performed on him (1 Samuel 16:13).

In the New Testament, oil is largely associated with healing as a point of contact for the Holy Spirit when praying for people in Jesus' name (Mark 6:13 and James 5:14-15). Demons (evil spirits) do not like consecrated oil – it burns them (spiritually speaking, as does holy water), when directed to use it by the Holy Spirit. Anointing can also refer to a spiritual process in which the Holy Spirit empowers a person's heart and mind with God's truth and love (1 John 2:20, 27). This helps them come to a better understanding of the truth that is contained within God's Word. It can be said that some believers are anointed when they speak, preach or that they have an anointing when they pray for people because the Holy Spirit moves. As disciples of Jesus Christ we all need an anointing from the Holy Spirit, for works of service and everyday living (Acts 1:8).

In Zechariah 4:14 the two 'anointed ones,' literally means in the original Hebrew 'sons of fresh oil.' Jesus is the Messiah – the 'Promised One' which means 'anointed.' Therefore a 'Christian' (follower of Christ) connotes 'anointed one.' On the day of Pentecost the followers of Jesus were anointed by the Holy Spirit for special service (Acts 1:2-8, 2:1-4, 14-21, see also Acts 4:27-33). Just as oil costs money to obtain, so the anointing given through obedience to the Holy Spirit will be costly in obedience (Acts 5:32). God will not tolerate sin in our lives and He will not fill dirty vessels (Isaiah 52:11b).

You can anoint Christians with any type of oil as oil on its own has no healing or special properties (though in the Old Testament a special compound of oil was prepared Exodus 25:6, 30:23-25, 37:29), it is what it symbolises and represents which is important, as in the communion service. The oil is used as a point of contact by faith. It is best to pray over the oil in Jesus Christ's name (asking God to bless and sanctify the oil) and then place a drop or two on the person's head, and pray in Jesus Christ's name that God would touch the person in their time of need, or heal them.

Oil Can Also be Used As
- A sign of honour and respect (Luke 7:36-46).
- A beauty treatment or moisturiser in hot and dusty climates (Deut. 28:40, Daniel 10:3 and Matt. 6:17).
- A sign of God's approval, to set apart for a specific work or service (Genesis 28:12-22, 1 Samuel 8:4-22, 1 Samuel 10:1, 1 Samuel 16:1-13 and 1 Kings 1:39).

Further study: Exodus 29:7, Exodus 30:21-33, Numbers 7:1-5, 2 Chronicles 23:11, Psalm 23:5, Psalm 45:7, Psalm 89:20, Isaiah 10:27, Isaiah 61:1, Ezekiel 16:9, Matthew 3:13-17, Luke 4:18, Acts 5:32, Acts 10:38 and 2 Corinthians 1:21-22.

Chapter Forty-Two

Laying on of Hands

'And it happened that the father of Publius lay sick of a fever and dysentery. Paul went in to him and prayed, and he laid his hands on him and healed him' (Acts 28:8).

The early church 'set before the apostles ['seven men of good reputation, full of the Holy Spirit'], and when they had prayed, they laid their hands on them' (Acts 6:3, 6).

"Why do some people place their hands on a person when praying for them?" The laying on of hands was very common in biblical times (Hebrews 6:1-2), and has great significance as a religious rite or ceremony. The laying on of hands speaks of imparting or transference as a point of contact (Leviticus 16:21). It is associated with the bestowal of Divine blessing upon a person (Genesis 48:14-20). It is also used as a special form of recognition, for a person who is set apart for God's service, commissioning (ordaining or appointing) them to Divine service or some special work (Numbers 8:10, Numbers 27:18-23 and Acts 13:2-3).

Jesus often placed His hands upon people, especially in relation to healing and deliverance (Matthew 8:3, 15, and 20:34). Jesus had so much power in Him that if people touched Him they could get healed (Matthew 14:36, Mark 5:28-30, Luke 1:31 and 9:27). Jesus also touched the children when praying a blessing on them (Matthew 19:13-15).

Christians often lay hands on people as a point of contact (Acts 19:11-12), for healing (Matthew 9:18, 25 and Acts 14:3), and for deliverance as the anointing of God flows. An impartation of the Holy Spirit (or a spiritual gift) can be received / imparted via the laying on of hands (Deuteronomy 34:9 and Acts 8:17). It cannot be bought, otherwise the sin of simony would be committed! (Acts 8:18-24).

Laying hands on someone is not a magic formula, but a point of contact. If you are going to lay your hands on individuals and expect to see results in Jesus' mighty name, you need to lead a holy, righteous life (Psalm 7:3, 1 Timothy 4:8-16 and James 5:14-18). You cannot impart that which you do not have, and individuals must seek God for themselves for their own anointing, though they can receive a measure from you.

'Do not neglect the gift that is in you, which was given to you by prophecy with the laying on of the hands of the presbytery' (1 Timothy 4:14).

The Laying on of Hands is Also Associated With
- The ordination of deacons, elders and ministers (Acts 6:1-8, Acts 14:23 and Titus 1:5). We are warned not to have ungodly elders and not to hastily appoint elders (1 Timothy 3:10 and 1 Timothy 5:17-22).
- The setting apart of missionaries (or other Christian workers) for Divine service (Acts 13:1-4).
- The impartation of spiritual gifts (Romans 1:11, 1 Timothy 2:8, 1 Timothy 4:4 and 2 Timothy 1:6).

Words of Wisdom
Do not allow just *anybody* to lay hands on you, see 1 Timothy 5:22a. You can politely decline. The laying on of hands is about imparting and transference of a blessing, healing, anointing or gifting. If the person who is praying for you is steeped in sin or 'possessed' by devils an ungodly transference may take place. In some larger churches only designated people can minister to others, often they are part of a ministry team. This is to protect the flock and visitors.

'Those who were sick with various diseases brought them to Him [Jesus] and He laid His hands on every one of them and healed them' (Luke 4:40).

Further study: Exodus 29:1-10, 15-21, Leviticus 1:3-4, 4:13-15, Numbers 8:9-12, Psalm 18:20-24, 24:4, Isaiah 1:15, Jer. 1:9, Mark 16:17-18, Luke 7:14-16, 22:50-55 and Acts 19:12.

Chapter Forty-Three

Inner Healing – A Wounded Spirit

'A merry heart makes a cheerful countenance, but by sorrow of heart the spirit is broken' (Proverbs 15:13).

'We do not lose heart. Even though our outward man is perishing, yet the inward man [soul and spirit] is being renewed day by day' (2 Corinthians 4:16).

At the point of conversion, there is the potential for complete healing and wholeness; but it is not always true that healing (physically or mentally) takes place automatically. In Christ Jesus, believers are a new creation (they have been born again), but issues from the past (hurts and memories, alongside present unconfessed sin), can still affect them and needs to be dealt with, often over a period of time when the person receives hands-on Christian ministry.

Inner healing concerns dealing with the scars from the past, healing a wounded spirit or soul. Wounds usually arise from one or two things: serious hurts or deep horrors. The hurt comes from rejection or being deprived of love. The horrors come from having experienced trauma, brutality, violence, sexual or physical abuse. If you have been involved in a car accident, your body will gradually heal, but you can still be traumatised in your spirit. The mind also finds a way of responding to life, based on past experience which includes repressing painful memories in the subconscious. Some people's past events are so painful that they shut them out and never wish to talk about the situation, even to the point of denial, "It never happened." Historical hurts are painfully recorded in the mind that can cause damaged emotions and can produce incorrect behavioural patterns. Often these events were encountered before the person became a Christian and so they had to find a way of dealing with the pain themselves, others have been caught up in accidents, wars, earthquakes, famines, terrorist attacks and other disasters and have seen or experienced terrible things.

Humans have five distinct functions, we are: physical beings, thinking beings, longing beings, choosing beings, and feeling beings (physical, rational, personal, volitional and emotional) which can be placed into three categories: the mind, the will and the emotions, which connect to the body, the spirit and the soul. The different capacities are not designed to work isolated from each other but as part of the whole, like a circuit board – you need all of them working together to have a workable system. The body and mind are so inextricably connected that what affects the mind affects the body and vice versa. For example, hatred, bitterness or unforgiveness can cause physical illness, likewise depression or low self-esteem can cause illness. If you are an unhappy person then your immune system will be weakened and harmful germs as well as harmful thoughts and emotions can invade your soul. When your spirit is in trouble your body can also be in trouble. What we think about affects the way we feel, and how we feel, affects the way we choose, and how we choose depends on our evaluation of what gives us a sense of inner intactness and a deep settled peace. Today a large number of illnesses are classified as psychosomatic, that is caused by psychological factors. If disease can come through the mind then a correct mindset can lead to health and wholeness (see Phil. 4:6-8). This is not mind over matter, but biblical thinking (1 Cor. 2:6).

Selwyn Hughes wrote: 'Some medical problems are purely the result of a physical ailment whereas others are the result of the mind passing on to the body its dis-ease (notice the hyphen).' John Wimber wrote: 'I define inner healing as a process in which the Holy Spirit brings forgiveness of sins and emotional renewal to people from damaged minds, wills and emotions.'[1] Jesus Christ came to heal the whole man, physically, mentally and emotionally (Isaiah 61:1-2 and Luke 4:18-19).

Scriptures on Health and Psychological Issues
- 'Anxiety in the heart of a man causes depression, but a good word makes it glad' (Proverbs 12:25).

- 'Hope deferred makes the heart sick but when the desire comes it is a tree of life' (Proverbs 13:12).
- 'A desire accomplished is sweet to the soul...' (Proverbs 13:19a).
- 'Even in laughter the heart may sorrow and the end of mirth may be grief' (Proverbs 14:13).
- 'A merry heart makes a cheerful countenance, but by sorrow of heart the spirit is broken' (Proverbs 15:13).
- 'A merry heart does good like medicine, but a broken spirit dries the bones' (Proverbs 17:22).
- 'The spirit of a man will sustain him in sickness, but who can bear a broken spirit?' (Proverbs 18:14).
- 'Like one who takes away a garment in cold weather and like vinegar on soda, is one who sings songs to a heavy heart' (Proverbs 25:20).
- 'There is one who speaks like the piercing of a sword but the tongue of the wise promotes health' (Proverbs 12:18).
- 'A wholesome tongue is a tree of life, but perverseness in it breaks the spirit' (Proverbs 15:4).
- 'The light of the eyes rejoices the heart, and a good report makes the bones healthy' (Proverbs 15:30).
- 'Pleasant words are like honeycomb, sweetness to the soul and health to the bones' (Proverbs 16:24).
- 'Whoever guards his mouth and tongue keeps his soul from trouble' (Proverbs 21:23).
- 'Do not be wise in your own eyes; fear the Lord and depart from evil. It will be health to your flesh and strength to your bones' (Proverbs 3:7-8).
- 'A sound heart is life to the body, but envy is rottenness to the bones' (Proverbs 14:30).
- 'For my life is spent with grief, and my years with sighing; my strength fails because of my iniquity' (Psalm 31:10).
- 'When I kept silent [non confession of sin] my bones grew old through my groaning all the day long...my vitality was turned into the drought of summer' (Psalm 32:3-4).
- 'There is no soundness in my flesh because of Your anger, nor is there any health in my bones because

of my sin. For my iniquities have gone over my head; like a heavy burden they are too heavy for me' (Psalm 38:3-4).

- 'I am feeble and severely broken; I groan because of the turmoil of my heart' (Psalm 38:8).
- 'As he clothed himself with cursing as with his garment, so let it enter his body like water and like oil into his bones' (Psalm 109:18).
- If you obey God (see Isaiah 58:6-10), 'The Lord will guide you continually, and satisfy your soul in drought, and strengthen your bones...' (Isaiah 58:11).

> '...He [Jesus] received them and spoke to them about the Kingdom of God, and healed those who had need of healing' (Luke 9:11).

Types of Hurt

1. We have hurt others: God, other people and ourselves: through personal sin or failure (the consequences of what we say or do). Sexual immorality, abortion, rebellion, dishonesty, anger and rage and all sin hurts God (and often yourself; you feel guilt and shame).

2. We have been hurt by others: abusive parents, (inconsiderate superior or church leaders etc.). It could be a sin of commission, they abused you (physically and or mentally), or a sin of omission, they never affirmed you, (or spent quality time with you). Often parents did the best with the knowledge they had. A relative, teacher, work colleague or a person may have made a negative remark or many persistent ones, which have damaged you, "You're no good," "You're ugly," "You'll never amount to anything" etc. The natural response when others hurt you is to hurt them through resentment or retribution (trying to get even), but this also hurts you. Anger and rage is also not helpful. There are also consequences for your forefathers' sins which need to be renounced (Ex. 20:4-5). This is covered in chapter 46.

3. A breakdown in relationship between God and man: children often see an authority figure that they identify with God, which could be positive, but sadly it is often negative. A domineering, heartless or stern father; a condemning male

teacher or pastor etc., are all images that can give a false impression of who God is. If you are a Christian, God is your Father and you are His child (John 1:12 and Romans 8:15).

Types of Emotions

Emotions are generally neutral, but how you apply the emotion can be positive or negative: anger can be godly or ungodly, fear of man is bad, but fear of falling over the cliff once you have climbed the fence is good. A woman who has been abused will probably have difficulty in having a meaningful relationship with a man. Emotions can be so repressed (that they are out of touch with a normal response to life) or they can control or overwhelm you, as an emotion can be out of proportion to the incident. If you walk through a field and see a rabbit, it will hop away, but if your car's headlights shine into the rabbit's eyes when it's crossing the road, then the fear will paralyse the rabbit and that is when the problem arises! Guilt, condemnation, unforgiveness, bitterness, godless anger, wrath, jealousy (Ephesians 4:26), rejection and malice etc. keep you from functioning how God would want you to (Ephesians 4:23-31 and Colossians 3:5-8).

It is important to remember that if you have a problem don't focus on the fruit, but deal with the root. Once the hurt has been dealt with, the emotions will come into line. Deal with the root then the tree will be healthy. An original hurt, like an infection if it is not dealt with can spread, grow and possibly endanger the rest of your body. The clearer your understanding of God the clearer your perspective will be not only in relation to God, but in relation to the whole of life.

'There should be no schism in the body...members should have the same care for one another. And if one member suffers, all the members suffer with it; or if one member is honoured, all the members rejoice with it. Now you are the body of Christ, and members individually' (1 Cor. 12:25-27).

How Is A Wounded Spirit Healed

- Acknowledge you have a problem. This is the most important step towards being made whole. Once the problem is acknowledged the solution is easier.

- Accept some of the responsibility (if you have destructive emotions) – you can either respond in forgiveness, or hatred and resentment which leads to bitterness, or you can choose to forgive and move on. This is not making light of the situation (and some people's lives are horrendous), but it is dealing with the consequences of continual emotional pain.
- Do you really want to be healed and set free? You may enjoy the sympathy (John 5:6b), or use the hurts you have received as an excuse to hurt others. This can be a hard question to answer, but be honest.
- Bring your problem to God (forgive those who have hurt you) and ask Him to heal you as whenever we do our part, God never fails to do His.

Counsellors and the Church

Counsellors often help a person to be able to deal with their situation in the short-term with the aid of looking for things. The Church can also help people to cope in difficult situations, but unless the root cause is dealt with the problems are not solved, just repressed for a time. In all Christian ministry the power and presence of God needs to be released. The Holy Spirit is the Counsellor and it is He who reveals issues, past sins or hurts which need to be dealt with (1 Corinthians 12:4-11). The healing of damaged memories and emotions is something that only God can do through the power of the Holy Spirit by the shed blood of Jesus Christ. God often uses Christian men and women to be the agents of His healing. If you need healing then your first point of call is your pastor, who should be able to pray with and for you, or your pastor may refer you to someone who is experienced in this area of Christian ministry.

'Counsel in the heart of a man is like deep water, but a man of understanding will draw it out' (Proverbs 20:5).

Further study: Proverbs 28:13, Matthew 11:29, Mark 11:25, John 14:27 and Ephesians 1:6-8.

Chapter Forty-Four

Receiving Inner Healing

Jesus said, "Come to Me, all you who labour and are heavy laden, and I will give you rest. Take My yoke upon you and learn from Me, for I am gentle and lowly in heart, and you will find rest for your souls. For My yoke is easy and My burden is light" (Matthew 11:28-30).

'Now may the God of peace sanctify you completely; and may your whole spirit, soul and body be preserved blameless at the coming of our Lord Jesus Christ' (1 Thessalonians 5:23).

Issues from the past need to be dealt with and this chapter looks at resolving inner healing: for those who have been wounded, have a damaged spirit or soul, or who need to receive forgiveness due to sin. The human mind will often act sinfully after a hurt (Proverbs 24:29). Our sinful reaction at being hurt is retaliation and this in turn hurts others. Guilt and condemnation often come due to unconfessed sin when there is no forgiveness. Condemnation will often bring fear resulting in good works as a way of trying to appease God. Humans have different ways of coping with painful memories: denial, repression, comfort eating, self-harm, becoming a workaholic or over achiever (to earn approval) etc. Often the life and soul of the party is a secret depressive; he or she is an extrovert in the crowd but depressed when alone, the over-the-top attitude is a façade to hide the inner hurt.

Scriptures on Health and Psychological Issues
* 'Bow down Your ear to me, deliver me speedily; be my rock of refuge, a fortress of defence to save me' (Psalm 31:2). [See also pages 204-206].

- 'The Lord is near to those who have a broken heart, and saves such as have a contrite heart' (Ps. 34:18).
- 'Why are you cast down, O my soul? And why are you disquieted within me? Hope in God, for I shall yet praise Him for the help of His countenance' (Ps. 42:5).
- 'In God (I will praise His Word)...I have put my trust; I will not fear. What can flesh do to me?' (Psalm 56:4).
- 'When you pass through the waters, I will be with you; and through the rivers, they shall not overflow you. When you walk through the fire, you shall not be burned, nor shall the flame scorch you. For I am the Lord your God, the Holy One of Israel, your Saviour...' (Isaiah 43:2-3a).
- 'And we know that all things work together for good to those who love God, to those who are called according to His purpose' (Romans 8:28).
- 'For our light affliction, which is but for a moment, is working for us a far more exceeding and eternal weight of glory.... For the things which are seen are temporary, but the things which are not seen are eternal' (2 Corinthians 4:17-18b).

The Road to Freedom
Jesus said to the paralytic at the pool of Bethesda, "Do you want to be made well?" (John 5:1-16). If you really want to be healed and set free from your hurts and distress (Psalm 143:4, 7), God will give you the grace, the strength and His healing touch to be set free as nothing is impossible with God (Luke 1:37), but there are conditions and things that you will need to do. If the devil has robbed you of your past, do not give him your future. Accept some of the responsibility for the way you are; you can either choose to respond in forgiveness or bitterness regardless of the circumstances. Bring your problem to God and ask Him to heal it, as whenever we do our part, God never fails to do His. Some issues and hurts are very deep and only under the light of the Holy Spirit can these issues be brought to the surface and dealt with. Often a time of ministry is needed when you will receive prayer, maybe deliverance and you will probably be cut free (spiritually speaking) from things in the past.

Being Set Free
1. What is my problem?
2. What have I done about it?
3. What do I expect the person ministering with me, and to me, to do about my inner hurts?
4. What do I expect God to do about my problems and inner hurts? Beware of hidden resentment (Psalm 139:23), and unforgiveness, and confess all known sin to God, including self-pity (Psalm 51).

Unforgiveness and Forgiveness
Doctors say that unforgiveness generates chemicals that directly affect your vital organs. These chemicals increase your heart rate, raise your blood pressure, tense your muscles, cause stress, disrupt your digestion and reduce your ability to think clearly. Those who do not have a clear conscience and / or don't forgive themselves and others are more prone to heart attacks, depression, stomach ulcers, hypertension and other serious illnesses. If you internalise stress and bottle things up inside of you, your blood pressure can soar, making you a prime candidate for ulcers and heart disease. Modern life confirms God's diagnosis that negative attitudes can cause us serious harm and even result in death through anxiety, neuroses, mental illnesses or even cancer. Michal, King David's wife was barren because of her bitterness and resentment towards her husband (2 Samuel 6:16-23). David's unconfessed sin caused a physical effect (Psalm 32:3-4). An inner healing can result in an outward healing as both are interlinked.

A preacher once said, "Unforgiveness is like digesting poison and waiting for the other person to die." By harbouring unforgiveness in your heart, you will be unable to receive God's forgiveness (Matthew 6:12-15). Also you will give demons a legal right to torment you (Matthew 18:21-35 especially verses 34-35). Trauma, anger, hatred, bitterness, fear or resentment etc. can also be entry points for demons to take advantage of you. King Saul and his jealousy of young David, gave an evil spirit an entry into his life (1 Samuel 18:1-16). Esau held anger towards Jacob for a long time because his brother tricked his father and Esau lost out (Genesis 27:36, 41 and 33:1-17). Yet Joseph the young man with a coat of many colours was able to forgive his brothers who wished him dead and sold him into slavery (Genesis chapters 37-45). If you know how much God has forgiven you, it is easier to forgive others, as what you have done to God by your thoughts, words and actions are far worse than what any person can do to you. Just think of all the sins that you have committed which people do not know about!

'We are to forgive others the same way that the Lord Jesus forgave us: unconditionally, freely, generously and without keeping a record of past wrongs. Then we will be free.'[1]

Scriptures on forgiveness (Matthew 5:23-24, 6:14-15, 18:35, Luke 17:3-4, Ephesians 4:32 and Colossians 3:13).

Ministry and Confession

It is important to show absolute love to the person you are ministering to and to encourage him (or her) that they are accepted by God (Ephesians 1:6-7). He also needs to work with you, cooperate and take responsibility for his past actions. Under the light of the Holy Spirit, He will reveal damaged areas (in your life) or the person who is seeking help and pinpoint situations which birthed the original hurt, as we are all products of our past. Be sensitive, ask questions (Proverbs 20:5) and work with the Holy Spirit. He may bring certain memories back to the person (or it may come through a word of knowledge or wisdom, or a picture etc.) to find the root cause of his pain or to remind him of past sinful actions or reactions.

The person who is confessing needs to fully vent their feelings (to get it off his chest), but this does not mean that he loses control of his emotions in blind rage – but talk about it. On the road to Emmaus, Jesus did not suddenly reveal Himself to the two disciples, but He fully allowed them to ventilate their hearts as they were overcome with grief (Proverbs 18:13 and Luke 24:13-32). A sudden revelation would have been inappropriate. To move too quickly with those feeling sorrow and grief, and not allowing them time to come to terms with their pain would have been wrong. To try to force people to feel better when they have not dealt with their pain properly is to make light of their condition. In Jerusalem, the disciples were confronted by Jesus in a sudden and dramatic way. They were not so much struggling with sorrow and grief as with confusion and unbelief and they should have known better (Luke 24:36-49). Peter was reinstated by Jesus around a campfire (John 21:15-17), it was the antidote to Peter's denial of Jesus around another fire (John 18:24-27). It is worth pointing out that Jesus had met Peter after His resurrection, but only when the time was right had He addressed the issue of his denial and thus reinstated Peter as a disciple.

After a time of ministry, you will need to ask for the healing of the memories and a fresh infilling of the Holy Spirit (especially after deliverance). This does not mean that the memory is forgotten, but that the pain is released from the memory so that negative harmful emotions cannot be manifested anymore. Often a release of repressed emotions will show, tears or sighs of relief, as the Holy Spirit comes and ministers to the person. Once the person is free from past hurts he will need to take responsibility for change, as Jesus said, "Go and sin no more" (John 8:11). The mind will continually need to be renewed along with attitude and actions. The person being ministered to may need to receive follow up (another meeting) and should know who they are in Christ Jesus, a son and heir, accepted in Him (Romans 8:15-17 and Ephesians 1:6-8). See also the following page.

It is unwise to minister to a non-Christian as he or she is not in a covenant relationship with Jesus Christ (Matthew 7:6, 12:43-45, 15:21-28 and Luke 10:17-20), however sometimes the result of being set free is that they surrender their lives to Jesus Christ. Where possible get your pastor's permission if you are going to minister to people from within the congregation, as he is responsible for them and over you (Romans 13:1-2). We are called to be in submission to those who are in authority over us (Titus 3:1, Hebrews 13:7 and 1 Peter 2:13-16).

Pronouncing Forgiveness

Pronouncing forgiveness is for those who are genuinely repentant but who are unable to accept their forgiveness (due to the seriousness of their sin) or for those who may have intellectually been forgiven yet still feel guilty. Members of the body of Christ need to pronounce God's forgiveness over the person's life. They may have reacted wrongly to life's situations – someone hurts them, they feel angry, they hurt others, they feel guilty. Openly declare the Lordship of Jesus Christ, renounce the devil and all his works, confess specific sins by name (Leviticus 5:5), as condemnation or guilt is due to specific sins having been committed. Confess and forsake sin and find mercy (Proverbs 28:13). Often people think that their problem is unique, but the enemy tries to isolate them and get them to believe that nobody else has committed that sin, or has that problem whereas some sins are quite common. It is helpful to mention if applicable, if you have struggled with the same issues. If God has forgiven you then you also need to forgive yourself; as in effect you are saying, "I know better than God." In Christ Jesus 'there is no condemnation' (Romans 8:1). A model prayer of pronounce-ment of the forgiveness of sins can be: "By the authority and power I have in the name of Jesus Christ, I break the power of guilt and condemnation over your life and pronounce the forgiveness of sins over your life in the name of the Lord Jesus Christ" (John 20:23 and James 5:16).[2]

Faith Building Scripture Declarations
- I am *redeemed* from the curse of the law (Gal. 3:13).
- I am *saved* by grace through faith (Ephesians 2:8).
- I am an *heir* of God and *joint-heir* with Christ (Romans 8:17 and Galatians 4:7).
- I am an *heir of eternal life* and *forgiven* (1 John 5:11-12 and Ephesians 1:7).
- I am *sanctified* and *justified* through Christ Jesus (1 Corinthians 6:11).
- I am *justified* and at *peace with God, more than a conqueror* (Romans 8:37 and Romans 5:1).
- I am *righteous* by faith in Jesus Christ (Romans 3:22 and 2 Corinthians 5:21).
- I am *healed by His wounds* (Matthew 8:17 and 1 Peter 2:24), and *victorious* (1 Corinthians 15:57).

Further study: Genesis 18:14a, Jeremiah 32:17, John 14:27, Romans 5:1-2 and James 5:14-17. Scriptures on healing: Exodus 15:26, Deuteronomy 7:15, Psalm 103:2-3, Proverbs 3:7b-8 and Isaiah 53:5, 10, 12.

Chapter Forty-Five

Soul Ties and Dominating Relationships

'...And the two shall become one flesh, so then they are no longer two but one flesh...' (Matthew 19:5b-6a).

'For rebellion is as a sin of witchcraft, and stubbornness is as iniquity and idolatry...' (1 Samuel 15:23a).

"What is a soul tie?" A soul tie is a spiritual link, a bond or connection that holds us into relationships with other people. In the Bible, a soul tie can be described as knit, cleave(d) or joined. Sometimes these words are not used, but the principle or spirit behind a situation or event can be seen. Soul ties can be godly or ungodly, positive or negative. Ungodly soul ties are a hindrance at best, and devastating at worst and need to be dealt with.

We Can Have Soul Ties With
- Family, as a result of our birth.
- We can develop them with other people, as a result of the decisions and choices we make, godly or ungodly friendships (1 Samuel 18:1-4).
- They can be forced upon us by individuals, unhealthy acquaintances who choose to take advantage or abuse us in various ways (2 Samuel 14:3 and 1 Kings 21:7-11, 25).
- We can enter into them via marriage or with sexual partner(s) with whom we become 'one flesh' (Genesis 2:24, 3:16, 34:1-3, 8 and 1 Cor. 6:15-17).

Godly Soul Ties
Godly soul ties are according to God's plan and purposes for mankind (1 Corinthians 6:17). We are made in the image of God and have free will; we can choose to have godly

friends or not (Matthew 7:12). Godly soul ties can be: husband and wife (Genesis 2:24), child with parent(s), brother and brother, sister and brother etc., the wider family circle (Judges 20:11 and Ruth 1:14); fellow believers (Acts 4:32 and Colossians 1:7-8); special friends or companions within the context of a healthy godly relationship (1 Samuel 18:1, John 13:25, John 15:13 and John 20:2).

Ungodly Soul Ties

Ungodly soul ties are contrary to God's plan and purposes as they control people, (often unknowingly) whether physically, emotionally or spiritually and can cause sickness (of the body, soul or spirit). It is wrong to manipulate, intimidate or dominate others. These traits are the tactics of the evil one and hallmarks of witchcraft practice, being rebellious against God's ways (1 Samuel 15:23a).

Ungodly soul ties are: premarital sexual partner(s) and or partners within adultery (1 Corinthians 6:13-18, Ephesians 5:30 and Hebrews 13:4); a child who tries to manipulate its parent(s) or vice versa, there is a difference between godly discipline and control; a parent who controls his or her child, when he or she is an adult; dominating relationships; abusive relationships i.e. sexual, emotional, mental, physical or psychological; a domineering friend, work colleague, manager etc., someone who has a hold over you.

People who have been damaged by others can bear unseen scars their entire life, whilst some feel beholden to the person, because their souls are tied / joined.

Sexual intercourse is a spiritual union where two become one. A part of you stays with them and a part of them resides with you. This is the strongest form of a soul tie.

Dealing With the Past

If you have controlled people in the past then you need to repent, ask God for forgiveness and release in Jesus Christ's name. You may need to apologise (in person, over the phone or via a letter, when and where appropriate) and or make amends (if and where possible) to the one whom you have hurt (Matthew 5:23-24 and Romans 12:2). If you are being controlled / manipulated by others then you will need to deal with the situation. Put a stop to it, as enough is enough. Be firm, polite and unwavering in your resolve.

Women who are abused by their boyfriend(s) can find it difficult to finish the relationship; this is because their soul has become connected and so they feel an emotional tie, a dependency (see Genesis 3:16 and Ephesians 5:30-33). King Solomon warns three times '...Do not stir up or awaken love until it pleases' (Song of Solomon 1:7b, 3:5b and 8:4b). '...For love is as strong as death, jealousy as cruel as the grave; its flames are flames of fire, a most vehement flame. Many waters cannot quench love, nor can the floods drown it. If a man would give for love all the wealth of his house, it would be utterly despised' (Song of Solomon 8:6b-7). Whilst this is talking about love (an emotional tie), a soul tie is a much stronger spiritual link.

Forgiving those who have taken advantage of you in a relationship (both men and women) is essential to help break an ungodly soul tie (Matthew 6:12-15), especially in relation to a sexual union. Items of affection (the devil's trinkets) from ungodly soul ties need to be destroyed e.g. photos, love letters (Jude 23), etc. or parted with, e.g. rings, gifts, clothes and other jewellery etc. It symbolises a break with the past and aids the release of your attachment and will help you to move on in the freedom of Christ Jesus.

> Jesus said, "When the Son sets you free, you are free indeed" (John 8:36).

Be Set Free

You need to cut and sever all ungodly soul ties (stop being used etc.). It is important to sever the spiritual 'umbilical cord' from those in the past. As long as you are connected in the soul with someone from the past, it is hard to move forward (2 Corinthians 11:20a). Forgive those who have wronged you. If you have blamed God for what has happened to you, ask Him to forgive you. If you have sinned, then repent. Renounce the devil and all his works and declare that Jesus Christ is Lord of your life. If you have committed wilful sexual sins e.g. premarital sex or adultery, and you are sincere, you can pray the model prayer of repentance on the next page. If you have been sexually abused or raped, you have not sinned, but have been sinned against, though you must forgive the perpetrator. This is not making light of the situation; forgiveness is not a feeling but a choice. We forgive because God has forgiven us. We forgive to release the perpetrator, and we too are released. If criminal law has been transgressed, justice still needs to prevail.

The model prayer below should be prayed aloud during a time of ministry in the presence of another Christian (or more) of your own gender (Isaiah 10:27 and James 5:16). Then have a member of the ministry team speak out the declaration over your life, as a release, a setting free from the past (see Isaiah 55:11, Ecclesiastes 4:12, Jeremiah 23:29, Matthew 18:16, Mark 11:24-25, 2 Corinthians 13:1, Ephesians 6:10-18 and Hebrews 4:12).

Prayer

Heavenly Father, I submit my soul, my desires and my emotions to Your Spirit. I confess all my consenting, promiscuous, premarital sexual activity with (name(s) e.g. Mary) and all willing sexual relationships outside of marriage as sin against You, and as a sin against my body; I confess all my ungodly spirit, soul, and body ties as sin and I ask You to forgive, cleanse and set me free in the name of Jesus Christ. Amen.[1]

Declaration

We come in the name of the Lord Jesus Christ and we break the ungodly body, soul and spirit ties between (e.g. John) and (e.g. Mary). We speak to anything that is ungodly and has come from dealing with (Mary), anything that has come into (John) we send it out in Jesus' name. Anything negative which has come into (John) through the establishment of the ungodly soul tie we send out in Jesus' name and anything that (John) gave into the relationship with (Mary) we now call back in the name of Jesus Christ, to be joined back to (John).[2]

Further study: Genesis 29:34, Isaiah 54:5, 1 Samuel 20:16-17, 1 Chronicles 12:17, Ecclesiastes 8:6, Amos 3:3, Matthew 19:4-6, 1 Corinthians 1:10, Ephesians 4:16, Colossians 2:2 and Colossians 2:8-10, 19.

Chapter Forty-Six

Sins of the Forefathers / Generational Curses

"...For I, the Lord your God am a jealous God, visiting the iniquity of the fathers on the children to the third and fourth generations of those who hate Me, but showing mercy to thousands, to those who love Me and keep My commandments" (Exodus 20:5-6).

'Whatever was written before [i.e. the Old Testament] was written for our learning...' (Romans 15:4).

The sins of the forefathers also known as generational curses go back to the third and fourth generation (up to thirty relatives) of your ancestors. They are the consequences of your ancestors' sins that could still affect you today. The consequences can come from your mother's and / or father's side of the family (Psalm 109:14); imagine your family tree with all its branches! The sins of the forefathers are like two interconnecting roads which wind in and out of each other (Exodus 34:7 and Jeremiah 32:18, 39b). In (and through) Jesus Christ, all curses can be broken and you can be released into the fullness of your potential.

The sins of our ancestors does not excuse sin, but may help explain it. 'That which has been is what will be, that which is done is what will be done, and there is nothing new under the sun' (Ecclesiastes 1:9). In the Old Testament, Israel (and other nations) were consistently punished by God, by war, raiders or famine etc. because of individual or national sins of their generation or from a previous generation (Joshua 7:25-26, Judges 2:6-20, 2 Samuel 21:1-14, 1 Kings 11:1-12, 16:34, 2 Kings 24:1-4 and Lamentations 5:7). For Israel, this eventually led to seventy years in exile (Jeremiah 17:1-10, 25:11-12 and Jeremiah chapter 52). Blessings and curses have taken effect since the beginning of time (Genesis 3:14-20) and is a spiritual law God set in motion that still affects our lives; it can be seen or unseen (Ecclesiastes 1:10-11, 3:1-8 and 7:8a).

Being Released

The Holy Spirit may show you specific things that you need to confess, renounce and repent of, even those of your ancestors or what the Holy Spirit reveals to you or those ministering with you. Generational curses can be broken in the name of Jesus and by the sword of the Spirit which is the Word of God. See the next chapter, Blessings and Curses.

1. Renounce any known sins of your forefathers and works of darkness such as idolatry, adultery, false religions, occult practices etc. (Leviticus 26:39-42 and Nehemiah 1:6).

2. Ask God to cleanse you and cut you free from any of your forefathers' sins or generational sins in the name of Jesus Christ and by His blood in declaration of the Word of God (Colossians 2:15, Hebrews 4:12, 1 John 3:8 and 4:4).

3. As a public declaration, state that you have been set free in Jesus' name and that you now want to receive your full inheritance in Christ Jesus (Matthew 12:37).

A Model Prayer of Release

Heavenly Father, I come in the name of Jesus Christ and covered by His blood [spiritually speaking, see Revelation 1:5] which He shed for me. I stand by faith and confess that Jesus Christ is my Lord and Saviour. I repent of any action, attitude, lifestyle or habit that does not glorify Jesus Christ. I confess and renounce every iniquity, transgression and sin that I, my parents or ancestors may have committed, known or unknown, willingly or unwillingly and which has brought poverty, bondages, dominations, afflictions or sickness into or over my life. I ask for forgiveness, cleansing and restoration and that You Father, will cut me free from any ungodly ancestral ties. I renounce the devil and all his works, influences, bondages, dominations, afflictions and infirmities in or over my life. I ask for the release of any godly anointing, finances or health etc. that may have been given away and or perverted or misplaced due to my sin or my ancestors' sin. I claim the release and freedom promised by Jesus Christ. Amen.[1]

- 220 -

Chapter Forty-Seven

Blessings and Curses

'I call heaven and earth as witness today against you, that I have set before you life and death, blessing and cursing; therefore choose life, that both you and your descendants may live' (Deuteronomy 30:19).

'All these things happened to them as examples and they were written for our admonition...' (1 Corinthians 10:11a).

Blessings and curses have been around since the beginning of time. It is a spiritual law that still governs our everyday lives, for better or for worse, seen or unseen (Ecclesiastes 1:9-11, 3:1-8, 7:8a and 2 Timothy 2:7). Obey the Scriptures and you'll get results; violate them and you'll get consequences. Some people have a continual walk of failure, like an unseen hand or a dark cloud over their lives (even some Christians) and no matter what they do, they cannot break free. This could be that they are living under a curse. Symptoms could be: accident-prone, continual sickness, financial problems, family history of depression, alcoholism or untimely deaths. These cases are examples where a curse could be taking effect on an individual and could be hereditary through the generational lines as in the previous chapter, Sins of the Forefathers / Generational Curses. On the other hand, those who are blessed walk in the light of success and fulfilment. This does not mean that Christians are immune from trials, discouragement, hardship, suffering or persecution, but we are meant to be the head and not the tail (Deuteronomy 28:13), and this is the realm into which all Christians should enter – victorious living in the will of God even through hard times. All curses can be broken in the name and power of Jesus Christ (Galatians 3:13-14 and Col. 2:15), though some are self-inflicted.

God works in addition and multiplication that is construction. The devil works in divisions and subtractions that is division. The main vehicle of both blessings and curses are words: spoken, written or uttered inwardly (Psalm 109:17, Prov. 13:3, 18:21 and Galatians 6:7). A curse could also affect us because of idolatry, witchcraft, false religions or sexual sins etc. When I speak, does my mouth bring forth fresh or salt water, life or death, blessings or curses? Do I edify and build up? (James 3:12 and 1 Peter 3:9).

Self-Inflicted Curses
- General habitual sinning, 'The curse of the Lord is on the house of the wicked' (Proverbs 3:33).
- Showing partiality to the law (the priests, Malachi 1:14-2:1-9).
- Robbing God in tithes and offerings (Malachi 3:8-12).
- In possession of accursed or defiled objects (Exodus 20:3-6, Deuteronomy 7:26, Deuteronomy 13:7, Joshua 6:18, chapter 7 and Isaiah 54:11).[1]

Spiritual Blessings
A spiritual blessing is the opposite of a curse and is an utterance which goes forth from your mouth and can come to pass to change a person, situation or event (Proverbs 18:21). It is not magic, witchcraft or 'name it and claim it,' but a God ordained possibility with biblical results. When you bless someone you are not operating in the physical but in the spiritual. As your tongue has the power to take or give life then you are sending forth blessings (God bless you means 'God make you whole / well,' see Matthew 9:21-22), or calling forth a slowdown or an entire stop to that which the enemy or others are trying to place over you, a situation or other. God blessed Adam and Eve and told them to be fruitful (Genesis 1:27-28).

God blessed the Sabbath day (Genesis 2:2). Rebekah was blessed by her brothers and sisters when she accepted a marriage proposal (Genesis 24:59-60). The patriarchal fathers and their relatives knew how to speak and impart a blessing. These utterances would often appear as prophetic, which came to pass but are not necessarily prophetic (Genesis 49:28). Generally the patriarchs used to place their right hand (symbol of authority and strength) on their eldest son's head and pronounce and decree a blessing. Blessings are non-discriminating as Jacob obtained Esau's blessing by deceiving the aged Isaac (Genesis 27:1-40). It is one thing to enunciate words but quite another when giving a blessing. Jacob (later known as Israel) blessed his grandchildren and knowingly placed his right hand on Ephraim's head (the younger) and placed his left hand on Manasseh's head and blessed (Genesis 48:9-20). King David blessed the people and then his household (servants, family etc.) when the Ark of the Covenant was returned (2 Samuel 6:17-20), but the enemy working through his wife did not like it (verses 20-23). King Solomon blessed the congregation of Israel and God (1 Kings 8:14-15, 55-61, c.f. Psalm 96:2). Parents asked Jesus to bless their children and He did (Mark 10:13-16 and Luke 24:50).

Boaz came from Bethlehem, and said to the reapers, "The Lord be with you!" and they answered him, "The Lord bless you!" (Ruth 2:4).

To Bless Means
1. To make whole, by speaking the word you have the ability to bless someone.
2. To ask and invoke God's Divine favour, for conditions, situations or circumstances to change.
3. To wish a person well, to speak wellness, "God bless."
4. To make happy and prosperous, asking God to prosper another or a situation.
5. To gladden, to glorify or praise. Jesus was anointed with the oil of gladness (Hebrews 1:9); glorify God through your situation, to praise, think on these things (Philippians 4:7-8).

Who to Bless
1. People, "God bless you."
2. Situations, instead of criticising something that you dislike, e.g. your job, ask God to bless it.
3. God, "Bless the Lord O my soul" (Psalm 134:1 and Psalm 135:19-21).

4. Those who persecute you (Romans 12:14), because if you do, bitterness will not be able to take root.
5. Bless your enemies (Matthew 5:44-48). God cannot bless sin but you can bless and be a blessing to sinful people, by being courteous, as 'a soft answer turns away wrath' (Proverbs 15:1). 'Do not repay insult for insult' (1 Peter 3:8-9), and 'if your enemy is hungry give him bread to eat' (Proverbs 25:21-22).
6. Bless Israel, pray for the nation and its citizens (Gen. 12:1-3, Num. 23:19-21 and 1 Chron. 17:22-27).

There are special blessings in Scripture that you can pray and pronounce over individuals or groups (see Numbers 6:24-26 and Deuteronomy 1:11, Romans 15:13, 2 Cor. 13:14, 1 Thessalonians 5:23, 2 Thessalonians 2:16-17 and Hebrews 13:20-21). Other blessings can be, may God bless you with: a listening ear, an obedient heart, abundance, a good marriage, fruitful loins, ability, creativity, faith, strength, good health, favour with God and man, protection, the work of your hands, wisdom and discernment etc.

Do not bless or give hospitality to a false teacher or cult member (the AV says 'do not bid him God speed' 2 John 10-11). Do not loudly proclaim a blessing early in the morning as it will be accounted as a curse (Proverbs 27:14). Do not ask God to bless something that is sinful, or a ministry or job which He has not ordained. God can do more than what we can think or imagine (Psalm 40:5 and Haggai 2:19).

How to Receive a Blessing
1. Bless Israel and you will receive a blessing (Genesis 12:1-3 and Genesis 27:29).
2. Ask God to bless you like Jabez did and God answered his cry (1 Chronicles 4:10).
3. You are blessed if you do not walk in the ways of the ungodly; but delight yourself in His Word (Ps. 1:1-3).
4. Bless God as He can forgive your iniquities, heal your diseases, crown your life with loving kindness and tender mercies and make you young! (Ps. 103:1-5).
5. Be faithful as 'a faithful man will abound with blessings' (Proverbs 28:20a).
6. Trust in the Lord, you will be blessed (Jer. 17:7-8).

7. Receive a blessing by not being offended because of Jesus – salvation is the ultimate blessing (Luke 7:23).
8. Invite those who are unable to repay you to your party or dinner (Luke 14:12-14).
9. You will be blessed if you wash the feet of Christians (John 13:1-17), NIV.
10. Bless those who speak badly of you (1 Peter 3:8-9).

Negative Versus Positive Comments

Negative comments such as, "You're ugly," "You're a failure," "You'll never change," or "You'll always be broke," etc. are ungodly comments which tear down a person's self-esteem and can be invoked as a curse, which can stay with them until they die, unless broken (Proverbs 11:9, 11, 12:18, 15:4, Matthew 12:35 and James 3:5-10). The receivers of these accusations often believe what has been spoken over their lives and live it (Proverbs 20:5 and Proverbs 27:19). 'As he thinks in his heart, so is he...' (Proverbs 23:7).

Positive comments such as, "Well done," "You've tried hard," "I believe in you," help instill confidence inside of a person and can invoke a blessing.

What Jesus Has Done

Jesus was punished that we might be forgiven and wounded that we might be healed (Isaiah 53:4-5 and 1 Peter 2:24). Jesus was made sin with our sinfulness that we might become righteous with His righteousness (2 Corinthians 5:21). Jesus died our death that we may share His life (Hebrews 2:9). Jesus became poor with our poverty that we might become rich with His riches (2 Corinthians 8:9). Jesus bore our shame that we might share His glory (1 Peter 3:18). Jesus endured our rejection that we might have His acceptance as children of God (Ephesians 1:5-6). Jesus became a curse that we might receive a blessing (Galatians 3:10-14), see also Isaiah chapter 53, Hebrews 2:9-10 and Hebrews 10:14.

If you are a Christian, covered by Jesus' blood (Revelation 1:5), who is walking in the light and not in darkness, being obedient to God and not in wilful sin, then people are unable to invoke or put a curse upon you (Proverbs 26:2). The devil is legalistic, so we must give him no right to have a legal stronghold over us; Jesus is our Advocate, He can plead our case before the Father (Proverbs 26:2, Isaiah 43:1-3a, 54:7, Zechariah 3:1-4, 1 Peter 2:9, 4:11, 1 John 1:5-10, 2:1-6 and 4:4). Live in all the fullness that God has for you. Reject any negative comments that are spoken against you, by the devil or people. Refuse to dwell on them and plead the blood over yourself (Ephesians 6:16-17 and Philippians 4:8, 13).

Breaking Curses

Renounce the devil and all his works; confess any known sin, especially unforgiveness. Declare and confess in the name of Jesus Christ and according to God's Word that you break all curses that are over your life in Jesus' name because you are a child of God (see Psalm 18, Jeremiah 2:11-13, 29:11, John 10:10 and Ephesians 4:11-13).

The model prayer below should be prayed aloud during a time of ministry in the presence of another Christian (or more) of your own gender (Isaiah 10:27 and James 5:16).

Prayer – Breaking Curses and Restoration

Heavenly Father, I come in the name of Jesus Christ and by His blood which He shed for me. I confess that Jesus Christ is my Lord and Saviour. I repent from all my sin and ungodly actions, attitudes, lifestyles or habits that does not glorify Jesus Christ. I ask for forgiveness, cleansing and restoration in Jesus' name. I renounce the devil and all his works, influences, bondages, dominations, afflictions and infirmities in my life. I confess and renounce every iniquity, transgression and sin that I, my parents, or ancestors may have committed, known or unknown and which has brought bondages, dominations, afflictions or infirmities into or over my life. I break all curses over my life in Jesus' name and claim the release and freedom as promised by Jesus Christ. Amen.[2]

Further study: Deuteronomy chapters 6-7, 11:26-29, 23:5, chapters 27-28, 2 Chronicles 32:14-33, (Numbers 5:17-31 and Psalm 109:18-19), Psalm 119:21, Proverbs 3:33, Ecclesiastes 7:22, Jeremiah 17:5, 29:16-22, Daniel 9:3-20, Malachi 2:1-9, 3:8-12, 4:4-6, Matthew 5:11, Ephesians 1:4, 1 Peter 3:9, 2 Peter 2:14 and Revelation 22:3.[3]

Chapter Forty-Eight

Deliverance – The Casting out of Demons

Jesus said, "These signs will follow those who believe: In My name they will cast out demons; they will speak with new tongues" (Mark 16:17).

'He who sins is of the devil, for the devil has sinned from the beginning. For this purpose the Son of God was manifested that He might destroy the works of the devil' (1 John 3:8).

Much of what happens in this world goes on in the unseen realms as the 'whole world lies under the sway of the evil one' (1 John 5:19). Demons also known as evil spirits or angels of darkness are agents of the devil. They work for him, are under him and seek to kill, steal and destroy anyone and everyone (John 10:10a). They seek to invade the body of Christians and non-Christians as a place to dwell. Demons can fight against our peace of mind and our physical well-being and generally try to harass and / or torment people (1 Samuel 16:14-16, Luke 13:11-13 and 1 Peter 1:13a). They can cause sickness (Luke 13:11, Mark 7:25 and 9:17), afflict people and cause destruction (Job 1:13-2:10), and hinder conversion (2 Corinthians 4:3-4). They can also plant evil desires (1 Chronicles 21:1), and can speak (Mark 3:11 and Mark 5:9). Demons can operate from within (Matthew 8:28-32) or outside of the human body (2 Corinthians 12:7), and can even be in animals (Matthew 8:31-32). Demons can be cast out of a person and / or off them – this is commonly known as deliverance, which some churches call exorcism.

Christians are commanded to resist the devil and to stand firm against him, whilst wearing the full armour of God (1 Peter 5:8-9 and Ephesians 6:10-17). If demons are attacking your mind (Mark 8:33 and 1 Peter 1:13a), you must resist them (James 4:7 and 1 Peter 5:8). If they are within or attached to a person (some people can see them in the spirit), Christians can expel, or cast them off (Mark 1:39). Christians have been given power and authority in the name of Jesus Christ of Nazareth to cast them out or off people. Jesus Christ is the 'King of kings and the Lord of lords' (Revelation 19:16), and He came to 'destroy the works of the devil' (1 John 3:8). Jesus has broken Satan's authority and all demons are subject to Him (Philippians 2:10, Colossians 2:15, Hebrews 2:14 and James 2:19). Jesus' authority has been passed onto Christians, disciples of Jesus Christ who are called to carry on His work (Matthew 10:8 and Matthew 28:18-20). The Holy Spirit who is in us is stronger than the devil (1 John 4:4).

Satan's Defeat
- Jesus 'having disarmed principalities and powers, He made a public spectacle of them, triumphing over them in it' (Colossians 2:15).
- 'They [Christians] overcame him [the devil] by the blood of the Lamb and by the word of their testimony...' (Revelation 12:11).
- 'And the God of peace will crush Satan under your feet shortly' (Romans 16:20).

The Influences of Satan and Demons
Whilst the devil is a defeated foe, he does have power in the permissive will of God and seeks to cause havoc where he can. He knows his end and is angry: 'And the devil, who deceived them was cast into the lake of fire and brimstone where the beast and the false prophets are. And they will be tormented day and night forever and ever' (Rev. 20:10).
- A 'distressing spirit *from the Lord* came upon [King] Saul' because of his persistent rebellion against the Lord (1 Samuel 19:9). See also 1 Samuel 16:14-15.
- The Canaanite woman's daughter was 'severely demon possessed' (Matthew 15:21-28).
- The Gadarene man with an unclean spirit, whom no man could bind, not even with chains (Mark 5:1-13).
- The 'devil put it into the heart of Judas Iscariot' to betray Jesus, one of the 12 disciples! (John 13:2).

- A 'daughter of Abraham' (thus a believer) crippled for eighteen years, bent over, kept bound by a spirit of infirmity (Luke 13:10-17). Abraham's children are known as believers (Luke 19:9-10 and Gal. 3:7-9).
- Satan desired to sift Peter as wheat (Luke 22:31-32), and he did deny the Lord three times! And repented.
- Peter said that Satan filled Ananias' heart so that he and his wife lied to the Holy Spirit. They were numbered among the believers (Acts 4:32-35). They sold a plot of land and *claimed* to have given all the money to the church, but kept some of the proceeds. Both were judged by God and died instantly within hours of each other (Acts 5:1-11).
- A slave girl with a spirit of divination, a fortune-teller, kept on proclaiming for many days that Paul and his workers were servants of the Most High God who proclaim the way of salvation. Paul was greatly annoyed and commanded the spirit to come out of her and within the hour the demon had departed (Acts 16:16-18).
- Demonic forces can attack Christians – hence why Paul said we should have on the full armour of God and take the 'shield of faith' by which we 'will be able to quench all the fiery darts of the wicked one' (Ephesians 6:1-17).
- The apostle Paul had received visions, revelations and had been taken up to the third heaven (2 Cor. 12:1-2). To keep him humble he was given 'a thorn in the flesh, a messenger of Satan to buffet me, lest I be exalted above measure' (2 Corinthians 12:7-10).
- Satan stopped Paul and others from visiting the church at Thessalonica. Paul wrote: 'We wanted to come to you, even I, Paul, time and again – but Satan hindered us' (1 Thessalonians 2:18).

The Presence and Nature of Demons

The presence and nature of demons can be known by two principle methods: If you have the gift of discernment, you will supernaturally know what is of God and what is of the devil (1 Kings 22:19-23, 1 Corinthians 12:10 and 1 John 4:3).

Secondly, by detection, simply observing what spirits are doing to a person, and seeing the symptoms (Mark 7:24-30 and Mark 9:17-22). Demons look for places to dwell in (Matthew 12:43). See Demonised Places... chapter 49.

Christians and godly people can have or be under the influence of demons (Job 26:4, Mark 1:23-24, 39, Acts 5:3, 2 Timothy 2:24-26 & James 3:14-16), though a true Christian cannot be completely taken over or 'possessed' (Luke 8:26-31), but Satan did enter Judas! (Luke 22:3-6 and Matthew 27:5). Demonic bondage can range from mild to severe and can cause hardness against the Good News (2 Corinthians 4:4), sinful behaviour (2 Peter 2:1-12), as well as apostasy and false doctrine (1 Timothy 4:1 and 1 John 4:1-3).

If you give demons a legal right to 'enter' or harass you, they will (Matthew 18:34-35 and 2 Corinthians 2:10-11). This can happen through sins of omission (neglecting something that should be done) or sins of commission (what you know is wrong but still do). Demons cannot touch you *if* you are living a pure and holy life, but if you are in *defiant wilful sin* then you give the enemy a *legal entry* to harass and to afflict torment on you.

'Whoever is born of God does not sin; but he who has been born of God keeps himself and the wicked one does not touch him' (1 John 5:18).

The devil always stands to accuse but the innocent who are washed in the blood of the Lamb can declare, "The Lord rebuke you Satan" – (see Zechariah 3:1-5), because our 'Advocate,' Jesus Christ 'is the propitiation for our sins' (1 John 2:1-2). Balaam, a false prophet who knew the demonic dark arts was hired to curse Israel by Balak, the son of Zippor. Balaam acknowledged that he could not go beyond the will of the Lord because of Israel's purity and position in God (Numbers 23:21-23).

Demons can also enter humans via the umbilical cord (our parents), sexual soul ties, our ancestors, kissing the dead (demons seek a place to dwell and cannot work through the deceased), emotional crisis, trauma, occult involvement and demonic orientated music (e.g. heavy metal, thrash or rave); the hypnotic beat is used in pagan worship to bring its worshippers to a frenzy, often allowing them to receive demonic trances, words or visions. If you continually get angry, lie or are violent (even if you are not physically harming anyone), you can be giving a demon a legal right to enter or oppress you (Acts 5:1-5, Acts 8:9-24, 1 Corinthians 7:5, 2 Corinthians 2:11 and Ephesians 4:25-27). Violent criminals and murderers are sometimes quoted as saying such things as: "Something took hold of me," "I was not in control," "A voice told me to kill her," etc., these are classic examples of someone who has been severely controlled or completely possessed / taken over by demons.

Healing or Deliverance?

There is no point praying for a person's healing, *if* they need deliverance. Is it a demonic problem or not? In the case of the man who had been blind from birth, Jesus told His disciples, the man nor his parent's had sinned, "but that the works of God should be revealed in him." Jesus spat on some clay, mixed it and put it on his eyes with the command to go and wash in the pool of Siloam. The man obeyed and came back seeing (John 9:1-7). No deliverance was needed, no demon or spirit of blindness was cast out. On the other hand, the woman who was bent over, crippled for eighteen years was kept bound by a spirit of infirmity (Luke 13:10-17). The Gadarene madman which no one could bind, did not need healing, but the unclean spirit cast out of him and Legion (meaning – for we are many) was cast into the herd of swine (Mark 5:1-13). In both these instances (and others within the Gospels), when Jesus cast the evil spirit(s) out, the person was delivered, set free and made whole.

Signs of Oppression or Possession

Signs of oppression or possession can be: Dark eyes because 'the lamp of the body is the eye' – your eyes are the window to your soul (Matthew 6:22-23), general lack of self control, addiction, hearing voices, (sometimes talking to them – fellowshipping or arguing with demons), feeling of evil from within or around them, aversion to Christianity, prayer, communion, Christian symbols (the cross), holy water, anointed oil, the name of Jesus Christ, inability to say the Lord's Prayer, or to renounce the devil and all his works, unnatural strength, sudden deafness, speaking in strangely, different voice or gobbledygook (demonic babble), NOT to be confused with the gift of tongues from the Holy Spirit.

Some Symptoms of Indwelling Demons Can Be:

- Emotional problems, which persist or recur: anger, resentment, rejection, gnashing of teeth etc.
- Mental torment / disturbances in the mind: confusion, paranoia, schizophrenia abnormal fear, tormenting voices, depression or frequent suicidal thoughts etc.
- Unclean thoughts: lust, sexual fantasy or addiction to pornography and all forms of unnatural sex.
- Outbursts or uncontrolled use of the tongue: rage, blasphemy, swearing or habitual lying etc.
- Addictions: nicotine, alcohol, food, caffeine, retail therapy, anorexia or compulsive exercise etc.
- Sickness (spirit of infirmity, John 9:1-3), or because of sin (Mark 2:5-11, Luke 13:11 and John 5:6-9, 14).
- Involvement in or former involvement in: false religions, religious errors, cults (Mormons, Jehovah Witnesses etc.), martial arts and yoga (part of the Buddhist religion), occult or witchcraft (Deut. 18:9-14, Isaiah 2:6, 1 Timothy 4:1 and 2 Timothy 3:5).

Please note: this list is not exhaustive.

Sins of the Flesh Versus the Demonic

Do not confuse the sins of the flesh (Galatians 5:19-21), with the demonic (2 Peter 2). There is the permissive will of God and whilst He is sovereign in the affairs of men, His sovereignty does not release us from responsibility. You cannot blame every problem on demonic forces and cannot cast flesh out of flesh. We must take responsibility for our lives, crucify the flesh, take up our cross daily, resist the devil and he will flee (Romans 7, Galatians 5:19-26 and 1 Peter 5:8-9). Negative emotions (e.g. bitterness, self-seeking and sensual wisdom) can be demonic (see James 3:13-18). Any area of your life that is not surrendered to Christ is fair game for the enemy. If we harbour anger, bitterness, envy, continual thoughts of an impure nature, living unholy lives etc. then we are inadvertently leaving the door wide open for a spiritual attack. Repent, be self controlled, walk in the Spirit and let the fruit of the Spirit grow in your life (Gal. 5:22-25).

Deliverance from Demons

As people with demons can range from mild to severe, there are several levels of ministry. There is self-deliverance, where an individual commands the demons to leave themself in the name of Jesus Christ. There is also deliverance during a time of ministry where other Christians cast them out or where the pastor and or ministry team prays with the person in need and casts the demons out. Some Christians have the gift of 'discerning of spirits' (1 Corinthians 12:10).

For anybody who needs deliverance he (or she) must confess all known sin, renounce the devil and all works of darkness and declare that Jesus is Lord of his life (Psalm 32:5, 139:23-24, Ezekiel 20:43, James 4:6-7, James 5:16 and 1 John 1:9). If he has any occult memorabilia it must be destroyed (Acts 19:18-19), alongside articles of affection (Jude 23). Unforgiveness, bitterness or deep-seated anger greatly hinders deliverance. For some people, the demons entry point into their lives is because of these negative sinful emotions that occurred because of an incident (Matthew 6:14-15 and 18:21-35). Once these emotions are dealt with (by forgiveness), the demons have no legal right to stay.

It is best that there are at least two Spirit-filled believers present praying for a person needing deliverance (Isaiah 10:27 and Mark 6:6). It is always best to explain to the person you are ministering to, what you will do as you go along to help put them at ease. Remind him (or her) that you are on his side and that he must work with you in his mind, commanding the demons to leave. Allow the Holy Spirit to guide you. He may want to give you a word of wisdom or knowledge or discernment (1 Corinthians 12:1-11). If possible learn from others who have had practical experience in the ministry of deliverance (Acts 19:13-15). Bind the strong man in the name of Jesus Christ and then cast out the demons in Jesus' mighty name. Command the demons to touch no one and never to return (Matthew 12:29-30, 18:18-20 and Luke 9:49-50).

Do not tease demons. Even 'Michael the archangel, in contending with the devil, when he disputed about the body of Moses, dared not bring against him a reviling accusation, but said, "The Lord rebuke you" ' (Jude 9). See also Zechariah 3:1-6). Allow Christ to deal with evicted demons. 'That at the name of Jesus every knee should bow, of those in heaven and earth, and of those under the earth, and that every tongue should confess that Jesus Christ is Lord, to the glory of God the Father' (Philippians 2:10-11).

Remember: the Scriptures (Christ's victory and the devil's defeat), the name of Jesus, His precious blood and who you are in Christ (you are a child of God and have been given authority). Allow the Holy Spirit to guide you (Joel 2:32, Psalm 18:2a, Mark 16:17a, Luke 10:19 and John 14:4). Deliverance sessions often last a few hours and those being ministered to may yawn, cry, sigh, cough, spit and can even vomit as demons flee. Have a box of tissues and a bin ready! Derek Prince said, "Lose your dignity for a time – loose your demons forever!" You may need to pray for a person several times until they are completely free. After each deliverance session spiritually cut yourself off (Ephesians 6:10-17). Ask for the cleansing of the blood of Jesus (on all concerned), and ask the Holy Spirit to come and fill them afresh (Luke 11:13, Acts 2:4 and Acts 8:14-16). If the delivered person continues in sin, they can become 'indwelt,' tormented or oppressed (Matthew 12:43-45 and Luke 11:24-26). To stay free: confess Jesus as Lord, resist the devil and live for God (John 2:5, John 14:15, Romans 10:9-10 and James 4:7).

It is unwise to minister to non-Christians as they are not in a covenant relationship with Jesus Christ. If they are delivered and continue in sin the latter end is worse than the beginning, the same as a Christian who backslides (Matthew 15:21-28, Luke 10:17-20, and 2 Peter 2:20). However, deliverance for some non-Christians can lead to conversion as can be seen in the Gospels with Jesus' ministry. The apostle Paul cast out a spirit of divination from a fortune-teller (an unconverted slave girl) because he was annoyed and distressed with her daily proclamations (Acts 16:16-18).

Further study: Isaiah 19:14, 54:7, Hosea 14:2, Luke 8:2, John 10:10a, Acts 5:16, 8:7, 16:16, 19:12, Romans 16:20, 1 Corinthians 5:5, Ephesians 6:12, Colossians 1:13-14, 1 Timothy 1:20, Revelation 2:13, 3:9, 12:9, 18:2 and 20:10.[1]

Chapter Forty-Nine

Demonised Places / Territorial Spirits

'God's intent was that now, through the church, the manifold wisdom of God should be made known to the rulers and authorities in the heavenly realms, according to His eternal purpose which He accomplished in Christ Jesus our Lord' (Ephesians 3:10-11), NIV.

'We do not wrestle against flesh and blood, but against principalities, against powers, against the rulers of this dark age, against spiritual hosts of wickedness in the heavenly places' (Ephesians 6:12).

"Can a building become an abode for demons / evil spirits?" Demons seek a place to dwell and are not just constrained to people, animals or buildings. There are various types of demons, some more powerful than others (just like angels, they have a hierarchy). They can also work over geographical areas and are known within the Bible as: territorial spirits, principalities and powers, strongholds, strong man, and rulers and authorities in the heavenly realms. The Scriptures give the names of some of these territorial spirits: 'queen of heaven' (Jeremiah 7:18), 'prince of Persia and Greece' (Daniel 10:13, 20), 'Satan's seat' (Revelation 2:13), 'Babylon a habitation of demons' (Revelation 18:2, implies a place to live). Legion's demons (within the Gadarene man) wanted to stay within their country/boundary (Mark 5:9-10), and so went into the swine.

You can have holy (Exodus 3:5 and Exodus 26:34), and unholy buildings or land. Unholy places have become defiled due to sin, often sites of occult or idol worship (Leviticus 18:25, Psalm 74:7, Psalm 106:36-39 and Jeremiah 16:18), and in these places demons can linger and make their abode. Land and buildings can become demonised through their use for: occult practices, false religions, idol worship, sins of the owners or previous occupiers or users, death (especially murders and sacrifices), sexual sins, curses, witchcraft or satanism etc. (see Leviticus chapters 17-20, 26:14-39 and 2 Kings chapter 21). These places may be: haunted houses, sites of atrocities, former site of pagan worship or buildings formerly owned *or used* by other religions (worshipping false gods – demon deities), occult activity, suicide, murder or sexual sins etc. Land and buildings can become demonised / defiled through sin. They can also be cleansed and consecrated for the glory of God.

If you enter a demonised / possessed / haunted / contaminated room or building, you may sense darkness, coldness or heaviness in the atmosphere. You could also be attacked spiritually with temptations, evil thoughts or unnatural sexual desires etc. The latter is an indication of what spirit is dwelling there and the type of sin that was committed within the room or building that gave it a legal right to enter/stay.

John Woolmer in *Healing and Deliverance* (1999) wrote: 'Scripture has little to say about spiritual problems in buildings, but the constant emphasis on 'destroying the high places' in the Old Testament seems to suggest that pagan and dangerous influences were liable to linger unless the places were thoroughly cleansed.'

'...Places where spiritual disobediences had taken place were a constant source of conflict in Old Testament times [Deuteronomy 12:1-4 – destroy the high places, on a mountain, hill and those under spreading trees. Smash the altars, sacred stones, burn their Asherah poles, cut down the idols and gods and wipe out their names from those places], and in Acts 19, Paul's ministry in Ephesus led many to burn their magic scrolls and to confess their occult deeds.'[1]

Territorial Spirits

The Old Testament abounds in references to evil places where false gods / demons were worshiped. They were known as high places, altars to a particular god, idols (of wood or stone), sacred images, pillars or poles, or sacred places such as spreading trees, green trees, groves and sacred or engraved stones (Leviticus 26:1, Numbers 21:28,

AV, Deuteronomy 12:2-4, 2 Kings 17:10-12 and Jeremiah 3:1-9). The nation of Israel was told by God to destroy these places when they entered the Promised Land of Canaan and to drive out the people, otherwise their evil practices would be a constant 'irritant in your eyes and thorn in your side' (Numbers 33:52-56 and 1 Samuel 15:18). Everything was to be destroyed and the plunder burned (Deuteronomy 13:15-17). Accursed objects (Joshua 6:18, 7:1), were also forbidden to be brought into their homes because of their association and connection with evil practices and demons, whilst even the silver and gold of the Canaanites was deemed an abomination (Deuteronomy 7:25-26, 13:17). The Canaanites worshiped idols and sacrificed to demons (Leviticus 20:3-5, 2 Chronicles 11:15 and Ezekiel 20:26). Archaeological excavations and finds have revealed that the Canaanites concealed their idols inside the walls of their homes for protection. These walls and idols were contact points for the demons, thus defiling the home. Leviticus 14:33-53 is about the cleansing or destruction of defiled homes.

In ancient times, it was a common belief that a god had rights over its territory. The Syrians believed that the God of Israel was the God of the hills and that if they fought in the plains they would be victorious (1 Kings 20:23). After Naaman the Syrian was healed, he asked for 'two mule-loads of earth' so that he could worship the Lord only and promised not to offer either burnt offerings or sacrifices to other gods. He wanted the soil so that he has the right *territory* to worship the Lord (2 Kings 5:17-18).

The Assyrians took captive the children of Israel and removed them from their homeland. People of other nations and religions repopulated Samaria (and other cities) and because they did not fear the Lord, God sent lions among them, which killed some of them. Some of the people spoke to the king of Assyria saying that the people 'do not know the rituals *of the God of the land...*' (v26), and so a priest who had been taken captive by the Assyrians was returned to his homeland to teach the people the rituals of the land (2 Kings 17:24-27).

Daniel wrote of the 'prince of the kingdom of Persia' who delayed an angelic messenger for twenty-one days who had come to inform Daniel. The messenger (an angel) had been helped by the archangel angel, 'Michael, one of the chief princes' against the 'kings of Persia' (Daniel 10:10-14).

The Gadarene man who made his dwelling among the tombs had an 'unclean spirit' (singular) and the demons (plural) wanted to stay in *their territory.* Jesus asked the unclean spirit its name, "Legion, for we are many." They 'begged Him [Jesus] earnestly that He would not send them out of the country.... Send us to the swine that we may enter them.' Jesus gave them permission to enter the herd of pigs of which there were about two thousand (Mark 5:1-14).

Defiled Structures

In the Old Testament, the temple was defiled many times and needed to be cleansed (2 Chronicles 28:22-25 and 2 Chronicles 29:3-36). Churches, organisations and structures can also become defiled and demonised due to all of the sins previously mentioned and through:

- Specific sins of the leadership, (pastors, elders etc.), freemasonry, deception, theft and adultery etc. (Num. 16:1-4, Num. 16:22-26 and Ezekiel 8:16, 11:1-12).
- Unbelief and the denial of the truths of God's Word, (Romans 14:23 and 2 Peter 2:1-3).
- False doctrine and beliefs (1 Timothy 4:1-3 and Revelation 16:13-14). Especially denying the gifts of the Holy Spirit or suppressing their use – thus insulting the Spirit of grace (Mark 16:17, 1 Cor. 14:39 and Hebrews 10:29). If you do not want the Holy Spirit in your midst, you may end up with evil spirits!
- Prior use of the land; former uses: occult worship sites, sites of execution/sacrifices martial arts centre or sex shop etc. (2 Kings 16:3-4 and 2 Kings 21:6-7).
- Sins of the denomination's leaders and legalism, being brought under bondage (2 Corinthians 11:20 and Galatians 2:4, see also Revelation ch. 2-3).

Please note: this list is not exhaustive.

Cleansing and Dedicating to God

It is always worth praying over items that you bring into your home (especially second-hand ones bought online), asking God to cleanse them in the precious blood of Jesus

Christ, as you do not know where they have come from, or their previous owner. Cleansing and dedicating is not a new doctrine but has deep roots.[2] Spirits of intrusion can damage items or cause them from functioning as they should, or your second-hand electronic gadget has just had its day!

When staying in hotels etc., always pray over the room. Command anything that is not of God to depart and ask God to cleanse the room in the precious blood of Jesus Christ. You do not know who the previous occupants were or the sins they may have committed whilst there.

When the temple and its utensils were made, they were anointed with oil and sprinkled with blood so that they could be consecrated for holy use (Exodus 30:26-29, Leviticus 40:9-11 and ch. 8). Dedicate items that you have purchased to the glory of God. Ask Him to bless them and the use thereof. Some people like to anoint valuable items with a dab of oil (see chapter 41) and ask God to cleanse the object in the blood, whether it is a car or just a new mobile/cell phone. (Please note that dedicating an item to the glory of God is not an alternative to maintenance and due care!). Some householders pour oil around their boundaries and dab it on their doorframes and lintels. Some also ask the angels to protect them / to keep guard, see Hebrews 1:14). However, neither is an alternative to efficient security and due care.

Cleansing of a Building or Land

If a leader(s) has given demons a legal right to defile a church; knowingly or unknowingly, only a fellow leader(s) who has God's appointed authority can evict the demonic intruders. The leader(s) needs to repent of the sin, whether committed by them or their predecessor(s). This will break the demons' legal right to stay. They need to be commanded to go in the name of Jesus Christ. If a room or building has become defiled, a Spirit-filled Christian can evict them in the name of Jesus Christ. Demons also hate praise and worship music and consecrated oil. In the Old Testament the re-consecrating or re-dedication of a building could take time (2 Chronicles 28:22-27 and 29:1-17). Command evil spirits to depart in the name of Jesus Christ of Nazareth, sprinkle holy water, use anointed oil (especially around boundary borders), take communion as a team, worship the Lord, play a worship CD on repeat at a reasonable volume! If the owners / occupants are not Christian, then one or other may be the problem as the demonic in them may attract others.

Jesus said, "I will give you the keys of the Kingdom of heaven; whatever you bind on earth *will be* bound in heaven and whatever you loose on earth *will be* loosed in heaven" (Matthew 16:19). The NIV margin notes of Matthew 16:19 reveal that *'will be'* can also mean *'or have been.'* John Woolmer wrote: 'If we accept the NIV margin note...then we can see that the binding of Satan is achieved in heaven. If this is correct, it underlines a point made by many writers that warfare prayer is only to be undertaken as a result of very clear instructions from the Lord.'[3] See also Psalm 119:89 and Psalm 135:6.

You cannot evict territorial spirits / principalities over a geographical area unless you have the anointing, authority and a direct command from God (Zechariah 13:2). You do not look for this type of work, God will show you, and only if you have been faithful, obedient and are an overcomer, having crucified the flesh. Principalities may have legal rights going back centuries and will not leave without a fight! Even the angel Gabriel needed help (Daniel 9:21-22 and Daniel 10:12-13, 20-21). He had a twenty-one day battle with the prince of Persia when Daniel the 'beloved' was in intercession. Do not go beyond your faith, your anointing and God's specific command.

Accursed Objects and Demons

People can unknowingly bring accursed or defiled objects into homes or churches etc. (Joshua 6:18 and 7:1). Often these objects are given or bought as souvenirs or presents from holiday destinations. Curses and demons can be attached to items such as woodcarvings, occult objects, facemasks, plaques etc. As food can be sacrificed to idols (and behind all idol worship there are demons, Acts 15:29 and 1 Cor. 10:20), therefore other objects can be defiled (Gen. 35:1-4 and Ps. 106:36-39). These objects need to be destroyed regardless of the value (Acts 19:19 and Jude 23).

Further study: Leviticus chapter 26, Deuteronomy chapter 28, John 3:18-19, 2 Cor. 2:10-11 and 1 John 3:18-21.[4]

Chapter Fifty

Epilogue

'Jesus died for all, that those who live should live no longer for themselves, but for Him who died for them and rose again' (2 Corinthians 5:15).

John the Baptist, in reference to Jesus said, "He must increase, but I must decrease" (John 3:30).

There are many steps in the Christian pilgrimage, but many small steps, over a lifetime equals a great distance travelled. The first starting block is conversion; to "repent" as John the Baptist thundered forth. Jesus said, "You must be born again" and as the Scriptures declare: 'There is no other name under heaven by which we must be saved.' The apostle Paul reiterated this principle of a new life in Christ Jesus, 'If you confess with your mouth and believe in your heart that God has raised Him [Jesus] from the dead, you will be saved.' But this is just the beginning; having been introduced to Jesus, we are called to become His disciples. After conversion, we are called to be baptised in water and baptised in the Holy Spirit (it does not matter in which order, and it differs between individuals). Being Jesus' disciples, we are called to progress from spiritual milk to meat and overcome sin, putting to death the carnal nature, so that we can become more Christ-like. After some years, God-willing, by His grace, mercy and by the training/leading of the Holy Spirit we will be able to confess that we are 'more than a conqueror.' One who is fully surrendered to the Master's will, knowing that 'without Him we can do nothing.'

We need to spend more time reading the Holy Bible and in prayer, which will enable us to get closer to God. We should be seeking God from day to day, trying to get to know Him and His ways. God should not be a stranger to us. We are told to 'seek first the Kingdom of God and His righteousness' (Matthew 6:33), and to 'delight yourself in the Lord' (Psalm 37:4). We should live each day as if it were our last, or as if Jesus was coming tomorrow, as one day soon He will! (See Matthew 24:27-51 and Matthew 25:1-13). Be ready for His imminent return.

Most Christians in their walk of faith will at one time or another ask the question, "How do I know if something is acceptable or unacceptable – OK or sinful?" The answer is that we have the Bible as our first port of reference and we have the Holy Spirit who will guide us into truth (for those willing to listen), or convict us (if we get it wrong), but we must be careful to listen to His small still voice. As a safety barrier for any uncertainty, always ask yourself: What would Jesus do in this situation? How would He react? What would He say? Would He visit certain establishments? If He did, what would He do – socialise or evangelise? Could a 'thing' form an ungodly habit? Can I thank God for it, or ask Him to bless it? Are you being secretive about it? Will it cause pain or hurt to other people? Don't just follow the crowd – sadly even in church, not every Christian lives a God-glorifying life. Also, something may be legal or socially acceptable in your country or state, such as abortion, adultery, homosexuality, euthanasia or social drinking, but it does not make it right in the eyes of God. When the Bible does not directly address an issue, then we need to look to the spiritual principle that can be applied. The Bible does not say, 'do not take harmful drugs,' but it does say 'your body is the temple of the Holy Spirit, do not defile it' (1 Cor. 3:16-17 and 2 Cor. 6:16). One wrong action could compromise or even ruin your testimony and possibly that of others, being a stumbling block.

As disciples of Jesus Christ, He should be the Lord of our lives, but often He is not. As well as the devil being our enemy, we struggle against the world and our flesh life. The flesh life loves attention and says that it has rights, such as, "I have the right to do this or say whatever." The flesh is naturally defensive and will fight back when in trouble. Spiritually we have to crucify the flesh with its passions and desires. Jesus said, "Not My will be done but Yours" (Matthew 26:42 and Luke 11:2). A preacher once said, "Those who claim to be a Christian, yet refuse to live as

Jesus commanded are denying and dishonouring Him. Jesus' pain did not end at the cross. It continues every time we put our interests before His."

A diamond is a highly valuable stone that needs to be cut and polished, so that light will truly reflect the beauty of the stone. It will undergo much change from when it was found in the depths of the earth and will become more valuable. Prior to conversion, we were dirty, but have since repented and have been spiritually cleansed by the blood of Jesus Christ (Hebrews 10:22 and Revelation 1:5). Whilst God at our conversion renews our spirit (it is our responsibility to renew our mind), we are called to walk in the newness of life, thus making us a highly valuable jewel (see Malachi 3:17). The more we give of ourselves to God, the better disciples we will become. God is the Master Potter and we are like clay in His hands, therefore we must allow Him to mould and transform us for the better (Jeremiah 18:6 and 29:11-13).

'Put off concerning your former conduct, the old man which grows corrupt...and be renewed in the spirit of your mind and...put on the new man...' (Ephesians 4:22-24a).

Dr. Kurt Koch in *Occult Bondage and Deliverance* wrote: 'There is a great difference between saying that we are prepared to live our lives according to the dictates of the Lord Jesus, and saying that the Lord can rule our lives for us. This is what He waits for – the command to take over. If we hope to stand in the battle, Jesus must become the Lord of our time, the Lord of our strength, the Lord of our wills, the Lord of our possessions, the Lord of our plans, and the Lord of our decisions. Jesus said in Matthew 11:27, "All things have been delivered to Me by My Father." We must ask ourselves, does this include us? Only when Jesus is our Lord will He protect us from the lordship of others.'[1] C.f. Romans 8:31 and 1 John 4:4.

Full Surrender

The flesh life and the issues from the heart can cause us problems that will alienate us from God. The deeper we want to go with God, the more we have to surrender to the Holy Spirit and obey Him (Psalm 51:17). We should love God with all our soul, strength, mind and heart (Mark 12:30), but how often if we are honest we do not! The Bible reveals that the heart is deceitful; where our treasure is, that is where our heart will be and what comes out of our mouth comes from the heart (Jeremiah 17:9, Matthew 6:21, 12:35 and 15:18). As disciples of Jesus Christ our hearts which are like stone need to be softened and made pliable (Ezekiel 11:19 and 36:26). When our heart is with God, He allows situations to happen to bring us closer to Himself to continually keep us humble and pliable. It is likened to a refiner's fire, who when smelting a metal has to get all the impurities out and only then has he got a pure metal, which is most valuable and fit to be used (Proverbs 17:3). All too frequently we have idols in our lives and don't even know it; it may not be a statue which we bow down to, but things that we put before God; they have a higher priority in our heart, our time, our affections or emotions (Ezekiel 14:3). We need to have an undivided heart so that we can fear God (Psalm 86:11). This can only truly be done when we give God our heart (Proverbs 23:26), and by doing this you unreservedly give yourself to Him.

Sixteen centuries ago, St. Augustine wrote: 'So it is that two cities have been made by two loves; the earthly city by love of self to the exclusion of God, the heavenly city by love of God to the exclusion of self. The one boasts in itself, the other in the Lord (2 Corinthians 10:17). The one seeks glory from men, the other finds its greatest glory in God's witness to its conscience. The one holds its head high in its own glory, the other calls it God 'my glory who raises high my head' (Psalm 3:3).'[2]

'...Present your bodies a living sacrifice, holy, acceptable to God, which is your reasonable service. And do not be conformed to this world, but be transformed by the renewing of your mind, that you may prove what is that good and acceptable and perfect will of God' (Romans 12:1-2).

The Bible speaks of our flesh life as 'the old man' which needs to be crucified, that is, put to death (Romans 6:6 and Ephesians 4:22). Physical crucifixion was an agonising way to die. Spiritual crucifixion is also very painful and can take years, or even decades to be truly dead to the world and its influences, but it all starts with a conscious decision that God can do more with your life than you can do on your own. We have to decide to put to death our carnal life and allow the Holy Spirit to completely fill us. We are called to take up our cross daily and follow Jesus (Matthew 10:38-39 and Mark 8:34-35). Many preachers have said, "We may have the Holy Spirit, but does the Holy Spirit have us?" What about you?

'Unless a grain of wheat falls into the ground and dies, it remains alone; but if it dies, it produces much grain. He who loves his life will lose it, and he who hates his life in this world will keep it for eternal life' (John 12:24-25).

Often hard and painful decisions will have to be made if we really want God's will (the best) for us. What is popular is not always right and what is right is not always popular. Beware of being stale or stagnant. Christian maturity is not about having grey hair or being old and wrinkly. It is being able to assimilate all that you know in and about Christ Jesus (alongside the teachings of Christianity as revealed in the Holy Bible) and the ability to use it with practical application.

Never forget that Jesus' commission was to die for mankind, yet He steadfastly set His face towards Jerusalem, knowing the pain and suffering He would have to endure (Matthew 16:21, 20:18, 23:37 and Luke 9:51). Full surrender to God comes at a high price, maybe higher than you're willing to pay (Luke 14:25-35). But it's worth it and the rewards and benefits will be glorious in this life and the next (Matthew 19:27-30).

Jesus was totally surrendered to the Father's will and was full of the Holy Spirit, moving in mighty signs and wonders to glorify the Father. With great power (an anointing) comes great responsibility. God will not release such power and authority to those who are not fully submitted to Him and totally dealt with to the very core of their being. This anointing is not given into the lives of those who are ungodly and unsanctified, but to the pure and holy, those who abide in the vine (John 15:1-11). Where there is inner division there will inevitably be outer ineffectiveness, therefore we must be fully surrendered and committed to the King and His cause. We need to fully and truly understand the concept of abiding in God, knowing that without Him we can do nothing (John 15:5), and let us not forget that Jesus only did the will of His Father (John 5:30). We can go as deep and as far with God as we choose to; the stronger the commitment, the deeper the relationship, the greater the anointing. Enoch walked with God (Genesis 5:24). Moses was desperate to see God's glory (Exodus 33:18). Peter's shadow healed the sick (Acts 5:15), and God worked unusual miracles by the hand of the apostle Paul (Acts 19:11).

To follow in the footsteps of Jesus, we have to fully surrender our lives to Him. There will be struggles and temptations; on occasions, life will be more than difficult and there will be trials, discouragements and misunderstandings. However, the rewards are out of this world and we have abundant resources to help us in our time of need. Jesus conquered all and has all authority, He is the head of the body (Colossians 1:18), and He will come back for a bride without spot or blemish (Ephesians 5:27 and Rev. 21:2, 9).

Jesus made Himself of no reputation and took the form of a servant (Philippians 2:7). As His followers we should be concerned with what God thinks of us (Acts 23:1 and Acts 24:16), as we live to serve Him with a loyal and undivided heart. A dead man cannot retaliate and likewise we should not retaliate or defend ourselves, but look to God to vindicate His own. Jesus did not make any defence when He was up before the High Priest and council members, but as a lamb is silent, He was led to His execution, to the cross of Calvary and prayed, "Father forgive them…" Jesus was innocent of all charges, but He accepted the humiliation and willingly died without a fight to take the punishment that we deserved so that we could go free and be reconciled back to God (Matthew 26:52-68 and Isaiah chapter 53). Therefore, let us live for Him – remember we will not only be judged by what we said and did, but also by what we did not say and did not do! Live fully for God and glorify Jesus Christ as a surrendered vessel through the power of the Holy Spirit.

Thank you for reading this book, please write a short (or long) review on your favourite review site, and give a shout-out on social media – thank you.

Other Books by Mathew Backholer

Christian Missions
- How to Plan, Prepare and Successfully Complete Your Short-Term Mission: For Churches, Independent STM Teams and Mission Organizations.
- Short-Term Missions, A Christian Guide to STMs: For Leaders, Pastors, Churches, Students, STM Teams and Mission Organizations – Survive and Thrive!

Christian Revivals and Awakenings
- Global Revival, Worldwide Outpourings, Forty-Three Visitations of the Holy Spirit: The Great Commission.
- Revival Answers, True and False Revivals: Genuine or Counterfeit? Do not be Deceived, Discerning between the Holy Spirit and the Demonic.
- Revival Fire, 150 Years of Revivals: Spiritual Awakenings and Moves of the Holy Spirit.
- Understanding Revival and Addressing the Issues it Provokes.
- Revival Fires and Awakenings, Thirty-Six Visitations of the Holy Spirit: A Call to Holiness, Prayer and Intercession for the Nations.
- Reformation to Revival, 500 Years of God's Glory: Sixty Revivals, Awakenings and Heaven-Sent Visitations of the Holy Spirit.

Christian Discipleship and Spiritual Growth
- Extreme Faith, On Fire Christianity: Hearing from God and Moving in His Grace, Strength & Power – Living in Victory.
- Discipleship For Everyday Living, Christian Growth: Following Jesus Christ and Making Disciples of All Nations.

World Travel
- Budget Travel, a Guide to Travelling on a Shoestring, Explore the World, a Discount Overseas Adventure Trip.

Social Media
www.facebook.com/ByFaithMedia
www.instagram.com/ByFaithMedia
www.youtube.com/ByFaithMedia
www.twitter.com/ByFaithMedia

Sources and Notes

Chapter One
1. *Unfolding Purpose – An Interpretation of the Living Tradition which is C.M.S.* by Max Warren, Church Missionary Society (CMS), 1950, page 4.
2. *Every Man a Bible Student* by Joe E. Church, Scripture Union and CSSM, 1938, 1961, page 11.
3. Ibid. page 11.
4. *Every Day With Jesus*, Mar/Apr 2006, CWR, 18 March.
5. *Every Man a Bible Student* by Joe E. Church, Scripture Union and CSSM, 1938, 1961, page 1.
6. *The Evangelist – His Ministry and Message* by W. P. Nicholson, Marshal Morgan & Scott, c.1940, page 88.

Chapter Two
1. Adapted from *Revival Fires and Awakenings* by Mathew Backholer, ByFaith Media, 2009, (Appendix F), pages 234-235.
2. *The Master and the Multitude* – the magazine of The Open-Air Mission October-December 2007, page 3.
3. *Understanding Revival and Addressing the Issues it Provokes* by Mathew Backholer, ByFaith Media, 2009, pages 177-178.
4. *China in Revival* by Gustav Carlberg, 1935, chapter three.
5. *Basic Principles of Biblical Counselling – Showing Care Through the Local Church* by Laurence J. Crabb, Marshall Morgan & Scott, 1975, 1985, page 54.
6. *Every Man a Bible Student* by Joe E. Church, Scripture Union and CSSM, 1938, 1961, page 1.
7. Ibid. page 7.
8. Ibid. page 3.
9. *The Set of the Sail* – A. W. Tozer, edited by Harry Verploegh, Kingsway and STL Books, 1986, pages 19-20.
10. *The Evangelist – His Ministry and Message* by W. P. Nicholson, Marshal Morgan & Scott, c.1940, page 92.
11. Ibid. page 97.
12. *God's Hell and Other Addresses* by W. P. Nicholson, Marshal Morgan & Scott, c.1940, pages 58-60.
13. *The Evangelist* by W. P. Nicholson, Marshal Morgan & Scott, c.1940, page 98.

Chapter Three
1. *The Rich Man and Lazarus – An Exposition of Luke 16:19-31* by Brownlow North, Banner of Truth, 1960, 1979, page 116.
2. *How to Bring Men to Christ* by R. A. Torrey, James Nisbet & Co., Limited, 1903, page 102.
3. *The Christian Counsellors Pocket Guide* by Selwyn Hughes, Kingsway Publication, 1977, 1983, page 19.
4. *The Churchman's Monthly Penny Magazine*, c.1845, page 50.
5. *Hot From the Preacher's Mound* by Stephen Hill, Together in the Harvest Publications, 1995, pages 72-73.
6. *The Evangelist – His Ministry and Message* by W. P. Nicholson, Marshal Morgan & Scott, c.1940, pages 111-113.
7. *The Teacher's Visitor,* No. 10, Feb. 1845 – Vol. II, pages 67-68.
8. *A Commentary on the Holy Bible with Practical Remarks and Observation by Matthew Henry* by Sir J. Bickerton Williams, Vol. I, Marshall Brother, c.1880, p.128.

Chapter Four
1. *Good News in Bad Times* by J. Edwin Orr, Zondervan Publishing House, 1953, page 232.

Chapter Five
1. *Full Salvation* by J. A. Broadbelt, Marshall, Morgan & Scott LTD., 1936, page 48.
2. *Every Day With Jesus*, Nov/Dec 2006, CWR, 6 Dec.

Chapter Seven
1. Inspired by a chapter within *The Set of the Sail* – A. W. Tozer, edited by Harry Verploegh, Kingsway and STL Books, 1986, pages 63-64.

Chapter Nine
1. *Hudson Taylor in Early Years – The Growth of a Soul* by Dr. and Mrs Howard Taylor, China Inland Mission, 1911, 1940, pages 372-373.

Chapter Ten
1. Short-term missions (STMs) are where Christians use their holiday (vacation) time often between college terms or a career break to go on a Christian mission trip; involving evangelising or humanitarian work and sometimes both. The duration is frequently from two weeks to a month, though can be as long as a year or two. See *How to Plan, Prepare and Successfully Complete Your Short-Term Mission* by Mathew Backholer, ByFaith Media, 2010.
2. See *Understanding Revival and Addressing The Issues It Provokes* by Mathew Backholer, ByFaith Media, 2009, chapter 18. Notably: Principles which Defy Logic, Biblical Paradoxes and God Defying Rules of Nature and Science.
3. *Hudson Taylor and the China Inland Mission – The Growth of a Work of God* by Dr. and Mrs. Howard Taylor, China Inland Mission, 1918, 1940, page 355.

Chapter Thirteen
1. *Every Day With Jesus*, Nov/Dec 2005, CWR, 14 Dec.

Chapter Sixteen
1. Largely drawn from *Revival Fires and Awakenings* by Mathew Backholer, ByFaith Media, 2009, chapter 21.

Chapter Eighteen
1. *Has God Given you a Mission?* by Geoff Green, (booklet) c.2006, chapter 5.

Chapter Nineteen
1. *Every Man a Bible Student* by Joe E. Church, Scripture Union and CSSM, 1938, 1961, pages 77-78.

Chapter Twenty
1. *Real Religion – Revival Sermons Delivered During His Twentieth Visit to America* by Gipsy Smith, Hodder and Stoughton, 1922, page 108.

Chapter Twenty-Two
1. *Candidates in Waiting – A Manual of Home Preparation for Foreign Missionary Work* by Georgina A. Gollock, Church Missionary Society, 1892, 1898, page 19.
2. *Missionary Education Helps for the Local Church* by Dick Pearson, Overseas Crusades inc., 1966, page 1.   3. Ibid. page 19.
4. *Candidates in Waiting* by Georgina A. Gollock, CMS, 1892, 1898, page 52.
5. Ibid. page 28.
6. *Real Religion – Revival Sermons Delivered During His Twentieth Visit to America* by Gipsy Smith, Hodder and Stoughton, 1922, page 111.

Chapter Twenty-Four
1. *The Personal Life of David Livingstone* by William G. Blaikie, London – John Murray, 1881, page 95.
2. *Missionary Education Helps for the Local Church* by Dick Pearson, Overseas Crusades inc., 1966, page 52.

Chapter Twenty-Six
1. *Candidates in Waiting – A Manual of Home Preparation for Foreign Missionary Work* by Georgina A. Gollock, CMS, 1892, 1898, pages 45-46.
2. *The Set of the Sail* – A. W. Tozer, edited by Harry Verploegh, Kingsway and STL Books, 1986, page 16.
3. *Candidates in Waiting – A Manual of Home Preparation for Foreign Missionary Work* by Georgina A. Gollock, Church Missionary Society, 1892, 1898, page 31.

Chapter Twenty-Eight
1. *Revival Sermons in Outline* edited by Perren, Revell, 1894, pages 73-74.
2. Ibid. pages 111-112.
3. *David Hill – Missionary and Saint* by W. T. A. Barber, Charles H. Kelly, 1899, pages 180-181.

Chapter Twenty-Nine
1. *Revival Sermons in Outline* edited by Perren, Revell, 1894, pages 65-69 & 71-72.
2. *How to Bring Men to Christ* by R. A. Torrey, James Nisbet & Co., Limited, 1903, pages 48, 68 and 100.
3. *Revival Sermons in Outline* edited by Perren, Revell, 1894, pages 88-89.
4. *How to Bring Men to Christ* by R. A. Torrey, James Nisbet & Co., Limited, 1903, chapter 12.

Chapter Thirty
1. *Frontier Evangelism – God's Indispensable Method for World Evangelism* by T. L. Osborn, T. L. Osborn Publication, 1955, 1962, pages 8, 14, 19, 39-40 and 122.

Chapter Thirty-Three
1. *How to Plan, Prepare and Successfully Complete Your Short-Term Mission* by Mathew Backholer, ByFaith Media, 2010, pages 183-184.

Chapter Thirty-Four
1. *Understanding Revival and Addressing the Issues It Provokes* by Mathew Backholer, ByFaith Media, 2009, page 158.

Chapter Thirty-Five
1. *Healing the Sick and Casting out Devils* by T. L. Osborn, 1955, T. L. Osborn Publication, pages 178-179.
2. *The Five Attributes of a Church in Revival* by David E. Carr, New Wine Press, 2006, page 68.

Chapter Thirty-Six
1. *Healing and Deliverance* by John Woolmer, Monarch Books, 1999, 2001, page 288.
2. *Power Healing* by John Wimber with Kevin Springer, Hodder and Stoughton, 1986, page 148.
3. *Healing Rays* by George Jeffreys, Elim Publishing, 1932, page 6.

Chapter Thirty-Eight
1. *Healing the Sick and Casting out Devils* by T. L. Osborn, 1955, T. L. Osborn Publication, page 47.
2. *Healing Through the Centuries* by Ronald Kydd, Henrickson, 1998, page 206, as cited in *Healing and Deliverance* by John Woolmer, Monarch Books, 1999, 2001, pages 208-209.
3. Based on *Power Healing* by John Wimber with Kevin Springer, Hodder and Stoughton, 1986, page 32.
4. *Power Healing* by John Wimber with Kevin Springer, Hodder and Stoughton, 1986, page 115.

5. *Dictionary of Pentecostal and Charismatic Movements* – Stanley M. Burgess and Gary B. McGee (editors), Patrick H. Alexander (associate editor), Regency Reference Library, 1988, page 351.
6. *Healing Rays* by George Jeffreys, Elim Publishing, 1932, pages 171-173.
7. Ibid. page 155.
8. Ibid. pages 157-158. (Healing Covenant is Ex. ch. 24, not 25, as Jeffreys' states).
9. Ibid. pages 167-168.
10. Ibid. pages 170-171.
11. Ibid. pages 157, 162-163 and 165.

Chapter Thirty-Nine
1. *Healing Rays* by George Jeffreys, Elim Publishing, 1932, page 97.
2. *From Refreshing to Revival* by Terry Virgo, David Holden and John Hosier, 1995, Kingsway Publications, page 50.

Chapter Forty
1. *The Heart of Revival* by Nicky Gumbel, Kingsway Publication, 1997, 1998, page 151.
2. *Good Morning Holy Spirit* by Benny Hinn, Thomas Nelson Publisher, 1990, 1997, page 123.
3. *Healing Rays* by George Jeffreys, Elim Publishing, 1932, pages 1.

Acknowledgment for chapters 43-49: The author has gleaned from the teaching and experience of others with whom he has worked and who have helped train and mentor him, especially hands-on ministry for which he is truly thankful. These individuals were from different organisations, denominations and ministries, and the teaching of Vineyard, Ellel Ministries, CWR and many others within the Charismatic Renewal (alongside the numerous Christian Conferences and weekend retreats) that have helped innumerable people; some of whom I sat under. The prayers of release within these chapters (which I have modified) have been widely circulated without accreditation or sources (by many), to whom I give thanks and credit.

Chapter Forty-Three
1. *Power Healing* by John Wimber with Kevin Springer, Hodder and Stoughton, 1986, page 95.

Chapter Forty-Four
1. *Project Pearl* by Brother David and Paul Hattaway, Monarch Books, 2007, pages 294-295.
2. The original source of this prayer is unknown but is based on John 20:21-23.

Chapter Forty-Five
1. The original source of this prayer is unknown but has been adapted for this book.
2. The source of this declaration is unknown but has been adapted for this book.

Chapter Forty-Six
1. The original source of this prayer is unknown but has been adapted for this book. For further study of Sins of the Forefathers / Generational Curses: Leviticus chapter 26, Numbers 14:18, Deuteronomy 5:9, Deuteronomy chapter 28, 1 Kings 14:22, 2 Chronicles 34:21-28, Nehemiah 9:1-2, Isaiah 65:7, Jeremiah 15:1-4, Jeremiah 16:11-13, 16-18, Ezekiel 5:5-12, Ezekiel 9:5-11, Ezekiel 18:2, Daniel 9:3-20, Amos 2:4, Zechariah 8:14-16, Matthew 27:25 and John 8:36.

Chapter Forty-Seven
1. People can unknowingly bring accursed or defiled objects into their homes or churches. Often these objects are given or bought as presents from foreign destinations. Curses and demons (evil spirits – 1 Timothy 4:1), can be attached to items such as woodcarvings, occult objects, idols, facemasks, plaques etc. As food

can be sacrificed to idols (see Acts 15:29 and 1 Corinthians 10:20), and behind all idol worship there are demons, then other objects can be defiled (see Genesis 35:1-4 and Psalm 106:36-39). Demons seek a place to dwell and are not just constrained to people, animals or buildings. You can have holy and unholy buildings or land (see Exodus 3:5 and Exodus 26:34). Unholy places have become defiled due to sin (often sites of occult or idol worship, see Leviticus 18:25, Psalm 74:7, Psalm 106:36-39 and Jeremiah 16:18). The Canaanites worshiped idols and sacrificed to demons (see Leviticus 20:3-5 and Ezekiel 20:26). They would hide their idols inside the walls of their homes for protection. These walls and idols were contact points for the demons, thus defiling the homes. Leviticus 14:33-53 is about the cleansing or destruction of defiled homes. Accursed or defiled objects in your possession need to be destroyed (burnt, broken, or thrown into a deep lake) and never sold, regardless of the value (see Acts 19:19 and Jude 23).

2. The original source of this prayer is unknown but has been adapted for this book.

3. For more information on blessings and curses see: *Blessing or Curse, You Can Choose!* by Derek Prince.

Chapter Forty-Eight

1. For further study on Deliverance – The Casting Out of Demons see: *Pigs in the Parlour* by Frank and Ida Mae Hammond; *Christian Set Yourself Free* by Graham and Shirley Powell and *Demons Defeated* by Bill Subritzky.

Chapter Forty-Nine

1. *Healing and Deliverance* by John Woolmer, Monarch Books, 1999, 2001, pages 36 and 343.

2. Cleansing and dedicating to the glory of God is not a new doctrine but very Scriptural. Historically, when Christianity came to Britain in the first century AD, the Romans (who invaded in AD 44 and stayed for four centuries) and subsequent missionaries were met by pagans, mostly druid worshippers and later, those who made allegiance with Rome and its gods. As Christianity began to spread, many places of pagan worship were either demolished (and a church was built on the site) or the old structure was converted into a church building. Either way, the ground and buildings were spiritually cleansed and consecrated to the glory of God. (St Paul's Church in London, England, is the fourth Cathedral built on the site of a Roman temple to the goddess Diana. The present Cathedral was rebuilt after the fire of London of 1666, and took thirty-five years to complete). In addition, new converts, Christians had to 'renounce the devil and all his works,' even traditional denominations such as the Church of England still practice this. The tradition remains, even if the understanding of previous generations has been lost.

3. *Healing and Deliverance* by John Woolmer, Monarch Books, 1999, 2001, p.103.

4. For further study on Demonised Land / Territorial Spirits see: *Reclaiming the Ground* by Ken Hepworth, *Redeeming The Land* by Gwen Shaw and *Needless Casualties of War* by John Paul Jackson.

Chapter Fifty

1. *Occult Bondage and Deliverance – Advice for Counselling the Sick, the Troubled and the Occultly Oppressed* by Dr. Kurt Koch (translated from German), Evangelization Publishers, c.1970, page 126.

2. *Saint Augustine and His Influences Through the Ages* by Henri Marrou, Longmans, 1957, page 124.

www.ByFaith.co.uk

www.MissionsNow.co.uk

www.RevivalNow.co.uk

ByFaith Media Books

The following ByFaith Media books are available as paperback and eBooks, whilst some are also available as hardbacks.

Christian Teaching and Inspirational
Tares and Weeds in Your Church: Trouble & Deception in God's House, the End Time Overcomers by R. B. Watchman. Is there a battle taking place in your house, church or ministry, leading to division? Tares and weeds are counterfeit Christians used to sabotage Kingdom work; learn how to recognise them and neutralise them in the power of the Holy Spirit.

Holy Spirit Power: Knowing the Voice, Guidance and Person of the Holy Spirit by Paul Backholer. Power for Christian living; drawing from the powerful influences of many Christian leaders, including: Rees Howells, Evan Roberts, D. L. Moody and Duncan Campbell.

Jesus Today, Daily Devotional: 100 Days with Jesus Christ by Paul Backholer. Two minutes a day to encourage and inspire; 100 days of daily Christian Bible inspiration to draw you closer to God. *Jesus Today* is a concise daily devotional defined by the teaching of Jesus and how His life can change yours.

Samuel Rees Howells: A Life of Intercession by Richard Maton is an in-depth look at the intercessions of Samuel Rees Howells alongside the faith principles that he learnt from his father, Rees Howells, and under the guidance of the Holy Spirit. With 39 black and white photos in the paperback and hardback editions.

The Baptism of Fire, Personal Revival, Renewal and the Anointing for Supernatural Living by Paul Backholer. The author unveils the life and ministry of the Holy Spirit, shows how He can transform your life and what supernatural living in Christ means. Filled with biblical references, testimonies from heroes of the faith and the experiences of everyday Christians, you will learn that the baptism of fire is real and how you can receive it!

Revivals and Spiritual Awakenings
Global Revival, Worldwide Outpourings, Forty-Three Visitations of the Holy Spirit: The Great Commission by Mathew Backholer. With forty-three revivals from more than thirty countries on six continents, the author reveals the fascinating links between pioneering missionaries and the revivals that they saw as they worked towards the Great Commission.

Revival Fire, 150 Years of Revivals, Spiritual Awakenings and Moves of the Holy Spirit by Mathew Backholer, documents in detail, twelve revivals from ten countries on five continents. Through the use of detailed research, eye-witness accounts and interviews, *Revival Fire* presents some of the most potent revivals that the world has seen in the past one hundred and fifty years.

Revival Answers, True and False Revivals, Genuine or Counterfeit Do not be Deceived by Mathew Backholer. What is genuine revival and how can we tell the true from the spurious? Drawing from Scripture with examples across Church history, this book will sharpen your senses and take you on a journey of discovery.

Reformation to Revival, 500 Years of God's Glory by Mathew Backholer. For the past five hundred years God has been pouring out His Spirit, to reform and to revive His Church. *Reformation to Revival* traces the Divine thread of God's power from Martin Luther of 1517, through to the Charismatic Movement and into the twenty-first century, featuring sixty great revivals from twenty nations.

Revival Fires and Awakenings, Thirty-Six Visitations of the Holy Spirit: A Call to Holiness, Prayer and Intercession for the Nations by Mathew Backholer. With 36 fascinating accounts of revivals in nineteen countries from six continents, plus biblical teaching on revival, prayer and intercession. Also available as a hardback.

Understanding Revival and Addressing the Issues it Provokes by Mathew Backholer. Many who have prayed for revival have rejected it when it came because they misunderstood the workings of the Holy Spirit and only wanted God to bless the Church on their terms. Learn to intelligently cooperate with the Holy Spirit during times of revivals and Heaven-sent spiritual awakenings.

Supernatural and Spiritual
Glimpses of Glory, Revelations in the Realms of God Beyond the Veil in the Heavenly Abode: The New Jerusalem and the Eternal Kingdom of God by Paul Backholer. In this narrative receive biblical glimpses and revelations into life in paradise, which is filled with references to Scripture to confirm its veracity. A gripping read!

Prophecy Now, Prophetic Words and Divine Revelations for You, the Church and the Nations by Michael Backholer. An enlightening end-time prophetic journal of visions, words and prophecies.

Heaven, A Journey to Paradise and the Heavenly City by Paul Backholer. Join one person's exploration of paradise, guided by an angel and a glorified man, to witness the thrilling promise of eternity, and to provide answers to many questions about Heaven. Anchored in the Word of God, discover what Heaven will be like!

Short-Term Missions (Christian Travel with a Purpose)

Short-Term Missions, A Christian Guide to STMs by Mathew Backholer. *For Leaders, Pastors, Churches, Students, STM Teams and Mission Organizations – Survive and Thrive!* What you need to know about planning a STM, or joining a STM team, and considering the options as part of the Great Commission.

How to Plan, Prepare and Successfully Complete Your Short-Term Mission by Mathew Backholer. *For Churches, Independent STM Teams and Mission Organizations.* The books includes: mission statistics, quotes and more than 140 real-life STM testimonies.

Budget Travel – Holiday/Vacations

Budget Travel, a Guide to Travelling on a Shoestring, Explore the World, a Discount Overseas Adventure Trip: Gap Year, Backpacking, Volunteer-Vacation and Overlander by Mathew Backholer. A practical and concise guide to travelling the world and exploring new destinations with fascinating opportunities.

Biography and Autobiography

The Holy Spirit in a Man: Spiritual Warfare, Intercession, Faith, Healings and Miracles by R. B. Watchman. One man's compelling journey of faith and intercession – a gripping true-life story. Raised in a dysfunctional family and called for a Divine purpose. Sent out by God, he left employment to claim the ground for Christ, witnessing signs and wonders, spiritual warfare and deliverance.

Samuel, Son and Successor of Rees Howells: Director of the Bible College of Wales – A Biography by Richard Maton. The author invites us on a lifelong journey with Samuel, to unveil his ministry at the College and the support he received from numerous staff, students and visitors, as the history of BCW unfolds alongside the Vision to reach Every Creature with the Gospel. With 113 black and white photos in the paperback and hardback editions!

Christian Discipleship

Extreme Faith, On Fire Christianity: Hearing from God and Moving in His Grace, Strength & Power – Living in Victory by Mathew Backholer. Discover the powerful biblical foundations for on fire faith in Christ! God has given us powerful weapons to defeat the enemy, to take back the spiritual land in our lives and to walk in His glory through the power of the Holy Spirit.

Discipleship For Everyday Living, Christian Growth: Following Jesus Christ and Making Disciples of All Nations by Mathew Backholer. Engaging biblical teaching to aid believers in maturity, to help make strong disciples with solid biblical foundations who reflect the image of Jesus Christ.

Historical and Adventure

Britain, A Christian Country, A Nation Defined by Christianity and the Bible & the Social Changes that Challenge this Biblical Heritage by Paul Backholer. For more than 1,000 years Britain was defined by Christianity, discover this continuing legacy, how faith defined its nationhood and the challenges from the 1960s onwards.

How Christianity Made the Modern World by Paul Backholer. Christianity is the greatest reforming force that the world has ever known, yet its legacy is seldom comprehended. See how Christianity helped create the path that led to Western liberty and laid the foundations of the modern world.
Celtic Christianity & the First Christian Kings in Britain: From St. Patrick and St. Columba, to King Ethelbert and King Alfred by Paul Backholer. Celtic Christians ignited a Celtic Golden Age of faith and light which spread into Europe. Discover this striking history and what we can learn from the heroes of Celtic Christianity.

Lost Treasures of the Bible: Exploration and Pictorial Travel Adventure of Biblical Archaeology by Paul Backholer. Join a photographic quest in search of the lost treasures of the Bible. Unveil ancient mysteries as you discover the evidence for Israel's exodus from Egypt, and travel into lost civilisations in search of the Ark of the Covenant. Explore lost worlds with over 160 colour pictures and photos in the paperback edition.

The Exodus Evidence In Pictures – The Bible's Exodus: The Hunt for Ancient Israel in Egypt, the Red Sea, the Exodus Route and Mount Sinai by Paul Backholer. Brothers, Paul and Mathew Backholer search for archaeological data to validate the biblical account of Joseph, Moses and the Hebrew Exodus from ancient Egypt. With more than 100 full colour photographs and graphics!

The Ark of the Covenant – Investigating the Ten Leading Claims by Paul Backholer. The mystery of the Bible's lost Ark of the Covenant has led to many myths, theories and claims. Join two explorers as they investigate the ten major theories concerning the location of antiquities greatest relic. 80+ colour photographs.

www.ByFaithBooks.co.uk

ByFaith Media DVDs

Revivals and Spiritual Awakenings

Great Christian Revivals on 1 DVD is an inspirational and uplifting account of some of the greatest revivals in Church history. Filmed on location across Britain and drawing upon archive information, the stories of the Welsh Revival (1904-1905), the Hebridean Revival (1949-1952) and the Evangelical Revival (1739-1791) are brought to life in this moving 72-minute documentary. Using computer animation, historic photos and depictions, the events of the past are weaved into the present, to bring these Heaven-sent revivals to life.

Christian Travel (Backpacking Style Short-Term Mission)

ByFaith – World Mission on 1 DVD is a Christian reality TV show that reveals the real experience of a backpacking style short-term mission in Asia, Europe and North Africa. Two brothers, Paul and Mathew Backholer shoot through fourteen nations, in an 85-minute real-life documentary. Filmed over three years, *ByFaith – World Mission* is the very best of ByFaith TV season one.

Historical and Adventure

Israel in Egypt – The Exodus Mystery on 1 DVD. A four year quest searching for Joseph, Moses and the Hebrew slaves in Egypt. Join Paul and Mathew Backholer as they hunt through ancient relics and explore the mystery of the biblical exodus, hunt for the Red Sea and climb Mount Sinai. Discover the first reference to Israel outside of the Bible, uncover depictions of people with multicoloured coats, encounter the Egyptian records of slaves making bricks and find lost cities. 110 minutes. The very best of *ByFaith – In Search of the Exodus*.

ByFaith – Quest for the Ark of the Covenant on 1 DVD. Join two adventurers on their quest for the Ark, beginning at Mount Sinai where it was made, to Pharaoh Tutankhamun's tomb, where Egyptian treasures evoke the majesty of the Ark. The quest proceeds onto the trail of Pharaoh Shishak, who raided Jerusalem. The mission continues up the River Nile to find a lost temple, with clues to a mysterious civilization. Crossing through the Sahara Desert, the investigators enter the underground rock churches of Ethiopia, find a forgotten civilization and examine the enigma of the final resting place of the Ark itself. 100+ minutes.